THE ROYAL SCHOOL OF NEEDLEWORK

BOOK OF
NEEDLEWORK
AND
EMBROIDERY

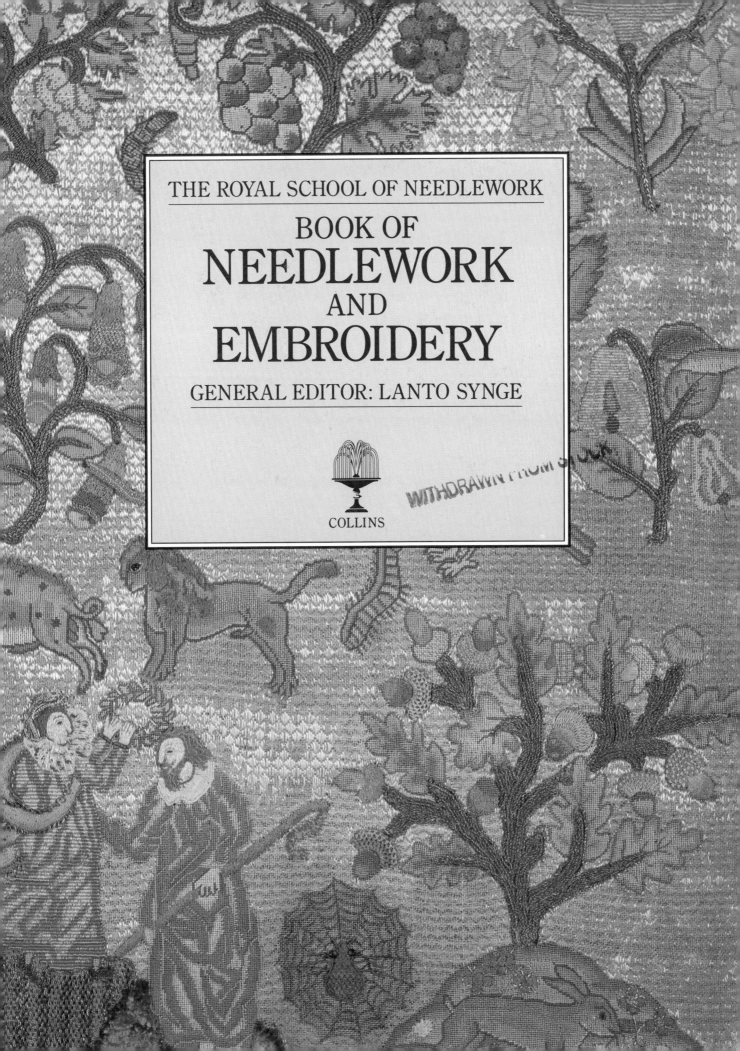

THE ROYAL SCHOOL OF NEEDLEWORK

BOOK OF
NEEDLEWORK
AND
EMBROIDERY

GENERAL EDITOR: LANTO SYNGE

COLLINS

First published in 1986 by
Wm Collins Sons & Co. Ltd,
London · Glasgow · Sydney · Auckland
Toronto · Johannesburg

This book was designed and produced by
The Oregon Press Ltd,
Faraday House, 8 Charing Cross Road,
London WC2H OHG

© The Oregon Press Ltd 1986

Editors: David Black and Raymond Kaye
Picture research: Simon Daffarn and Annabel Moeller
Design: Yvonne Dedman
Production: Hugh Allan

British Library Cataloguing in Publication Data
Synge, Lanto
Royal School of Needlework
book of needlework and embroidery
1. Embroidery—History
I. Title
746.44'09   NK9206

ISBN 0-00-411710-7

Filmset by SX Composing Ltd, Rayleigh, England
Printed and bound by Printer Industria Gráfica SA.
Barcelona, Spain D.L.B. 11493–1986

746.4
C2106037
CE.

Half-title: Detail from a crewelwork curtain, one of a set
of four, in polychrome wools, its design derived from
Chinese lacquer and wallpaper. English, *c.* 1700.

Title page: Detail from a canvas work panel showing a number
of spot motifs of plants, animals and insects. English, *c.* 1610.

Contents page: Detail from a fine-quality filet and whitework
cover with bobbin lace border. French, *c.* 1600–25.

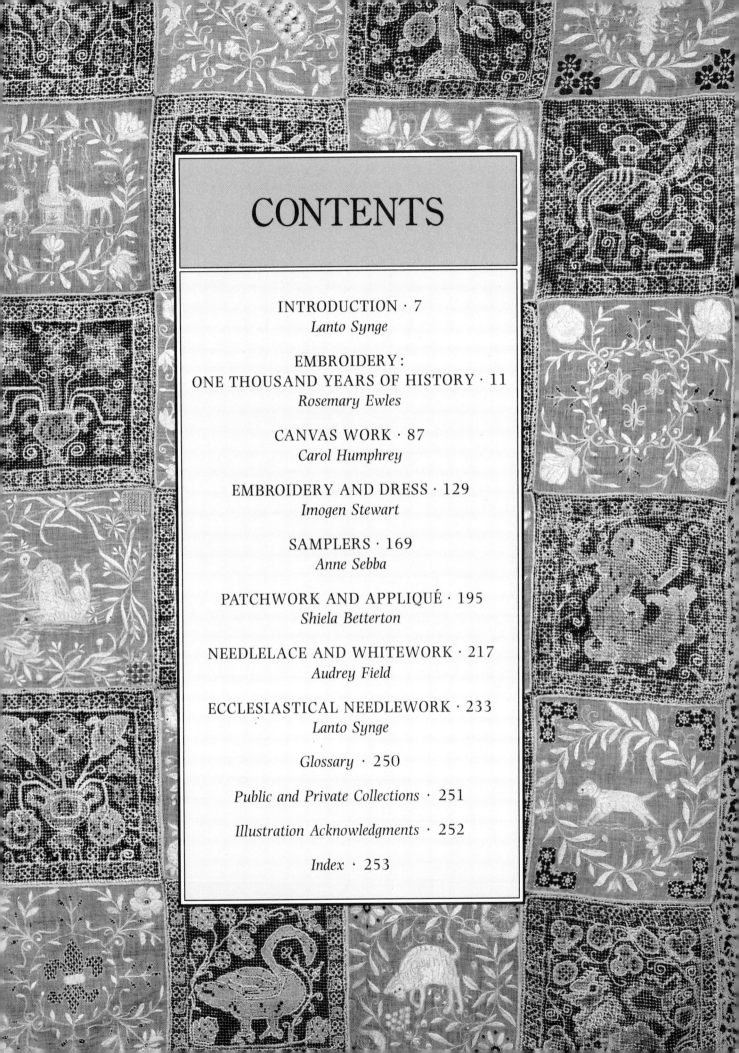

CONTENTS

edvardus vii dei gra brit
omn rex fid def ind imp
E R
dieu et mon droit

INTRODUCTION

LANTO SYNGE

Even a brief visit to a great museum, such as the Victoria and Albert Museum in London, affords an opportunity to see a wondrous variety of textiles, and immediately the viewer realizes how decorative fabrics have been a very significant feature throughout history and into the present, in military, household, ceremonial, sporting and many other circumstances. Woven tapestries, made on looms, were used as large hangings but a colossal variety of smaller articles were of needlework, individually embroidered for a very wide spectrum of uses. On entering the Victoria and Albert we soon see, for example, a magnificiently embroidered Mogul hunting coat: Japanese tobacco pouches with complex imagery in needlework; sumptuous court costumes of mid-eighteenth century society ladies, heavily wrought with gold and silver; small domestic samplers of all periods recording the early sewing efforts of children; large and relatively coarse crewel embroidered hangings, made entirely of home-produced materials to shelter and enhance draughty oak beds. There are examples in many rooms of different cultures and nationalities. The furniture galleries display embroidered pictures of silk, wool and appliqué, sometimes combined with other materials such as shells, and also a large amount of canvaswork for chair seats, bed and wall hangings, firescreens, boxes and other objects. The realization soon dawns that although there is a lot of needlework to be seen, it represents only the tip of an iceberg, being the surviving remains of a large, highly perishable corpus of artistic industry. In distant corners of the museum the visitor can inspect early Buddhist embroidered hangings and wonder in amazement how such articles have lasted, admittedly in drier climates than the British, for over one thousand years.

My fascination for the subject began as a child. I clearly remember how, when I was once laid up in bed, I tried to embroider a few small motifs drawn out on an old piece of linen by my mother. Like most needleworkers I had been inspired by the previous generation. My grandmother had been an excellent sewer of all kinds and left behind her after her death some very original tablecloths, a tea cosy and garments: all eminently typical of her period, but in her case unusually inventive. My other grandmother and grandfather were medical missionaries in China and they were sometimes given interesting pieces of embroidery by grateful patients. One of these Chinese embroideries was a long emerald silk panel embroidered with a continuous frieze of birds, flowers and butterflies. It was made in about 1890 and was said to be for the bottom of a mandarin's robe. Many years later I was given this piece and I had it framed for safety; it still fascinates me, although my

1. *(opposite)* Heraldic panel: the coat-of-arms of Edward VII made at the Royal School of Needlework. Gold and silver threads on a crimson background of long and short stitches.

2. *(above)* A panel of modern needlework based on a traditional form of design of the first half of the eighteenth century. Worked by Peter Maitland.

taste has since broadened and subsequently focused in again on European, especially English needlework, which is softer in colour and on the whole broader in metaphor.

On arriving in London to work for an antiques business I found myself in the hub of the trade and in a place where I saw a quantity and variety of fine textiles. I was expected to get to know the museums, and one of my greatest joys was visiting country houses. I therefore had every chance to familiarize myself with periods and styles, and gradually develop preferences which soon turned into an almost consuming passion. My first, inexpensive, acquisition was an early nineteenth-century sampler, moth-eaten but still retaining remarkably fresh colours. A few months later a much more un-likely item augmented my collection: a priest's stole of about 1730, with a gold background and with floral embroidery. I loved the technique of the work and the soft colouring. My next discovery set me on a course that left me almost besotted by the strange allure of needlework. The shop acquired a pair of late-seven-teenth-century English bed curtains of fine polychrome crewelwork. These were densely embroidered in chain stitch and depicted flowering oriental shrubs, exotic foliage, Chinese pheasants and large mythical birds with crested heads and flowing tail feathers (see p. 1). The design, although made in England, clearly reflected complementary patterns from Chinese wallpapers and Coromandel lacquer screens, each of the highly deco-ative kind that was made for export to Europe from the second half of the seventeenth century onwards.

When these bed curtains arrived in the shop, I fell in love with them and, my plight being observed, I was generously allowed to buy them, paying a small sum out of my wages each week. My excitement and interest in needlework was even further increased when I did some research and discovered two more larger curtains which together made up the complete set of four that had clearly been produced for a great state bed. It later transpired that they are virtually identical to the curtains on a magnificent bed at Houghton Hall, Norfolk, and the two sets must have been made together. The fascinating riddle now to be solved is whether all this particularly spectacular embroidery was professionally made and, if so, in whose workshops and where. The designs must certainly have been drawn out by professionals and it seems unlikely that the fine quality chain stitch embroidery was done by the ladies of a household. The Houghton bed has elaborate upholstery shapes and the needlework includes complex heraldry, which further suggests the unlikeli-ness of amateur workmanship.

That then is how my interest in this subject began. The field is almost limitless once you are involved in it and the dimensions, historically, nationally and inter-nationally, and in many different cultures, are totally absorbing for an enthusiast. An interest in looking at or collecting pieces from the past is in itself worthwhile, but is also essential as a background for the practice of modern embroidery (1, 2). It is in this respect that the traditions of the Royal School of Needlework are so valuable.

The Royal School of Needlework

In the wake of a renaissance of artistic design and a new interest in worthwhile craftsmanship, the School of Art Needlework, later known as the Royal School of Needlework, was founded in London in 1872. Under the presidency of Queen Victoria's daughter, Princess Christian of Schleswig-Holstein, its purpose was 'to supply suitable employment for poor gentlefolk' both in the restoration of old needlework and the creation of new. The committee consisted of distinguished and high-minded ladies such as Lady Marion Alford whose book, Needlework as Art (1886), epitomized the serious approach to the subject. The school employed over a hundred women and undertook commissions, working to designs by leading painters including Edward Burne-Jones, William Morris, Lord Leighton and Walter Crane. Prepared works were supplied for ladies to work in their own homes and the provision of set pieces soon became a substantial business and source of income. An 1880 advertisement for these indicates the practical nature of the pieces chosen for art needlework. Hangings, bed-covers, curtains, screens, tablecloths, cushions, chair-back covers and all sorts of borders were advocated, but the school also listed designs and materials for more curious accessories:

Tennis Aprons, Folding Screens, Kettledrum D'Oyleys, Photograph Frames, Bellows, Opera Cloaks, Piano Panels, Babies' Head Flannels, Knitting Pockets.

In fact the craze for art needlework would seem almost to have eclipsed the abundant Berlin work. An amusing cartoon in Punch, entitled 'Sweet Little Buttercup, or Art Embroidery 1879', depicted a languid female dressed in a garden of embroidery and surrounded by admiring animals in human clothes.

The Royal School of Needlework, however, persisted in its serious aims, and in giving training and employ-ment to the 'penurious women of gentle birth' as intended by its founders it encouraged high standards of workmanship. The quality of work produced was

3. A view of one of the workrooms in the Royal School of Needlework, London.

carefully checked and the school's success led to the formation of other needlework societies, such as the Decorative Needlework Society, The Ladies' Work Society and, among smaller organizations, the Wemyss Castle School in Scotland.

By the end of the century the Royal School was generally esteemed as a national institution, holding extensive exhibitions and having a wide influence. The start of a new building for it in 1899 was celebrated as something of a minor state occasion. The Prince of Wales laid the foundation stone, the Life Guards were paraded, the Royal College of Music performed and the Bishop of London offered a prayer before a rendering of The Old Hundreth. That building was in Exhibition Road, Kensington. Later, the Royal School moved to a nearby site in Prince's Gate, where it still is (3). It has continued to enjoy royal patronage and has had a tradition of undertaking such important commissions as the making and embroidery of coronation robes, including the one for HM Queen Elizabeth II. The most significant work made by the Royal School in modern times must, however, be the Overlord Embroidery, commissioned by Lord Dulverton, as a permanent memorial and record of the effort made by the Allies to liberate occupied Europe during the Second World War. This project is discussed later in this book (see page 201).

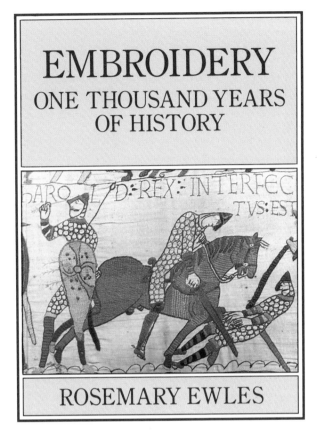

EMBROIDERY
ONE THOUSAND YEARS OF HISTORY

ROSEMARY EWLES

Those European embroideries that have survived to create a picture of the craft from the ninth to the fifteenth centuries are primarily ecclesiastical; and their survival has usually been due to their preservation in the treasuries of the churches for which they were originally made or to which they were later presented.

Our knowledge of the secular embroidery of the earliest centuries is more dependent upon documentary references and paintings, although these only provide evidence of the luxury textiles which enhanced the homes and persons of the court and aristocracy. We can but guess that embroidery had an important place within an ancient tradition of textile working in the home for domestic use. In much of Europe this would necessarily involve the use of locally produced wool and linen.

Embroidery was of course only one method of patterning fabric. The dyeing and weaving of textiles, particularly that most luxurious and iridiscent of fibres — silk — had reached a high level of development by the eleventh century in the Near East, Byzantium, Italy and Spain. The making of these patterned-weave silks represented one of the most sophisticated technologies which these countries had achieved. By the time these silks reached their markets, they were able to command extremely high prices.

1. *(opposite)* Detail of the Jesse cope, showing the Virgin and Child. English, 1295–1315. *(See also p. 237)*.

2. *(above)* Detail of the Bayeux Tapestry, showing the death of King Harold. Probably English, *c.* 1070.

For this reason patterned silks, although mechanically produced, enjoyed greater prestige than embroidery which depended entirely upon manual skill. This factor, which seems surprising today, has been reflected in the imitating of woven silks by embroiderers in many areas of Europe and the Near East at various periods. However, embroidery remained unrivalled for the adaptation of particular motifs to a shaped textile, for the emblazoning of arms and badges upon textiles of battle and ceremony, and, above all, for the depiction of religious narrative upon textiles for the church. When temporal or divine power was to be symbolized in the encrustation of fabric surfaces with gold, pearls and precious stones, it was embroidery that served the purpose.

The absence of a textile industry producing patterned-weave silks was no doubt a contributory factor in the emergence of a major embroidery industry in medieval England. Apart from the manufacture of fine wool cloths, many of which were exported to Italy for finishing and dyeing, this country did not in other respects command a trade in luxury textiles. While medieval embroideries survive from all other European countries, the oldest are attributed to England. During the thirteenth and fourteenth centuries English church embroidery enjoyed the highest reputation among foreign contemporaries.

The Reformation of the English Church in the early sixteenth century gave rise to the destruction or re-use for secular purposes of the greater part of the treasury of medieval embroidery which had accumulated in

England itself, and what escaped the reformers finally fell prey to the iconoclasts of the seventeenth century. Much of what remains of this great phase has survived in continental church treasuries.

Anglo-Saxon Embroidery

The earliest, and the oldest extant European embroidery, is a fragment of a vestment of about AD 850 at Maaseik in Belgium. Although in very poor condition it illustrates the sinuous and intertwined line incorporating animal forms which is characteristic of the Irish-Northumbrian School of manuscript painting, and has therefore been attributed to England. It is worked in surface-couched gold thread and coloured silks, and was formerly ornamented with pearls.

Within about fifty years we come to a much better documented set of Anglo-Saxon embroideries in the stole and maniple discovered in the tomb of St Cuthbert in Durham cathedral in the nineteenth century (3). Inscriptions incorporated into the design record that they were commissioned by Aelfflaed, the wife of Edward the Elder, for use by Bishop Frithstan of Winchester (909–31). Aelfflaed herself died in AD 916 and this enables us to place these embroideries within the seven-year period 909–16.

The stole and maniple were in all possibility made in the capital of Winchester. They bear a series of figures of ecclesiastics, saints, and prophets, set one above the other with, alongside, inscriptions of their names, and above and below, fleshy acanthus scrolls. The whole surface of the fabric is covered by the embroidery, which uses stem and split stitch for the figures and surface-couched gold thread for the ground. These fragments bear eloquent witness to the standard of embroidery in England at this early date, and the classical elements expressed in the figures and leaf ornament suggest that English artists were attuned to Carolingian influences from abroad.

There are references to embroidery in England from the seventh century but they do not enable us to gain a clear picture of those who most commonly embroidered: whether they were male or female, lay or cloistered, or indeed of noble blood. Chroniclers do make reference to particular noble women and nuns who were famed for their embroidery, but in commenting upon the talents of these individuals they may have been taking for granted among their readers knowledge of the existence of many humbler lay professionals. One Eanswitha, an embroiderer of Hereford, seems to have been such a secular figure who in AD 802 was granted a lease of a 200-acre farm for life upon condition that she would 'renew and

3. Fragments of the maniple of St Cuthbert; stem and split stitch with surface couching. English, 909–16.

4. Coronation mantle of the Holy Roman Emperors, probably made for Roger II of Sicily. Palermo, *c.* 1133.

scour, and from time to time add to, the dresses of the priests who served in the cathedral church'.

It was probably true throughout the Middle Ages that embroidery was carried out in a wide variety of circumstances. It had a strong domestic base, as with all crafts by which women had long provided for the needs of the home. It required no elaborate equipment, and could equally well be carried out in a town house, convent or queen's chamber. There was no stigma attached to manual labour if it were devoted to spiritual ends. The confessor of Queen Margaret of Scotland (1045–95) wrote that her chamber 'was like the workshop of a heavenly artist, there copes for singers, chasubles, stoles, altar cloths and other priestly and church vestments were always to be seen'.

The monastic communities, which multiplied and grew in importance throughout the period, were highly influential centres where the following of a holy Christian rule found no conflict with a life of useful manual work. As such these religious communities nurtured the artists and craftsmen who formed current artistic taste. Through travel, and contact with their mother houses on the continent, they were also the focus for assimilation of artistic influences from abroad.

The medieval artist was skilled in many techniques. St Dunstan (924–88) was a famous metalsmith, an illuminator, and 'designed embroideries for the pious Aedelthrym to execute'. Because of the close relationship

between works of art in different techniques, we must see the surviving embroideries of medieval England, and of Europe in general, as intimately connected in both style and iconography to the spirit of contemporary painting, and to other narrative media such as stained glass.

5. Silk mitre, showing martyrdom of St Thomas of Canterbury. English, late twelfth century.

The Bayeux Tapestry

Although commissioned by William the Conquerer's brother, Odo, Bishop of Bayeux, as a justification and a celebration of the Norman victory over the Anglo-Saxons, the Bayeux Tapestry is now assumed to be of English workmanship. It has been stylistically connected with the Canterbury School of manuscript painting.

Worked upon linen using coloured wools in laid and couched work and in outline stitch, it is indicative of the existence of a different class of embroidery from the gold-enriched church work at Durham. This is embroidery on a bold scale, the technique admirably suited to the textile's great size and to the economy of the drawing style. Although it is almost as familiar an artistic image as the Mona Lisa, no one actually seeing it for the first time can fail to be convinced afresh that this 1000-year-old embroidery still represents one of the greatest achievements of the craft (2).

It is known from contemporary texts that narrative embroideries of this type illustrating military episodes were not uncommon in Anglo-Saxon churches and houses. The Bayeux example, by accident of history, is the only one to come down to us. It is perhaps also a useful indication, on a grand scale, of the secular furnishing embroidery of the period, employing as it does the readily available materials of linen and wool. It foreshadows the bright and durable crewelwork hangings of the seventeenth and eighteenth centuries.

Church embroidery, and embroidery for the royal court, required the costly input of imported silk cloth and thread, and metal threads which were either pure beaten gold or gilded silver twisted around a fibre core. The application of pearls, precious stones, and gold medallions was common. Only the best would suffice for the Church. The illiterate laity might not understand the finer points of theological doctrine, but the splendid and lavish decoration which accompanied the liturgy was proper token of the awesome power of God manifested in His church on earth.

Between 1239 and 1244 King Henry III commissioned many vestments and church furnishings from an embroiderer named Mabel of Bury St Edmonds, as is shown by payments made to her for the work and to buy materials. For a chasuble and offertory veil ordered in 1239 Mabel was paid £10, the greater proportion of which would have been for materials, and she subsequently received two further payments of 100 shillings and 5 marks to complete, presumably the same, chasuble. At this period a small tenant farmer with a farm of about 20 acres would have had a reasonably comfortable existence on an income of £4 a year.

Despite variations in design, and to some extent in technique, the luxury embroideries of the Middle Ages all made use of silk and gold thread. A magnificent work produced some sixty years after the Bayeux Tapestry, and illustrative of a very different decorative tradition within Christendom, is the coronation mantle of the Holy Roman Empire, made in about 1133 in the Arab workshops of Palermo for the new Norman King of Sicily, Roger II (4). This is one of a group of Norman–Sicilian textiles and goldwork now in Vienna which were produced in established Islamic ateliers to meet the needs of a Christian ceremonial tradition. The double motif of a lion felling a camel with a date palm between is an ancient one here expressed in Saracenic form, and is worked in couched gold and pearls on a red satin ground.

At the same moment that this splendidly barbaric textile swathed the shoulders of a Norman Christian monarch at one extreme of Europe, Norman influence in Anglo-Saxon England was encouraging the adoption of the still formality of the Romanesque style in embroidery. This can be seen in surviving twelfth-century English pieces such as the fragments associated with St Thomas of Canterbury, now at Sens cathedral, France, and Erdington abbey, Birmingham (1140–70); the pair of buskins and an amice apparel from Archbishop Hubert Walter's tomb at Canterbury (1170–1200); and a fragment with a mounted knight at St John's Seminary, Wonersh, Berkshire (1180–1210). The designs of these embroideries are formal and often geometric, using roundels and diaper patterning. Animal forms are stylized and human figures have a solemn hieratic stillness. the mitre (5) is one of four in this style which survive, all showing embroidered versions of the death

of St Thomas of Canterbury. Historian Dr Agnes Geijer has suggested that they are 'the remains of an extensive serial production intended for distribution as propaganda for the cult of St Thomas'. This would indicate a workshop at Canterbury geared to producing many similar embroideries for a general market rather than to specific commission.

In technique all these embroideries show a development which is to characterize the best of English ecclesiastical work for the next 150 years. This is the use of underside couching for the metal threads. By this method the couching thread is used under the textile rather than on top, and pulls through tiny loops of the gold thread to secure it at the back. It has the effect of producing a uniformly smooth surface to the gold at the front and of breaking the resistant stiffness of the gold thread with hundreds of tiny hinges. This enabled the surface, particularly on vestments, to be liberally covered with gold thread while retaining the essential flexibility of the textile.

The skill of this technique can only produce wonder in the modern viewer: the metal threads are of a fineness rarely seen again in the history of embroidery (indeed this is one reason why it is well-nigh impossible to reproduce the effect today), and the minuteness of working, often using the couching stitches to produce geometric patterning within solid grounds, shows masterly manipulation of materials. In this group of twelfth-century embroideries we can see the technique well-established and, while it was by no means to be confined to England in the following 200 years, the facility with which it was practised by English embroiderers was perhaps one element in the international success of *opus anglicanum*.

6. Altar frontal, worked by Jacopo di Cambi in silks and silver-gilt threads, depicting the Coronation of the Virgin, with saints. Florence, Italy, *c.* 1336.

Opus Anglicanum

The term *opus anglicanum* (English work) was the usual designation of English church embroidery in medieval inventories. There are many references to successive popes either ordering vestments of *opus anglicanum* or receiving them as gifts. The historian Matthew Paris, writing of the year 1247, relates an anecdote concerning Pope Innocent IV, who having noticed that the vestments of certain English priests were 'embroidered in gold thread after a most desirable fashion', enquired after their origin. Learning that they were English, he sent letters to all the Cistercian abbots of England requesting that he be sent without delay 'those embroideries of gold which he preferred above all others, and with which he wished to decorate his chasubles and copes, as if these acquisitions would cost him nothing. This command of my Lord Pope did not displease the London merchants who traded in these embroideries and sold them at their own price.' So, we already have evidence at this early date of an established entrepreneurial trade in these textiles.

Whatever the outcome of the particular papal imperative related above, English work was very well represented in Rome by the end of that century. The Vatican Inventory of 1295 lists, among the *opus romanum* and *opus florentinum*, no fewer than 113 vestments and church furnishings of *opus anglicanum*: far outnumbering any other type of embroidery. Since, as we have seen, the techniques and materials used in

7. Linen burse showing the Coronation of the Virgin and the Crucifixion. English, *c.* 1310–40.

English embroidery did not significantly differ from those used in luxury embroideries in Italy itself at this period, it is interesting to speculate upon the special appeal of this work in southern Europe.

We can see from surviving examples that it exhibited the great technical assurance and refinement which reflect a long-established and flourishing craft tradition (7). By analogy, Chinese embroidery has always had something of this appeal to the West. The cost of imported decorated fabrics had stimulated the English embroidery industry into a high level of production for the home market, and when the export market was favourable, it was geared to supply the demand.

The Gothic Spirit

Superb quality of execution was married, during the thirteenth century, with designs which represented a fundamentally new artistic style. The Gothic style originated in France during the second half of the twelfth century and was rapidly transmitted to other European countries, particularly those to the north. In England, which had close political and ecclesiastical links with France, a style developed of manuscript illumination of a freshness and vigour which, in the early period, superseded that of France.

By contrast with the dignified symmetry and iconographical abstraction which characterized Romanesque design and representation, the Gothic spirit was conveyed in dynamic line and a new consciousness of the natural world. Although not realistic in terms of three-dimensionality or perspective, in its naturalistic detail and concern with emotional drama, it was closer to ordinary human experience than the ideals of Romanesque art. Gothic art found its appeal in a social climate which sought points of human contact in spiritual life: the humanizing tendency is also evident in new themes and subjects in church iconography. The life and maternal qualities of the Virgin Mary, the legends of the saints, an emphasis upon narrative cycle and genre detail: all these topics are given increasing emphasis and are conveyed in emotional terms ranging from lyrical devotion to tense excitement and grief.

This change was partly a reflection of doctrinal tendencies, but equally signified the interests of a growing middle class whose wealth was increasingly dictating the nature of commissions for the Church. Secular patronage demanded a religious art which was intelligible to the layman and which found sympathy with its own realistic and practical attitudes.

The early flourishing of a school of Gothic illumination in England was naturally echoed in embroidery, as the closest medium in which this expressive style might be utilized. The artists of illuminated books were in any case inevitably involved with embroidery design. We can therefore imagine that it was a combination of an early, developed Gothic style with superb technique which marked English vestments out for attention on the continent.

Surviving examples of Italian embroidery of around 1300 show that Roman and Florentine embroiderers had reached a stage of equal technical virtuosity. The altar frontal (**6**) signed by Jacopo di Cambi, made in Florence in about 1336, shows that, if anything, Italian embroidery could be even more lavish in its use of gold thread and decorative patterning. The split stitch used for the figures and draperies exactly conveys the sensitive shading of the artist's drawing. Yet in this, as in similar Venetian and Roman frontals of the period, the figure drawing exhibits an almost Byzantine calm and dignity very different from the drama and movement of the English Gothic embroideries.

Opus anglicanum reached its zenith in the first half of the fourteenth century. The geometric elements used to enclose figures and scenes seen on the Syon cope (**8**) developed into the scrolling, foliate compartments seen on those on the Jesse cope, also in the Victoria and Albert Museum (**1**), and finally into the elaborate architectural arcading of the copes now in Bologna (Italy) and Vich (Spain).

The production of embroidery by this date was increasingly concentrated in the hands of lay professionals; embroiderers and merchants who were both men and women. During the thirteenth century guilds of embroiderers appeared in many European cities and both young men and women were apprenticed to the craft. As time went on, however, the growth of formal controls and monopolies tended in general to favour male craftsmen in all fields. By the fifteenth century in England, women embroiderers were paid less than their male counterparts. When the Broderers' Livery Company was finally incorporated in 1561, all its officials were men, as was the case in Italy and France. It is male names that were recorded in connection with important commissions, or as appointed embroiderers to court and nobility. Women, while still no doubt involved in professional work, had by 1600 slipped into anonymity.

Secular Embroidery

We have so far concentrated almost entirely upon embroidery for the Church, but there are a few surviving examples which give an indication of how the same techniques – of silk split stitch combined with laid gold thread – were used upon rich objects for secular use.

The records of every European country show that royalty, nobility and the rising gentry commissioned embroidery for costume, domestic furnishings, horse trappings, tents, flags and banners, and that this was frequently lavish and of the most costly materials. The single most expensive item of English furniture recorded during the Middle Ages was Queen Philippa's bed with hangings of green velvet embroidered with sea sirens, which cost the sum of £203. The intrinsic value of such

8. The Syon cope. Silver-gilt and silver threads and coloured silks in underside couching with split stitch on a linen ground. Originally a chasuble, but later reduced in size and the heraldic orphrey and borders added. English, *c.* 1300–20.

9. Detail of the orphrey of the Butler Bowden cope. English, 1330–50.

10. (*opposite*) Red velvet heraldic panel, one of two converted into a chasuble. English, mid-fourteenth century.

textiles was so great that it was perfectly acceptable for owners to give or bequeath them for church use. In 1398 John of Gaunt bequeathed bed hangings of cloth of gold embroidered with roses and ostrich feathers for use on the high altar of St Paul's cathedral.

There is probably a similar story behind the magnificent heraldic panels in the Musée Cluny in Paris, (10) which date from the mid-fourteenth century, and are embroidered with couched gold thread on red velvet. These may represent a horse trapping later converted into a chasuble. The heraldic leopards are set against a field of foliage enlivened with small lay figures. The embroidery has been attributed at various times to France, the Lower Rhine region, and to England.

A number of fourteenth-century purses survive from France, which seems to have specialized in their manufacture. The Parisian embroiderers' guild regulations of the thirteenth century refer, among various classes of worker, to the 'makers of Saracen purses', indicating that these flat, square or triangular purses were considered an Eastern fashion. They frequently depict romantic or chivalric scenes such as a pair of lovers, now in Hamburg (11), executed in laid gold thread, with silk split stitch used for the figures. Although small objects, these purses provide a glimpse of the delicate craftsmanship and elegant stylishness which must have typified much secular embroidery of the period.

Other Techniques

As distinct from the techniques used on these pieces, there is good evidence of the established use of other embroidery techniques in the later Middle Ages. An altar frontal from Bamberg cathedral of c. 1300 is solidly worked with rows of fine chain stitch in coloured silks and gold thread. Secular hangings from Lower Saxony, showing scenes from the popular Tristam legend, are worked in coloured silks using *Klosterstich* (convent stitch), in which a thread is couched with another of the same colour. *Klosterstich* hangings in both silk and wool continued to be an important feature of Swiss and German embroideries until the seventeenth century. They were frequently imitative of tapestry-woven hangings, providing a further example of domestic and convent embroiderers copying more expensive, professionally made textiles in other techniques.

All-over embroidery which was counted over the threads of the ground fabric (what we would call canvas work embroidery) was also to become an important method of imitating tapestries and pile carpets. Stitches which may be classed as part of the canvas work repertoire seem to have been in common use in medieval Europe. An outstanding set of vestments of the mid-thirteenth century, executed at the convent of Göss in Austria, are of all-over silk embroidery which is primarily slanted gobelin stitch. The English stole (12) dates from between 1290 and 1340. It is worked in long-armed cross stitch, a technique to be much in evidence from the sixteenth century, particularly in Italy and the countries bordering the Mediterranean.

Quilting, that is, the inserting of wadding between two layers of fabric, and stitching through all thicknesses to keep the wadding in place, is an ancient technique which derived from the need to make textiles warmer and thicker. The wadded bed quilt still reflects this function. Quilting is also known to have been used

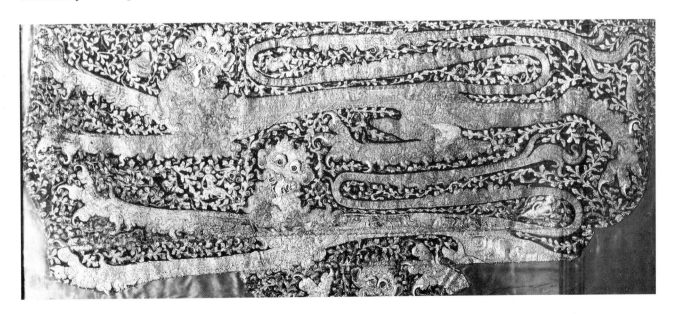

as an adjunct to armour, both to provide additional protection and to prevent chafing. It is not surprising to see that the decorative qualities of quilting were being exploited at an early stage, as is shown by the remarkable Sicilian cover of about 1400, which is now in two pieces: one in the Victoria and Albert Museum, London, and the other in the Palazzo Davanzati, Florence (13). It is an enormous textile made from two layers of linen wadded with wool, and illustrates scenes from the Tristam legend within square compartments, each described in the Sicilian dialect.

Whitework embroidery too must have had a long existence as suitable for ornamenting linen which was regularly washed. During the Middle Ages Switzerland and Germany produced professional whitework embroidery in such quantity, that this technique was designated *opus teutonicum* in medieval inventories. White embroidered church linen comprised such items as altar cloths, chalice veils and large Lenten veils intended to act as curtains to conceal the high altar from the choir and congregation during Lent. The fourteenth-century Swiss cover (14) is a table cloth probably for secular use, and shows a wide variety of surface stitches, including blocked satin, brick and interlacing.

Embroideries in linen and wool used materials local to Europe, and were accordingly less expensive textiles devoted to humbler purposes than the work in silks and gold thread. This type of embroidery shows the first distinct evidence of a convent and domestic tradition developing along different lines from that of professional work. The former embraced a wide variety of stitches and techniques which could be employed to meet changes in secular fashion; the latter drew to itself primacy in the field of the metal thread embroidery and fine painterly silk work which continued to characterize embroidery for church and civic ceremonial.

Late Gothic Embroidery

By the late fourteenth century we have a far greater range of surviving European textiles by which to appreciate the various schools of Gothic church embroidery. One particular group which might be singled out as particularly expressive of the Gothic ideal are those embroideries, mainly chasuble orphreys, produced in Prague under the patronage of Charles IV of Bohemia. They are characterized by large figure groups worked in

11. *(opposite)* Embroidered linen purse with romantic scene. French, fourteenth century.

12. *(right)* End of embroidered linen stole using long-armed cross stitch. English, 1290–1340.

13. Detail of linen cover wadded with wool. depicting the story of Tristam. Sicily, *c.* 1400.

14. *(below left)* Detail of a linen tablecloth. Swiss, fourteenth century.

15. *(below right)* Embroidered chasuble. Bohemia, *c.* 1380–90.

split stitch, usually on plain gold grounds. The silk embroidery is so fine as to lose nothing of the artist's original shading. The orphrey cross (15) (mounted upon a later chasuble) is one of the loveliest examples of this school, despite having been cut up and re-aligned. The Virgin, crowned and supported by two angels whose wings extend into the branches of the orphrey, holds up a lively Christ Child. The lower part of the cross contains a gentle Annunciation. Both are masterly compositions of curving line; their scale, and the soft gradations of light and shade, produce an effect of dramatic immediacy.

There is no doubt that the designs of such professional embroideries were generally provided by artists. The romantic notion that medieval and later embroideries were entirely the product of one brain and hand is one that has arisen from late nineteenth century theories of what constituted 'good craft'.

In *The Book of the Art* of 1437 the Italian painter Cennino Cennini instructs painters that they will be sometimes called upon to provide embroideries with various sorts of designs. He describes how the design should be drawn onto the cloth with charcoal, over-drawn in ink, and then wetted so that the shadows, executed with a soft miniver brush, would be subtly graded. He also gives instructions for designs on velvet.

Threads of Gold

English church embroidery declined in quality during the latter part of the fourteenth century as the patterned silks of Italy rose in popularity and in availability. With their products less in demand the embroiderers attempted to speed up production by adopting simpler techniques. Underside couching was generally abandoned by 1450, and mass production was assisted by embroidering many small motifs for application to imported Italian velvets. The celebrity which the English arts, and particularly embroidery, had enjoyed in the thirteenth century was dissipated by the fifteenth century. The market had changed, and the industry, suffering from the social and economic effects of plague and sustained warfare, was unable to adapt.

Supremacy in this field was transferred to the embroidery workshops of Flanders, whose style and technique had great influence in Europe from 1450 to 1550. The English cope hood of about 1460–90 (16) already shows the influence of the Flemish drawing style in its perspective and heavy, massed draperies. Flemish embroidery production was stimulated by the patronage of the highly cultured and extravagant court of the Dukes of Burgundy. It was probably a commission from Duke Philip the Good which initiated the creation of the most magnificent set of embroideries to emanate from these workshops.

The mass vestments of the Order of the Golden Fleece, first mentioned in an inventory of the Order in 1477, are thought to have been made over the period 1425–75 and consist of copes, dalmatics, a chasuble, altar frontal and dossal. It is assumed that they are the work of a Brussels workshop. They show the use of a new goldwork technique which enabled embroidery to reach the heights of pictorial accuracy (17), and to render light and perspective in such a way that the naturally reflective surface of the stitches contributed to the illusion. This technique was *or nué*, or 'shaded gold', in which the gold threads were laid horizontally across the surface of the fabric cartoon, and couched down with coloured silk threads using vertical stitches. The stitches were most densely placed where shadow was deepest, and most widely spaced over the high lights, so that the image was created in gold light and coloured shadow. The realism which could be achieved by this method is well illustrated in the Brussels Mass Vestments. The saints in their architectural niches, and the Virgin enthroned upon the hood, have a startling three-dimensional quality: we are seeing Flemish

16. Cope hood using split, brick, and long and short stitches with couched work. English, *c.* 1460–90.

17. Mantle of the Virgin, from the mass vestments of the Order of the Golden Fleece. Netherlands, probably Brussels, mid-fifteenth century.

panel painting rendered into a flexible medium. This set of vestments also retains its seed pearls and semi-precious gem stones, providing us with a rare glimpse of late medieval church embroidery in pristine condition.

The *or nué* technique was to be seen in the embroideries of other major European countries from the late fifteenth century, and remained an important part of the professional embroiderer's repertoire into the eighteenth century. Its suitability for the rendition of three-dimensionality and perspective naturally found favour in Italy, where painters were exploring a much more substantial realism than that of the Gothic North. Thus we have surviving examples of Italian *or nué* embroidery worked after designs by Pollaiuolo, Botticelli and Andrea del Sarto.

The Catalan altar cloth in the Chapel of St George in Barcelona (18) was worked in about 1460 by Antoni Sadurni. It already shows the confident use of *or nué*, but with added realism created by padding. In the central figures of St George and the Dragon, painterly realism

18. Altar frontal by Antonio Sadurni. Barcelona, *c.* 1460.

has been extended to sculptural realism. A growing taste for raised effects is noticeable in late medieval European embroidery, and is a marked feature of both fifteenth- and sixteenth-century metal thread work; taken to its greatest extreme in south and east Germany, Austria, Hungary, and Poland, where gold thread was laid over almost completely rounded carved wooden forms applied to vestments and civic badges.

THE SIXTEENTH CENTURY

By 1500 the North Italian city states represented a high concentration of the most advanced capital enterprise in Europe. Their merchants and bankers commanded enormous wealth, and financed most of the royal courts of Europe, including the Papacy. The patronage of this powerful upper middle class played a significant role in stimulating and directing the artistic and intellectual impulses which constituted the phenomenon known as the Renaissance.

It was a social process in which the largest cities of northern Europe were not far behind: the Renaissance ideals which glorified the individual seemed appropriate to all coming men with a desire to impress the world with their wealth and status. During the sixteenth century this wealth was to be increasingly devoted to secular purposes: towards providing more comfortable and splendid houses, and lavish personal show. The unprecedented demand for luxury goods created by these conditions included embroidery. It was used for wall and bed hangings, cushions, upholstery, table covers and table carpets, and, in the elaborate formal costume of the latter half of the sixteenth century, embroidery had an importance hardly equalled in the subsequent history of dress.

Italian painters were primarily concerned with three-dimensional and spatial realism, and while the significant developments in this direction were translated to some extent into other media (including, as we have noted, into embroidery through the use of *or nué*), pictorial representation in the crafts became, on the whole, subservient to surface ornament. Realistic narrative scenes in embroidery, for example upon vestments, were confined to cartouches and roundels within a scheme of decorative patterning. Up to this point embroidery, always reliant for its designs upon the lead taken by contemporary artists, had been closely in the vanguard of the predominant painterly style. The bifurcation of fine art and applied ornament which occurred during the Renaissance inevitably took embroidery the way of the latter. It also tended towards the demotion of the craftsman to artisan level, while the

esteem given to the art of painting elevated its practitioners to new social heights. Although embroiderers would continue to imitate paintings in future centuries, painters rarely again designed specifically for the medium of embroidery.

Influential Designs

The sixteenth century was a great pattern-making age, and one in which artists showed wide eclecticism in their use of sources for ornament. The most innovative themes naturally stemmed from Italy. The 'grotesque' style was derived from the interior decoration of Roman private houses excavated in the late fifteenth century amid enthusiasm for exploring Italy's antique past. The wall paintings revealed were in a hitherto unknown style, and were copied by Raphael in the decoration of a loggia in the Vatican Palace. Named 'grotesque' from their discovery in what appeared by then to be caves or grottoes, these designs were rapidly adapted for more general application. The style was composed of linear patterns incorporating acanthus leaf and swags, architectural detail, medallions, urns, and semi-fantastic animal and human forms. It became the mode by which the classicizing tendencies of Italian art were first assimilated into Northern ornament. In France the grotesque style was highly popular for embroidered hangings and bed furnishings from the 1540s (**23**). The usual technique employed was that of applying the motifs, which were cut from a light coloured satin, onto a darker satin ground, and working the outlines and details in stitchery.

The grotesque style produced the effect of a formally symmetrical, but airy, linear design. To this influence was added ornament taken from Moorish, Turkish and Arab art which Italian craftsmen absorbed through the trading centres of Genoa and Venice. It was a moment when the heritage of Islamic non-figurative design found great receptiveness in Europe. From these sources derived 'mooresque' and 'arabesque' ornament, both essentially repeating, linear and interlaced. The geometric designs of imported Eastern carpets were also of influence in the textile field, and were added to this rich mixture along with the inherited medieval tradition of diapered, and scrolling floral, ornament.

Early Pattern Books

Such patterns were transmitted to countries like England not only through the importation of Italian luxury goods and Italian craftsmen, but also, for the first time, through the medium of print. In the field of embroidery, as in every other aspect of cultural life, the printed page made it possible to disseminate ideas with unprecedented rapidity, and to a much wider audience.

Books were published containing patterns intended for use in various crafts. The earliest, surviving, publication containing designs specifically for embroidery appeared in Germany in 1524, and was soon followed by others in Italy, France, and England. An English example was *Morysse and Damashin Renewed and Encreased. Very Profitable for Goldsmythes and Embroyderars* published by Thomas Geminus in 1548 (19).

19. Page from *Morysse and Damashin Renewed and Encreased. Very Profitable for Goldsmythes and Embroyderars.* Thomas Geminus, 1548.

20. *(left)* Four linen borders. The widest is worked on a loosely woven linen mesh *(buratto)*. Italian, seventeenth century.

21. *(opposite)* Detail of an insertion of lacis (knotted linen mesh darned with linen thread). About 130 mm (5 in) long.

Far more similar embroidery pattern books were no doubt published, but most have been destroyed because their pages were removed and used as designs to be pricked and pounced onto fabric.

They frequently contained designs for repeating borders combining elements of the grotesque, arabesque, or simply geometric styles. This class of border pattern was widespread in sixteenth- and seventeenth-century Europe, and endured even longer in peasant embroidery. The designs were adapted to edge a shirt or handkerchief, or to border sheets and covers, and were commonly worked in one colour of silk using stitches suited to linear pattern, such as double running. Italian examples often show the ground solidly worked in cross or long-armed cross stitch, and the design voided (20).

Other embroidery pattern books contained designs on a squared ground for use in counted thread embroidery, or for lacis – darning on a hand-knotted square net mesh (21). This latter whitework technique had been used during the Middle Ages but enjoyed renewed popularity during the sixteenth and early seventeenth centuries as insertions for domestic and church linen covers.

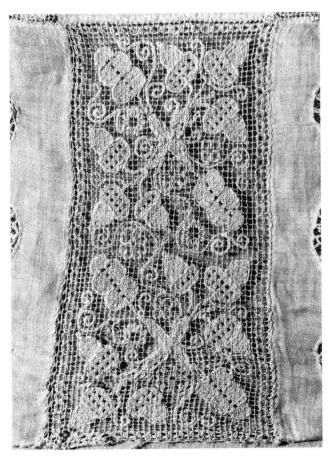

A significant feature of most pattern books was that they were intended for the amateur embroiderer. This is reflected in flowery dedications to noble women of the day. The Venetian, Federico Vinciolo, whose popular *Singulaires et Nouveaux Pourctraits pour les Ouvrages de Lingerie* of 1587 ran to more than ten editions, was personal designer to Catherine de Medici, Queen of France, and supplied patterns for her own needlework. His book was dedicated to his royal mistress. Noble embroiderers had been frequently noted by medieval historians, usually in connection with service to the Church, but the notion of the needlewoman of rank was now something subtly different. It has often been said that this century truly sees the rise of the amateur embroiderer, and indeed, changing economic and social arrangements as exemplified by guild rules were tending to exclude women from the professional practice of the craft. At the same time opinion regarding appropriate education and rightful occupation for women not forced to labour for their bread approved the practice of embroidery at home. Rozsika Parker, in her recent study of the history of attitudes to embroidery and embroidering women, quotes a significant statement by the Italian, Federico Luigini, writing in 1554:

> The needle belongs to all women both high and low, but where the poor find only utility in these arts, the rich, the noble, and beautiful lady wins honour also.

From this period skill in embroidery became the mark of the cultured gentlewoman, a status to which every merchant's wife aspired.

It is nevertheless sometimes extremely difficult to assign surviving sixteenth-century secular embroideries to the hand of either professional or amateur, unless it is a piece which bears all the hallmarks of a sizeable commission. There is little divergence between the designs and techniques of each at the level of embroidery for costume and the home. The court, and most major households, employed the services of professional embroiderers, or pattern drawers, if not permanently, then at least on an occasional basis, and these individuals might oversee and partake in the embroidery projects embarked upon by the lady of the house.

English domestic embroidery of the second half of the sixteenth century was of a richness and character unrivalled on the continent; perhaps still partly due to the lack of a native silk-weaving industry. The tradition of ecclesiastical embroidery had come to an abrupt halt with the Reformation and, despite a brief revival under Archbishop Laud in the early seventeenth century, went into abeyance for over 300 years. Many of the old church embroideries which escaped destruction were sold off to be re-used for their rich materials. A later historian of the period recorded that:

> Many private men's parlours were hung with copes instead of carpets and coverlids . . . it was a sorry house and not worth naming which did not have something of this furniture in it, though it were only a fair, large cushion made of a cope or altar cloth.

A late altar frontal (**22**) illustrates the techniques commonly in use at this time. It was commissioned by Sir Ralph Nevill in 1535–55 and shows himself and his family kneeling either side of a crucifixion. The technique, developed in the fifteenth century, of applying individually worked motifs to a velvet ground, is also seen in contemporary civic pieces such as livery company funeral palls.

Little English embroidery survives from the first half of the sixteenth century, by comparison with the relatively numerous examples of Elizabethan and Jacobean embroidery. However, the new art of portraiture enables us to see something of how embroidery was being employed on fashionable dress in the earlier years of the century.

22. (*above*) Detail of an altar frontal showing Sir Ralph Nevill and his sons. English, 1535–55.

23. (*right*) Bedhead in the 'grotesque' style. French, *c*. 1550–60.

The miniature of Margaret Throckmorton, Mrs Robert Pemberton, painted by Hans Holbein in about 1536 (24), illustrates the fashion for monochromatic, linear or geometric embroidery, here used on the collar and cuffs of the linen chemise. It can be seen in many portraits of both men and women from this date, and grows in importance as the display of white linen against deep-toned velvets and figured silks becomes more marked. The designs used in this portrait are typical of the type found in early pattern books, owing something to Italianate border designs and something to North European geometric tradition. The technique most commonly used for this embroidery was double running stitch, sometimes called Holbein stitch after the artist who so often recorded its use.

24. Miniature of Margaret Throckmorton showing geometric blackwork on the collar and cuffs. Hans Holbein, c. 1536.

A boy's shirt of about 1540, in the Victoria and Albert Museum, has very similar embroidery to that on Mrs Pemberton's chemise, but is worked in blue silk using cross stitch, and the running, interlaced pattern incorporates columbine heads (*see p. 131*). Increasingly English embroiderers transformed formal Italianate ornament into traceries filled with recognizable flowers. These border patterns continued in popularity well into the seventeenth century (25), and were still recorded upon young girl's samplers long after they had ceased to have any practical use.

The favoured colour combination for this work was black silk upon white linen, which provided the greatest dramatic contrast. By Elizabeth's reign 'blackwork' embroidery was no longer confined to borders but had expanded into the all-over, coiling stem patterns so characteristic of Elizabethan and Jacobean embroidery. The sleeve (26) is typical of one class of blackwork in which fine detail and shading were achieved with the use of speckling stitches within outlines made with line stitches. In other, more formal, patterns intricate fillings were created using minute, counted, straight stitches (27). The marked taste for monochromatic embroidery was no doubt influenced by the proliferation of printed design which was still a recent enough phenomenon to be considered a novelty to be enjoyed. This connection is given weight by a fragment of linen in the Victoria and Albert Museum which is printed with an all-over design of animals, birds and flowers, and partly embroidered with black silk.

Elizabethan Embroidery

The designs used in Elizabethan embroidery, with their closely scrolling floral patterns, were quite unknown on the continent. The prevailing style in Italian and French embroidery incorporated floral motifs, but these were highly stylized and regimented within formal patterns. Professional embroiderers in these countries favoured completely abstract schemes of scrollwork arranged in repeats which reflected woven silk designs. This is well illustrated by the Italian chasuble of about 1600–1629 (28) which epitomizes a formality in continental ornament which would continue to balance and control even the exuberant floral blooms of the Baroque.

By contrast, English embroidery exhibited a busy informality (29) and was crowded with detail which included flowers, animals, birds and insects. Embroiderers turned not only to books of ornamental pattern but also to herbals and bestiaries. The latter brought together extant knowledge (and some fantasy) about the physical world, and were full of pictures providing a rich source of subject matter for the amateur. Two of the most widely used books were John Gerarde's *Herbal or Generall Historie of Plantes* (1597) and Konrad von Gesner's *Historia Animalium* (1560). Individual motifs taken from such books, particularly small flower sprigs or 'slips', were worked separately and applied to silk or velvet in much the way that professional embroiderers had been doing since the previous century. The usual technique employed was canvas work in silk using tent stitch. Once attached, the perimeter of the motifs was overlaid with a thick silk thread, couched down to conceal the edges, and finer details of stems or insect legs might be worked over onto the ground fabric with stem stitch. Applied slips were usually used for furnishing textiles such as cushion covers (30) and hang-

25. *(above)* Linen handkerchief embroidered with silk. English, *c.* 1600.

26. *(above right)* Panel for a sleeve. English, *c.* 1600.

27. *(below)* Man's linen nightcap, trimmed with gilt bobbin lace edged with spangles. English, early seventeenth century.

28. *(below right)* Chasuble of Bishop Madruzzo of Trento. Italian, *c.* 1600–29.

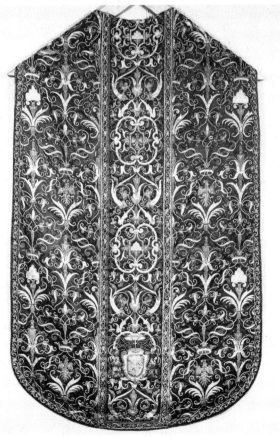

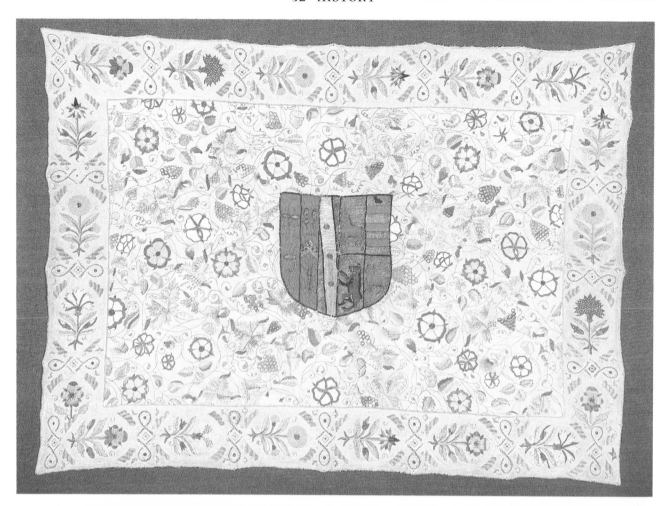

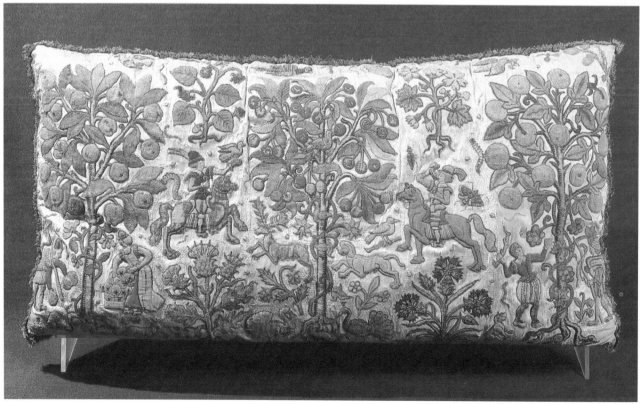

29. *(opposite above)* Cover with arms of Grenville impaling Bevill. English, *c.* 1592.

30. *(opposite below)* White satin cushion. English, *c.* 1575–1600.

31. *(right)* Velvet bed hanging. English, Hardwick Hall, late sixteenth century.

ings (**31**), although the same growing sprigs of flowers were also embroidered directly onto silk grounds using other techniques in costume embroidery.

Motifs in general contained a wealth of symbolic meaning which could be 'read' by the contemporary viewer at a period when allegory and allusion were literary and artistic conventions. The choosing of emblematic designs and 'impresas' – personal badges conveying symbolic meaning – was, one senses, as much a part of the pleasure of amateur embroidery as the stitching itself. In this one might turn to such books as *Choice of Emblemes* published by Geoffrey Whitney in 1586, or Claude Paradin's *Devises Héroïques* of 1557.

The Art of Canvas Work

Mary Queen of Scots, so recently Queen of France, turned to this latter French book for some of the designs she used in working part of the set of hangings now, in the main, preserved at Oxburgh Hall in Norfolk. She is one of the most famous examples of the noble embroideress. Brought up in France from the age of six, her mother-in-law to be was Catherine de Medici, who had herself received a convent training in needlework. Embroidery was obviously one of Mary's few solaces

during her twenty-year imprisonment in England, and it was fortunate that at least some of her custody was spent in the company of the equally prolific embroiderer Bess of Hardwick, Countess of Shrewsbury. Mary had brought her personal embroiderer, Pierre Oudry, with her from France and he may have assisted her in adapting designs and drawing them onto canvas.

The medallions and panels of the Oxburgh hangings are all worked in tent stitch using coloured silks on linen canvas. Many are directly taken from Paradin's emblem book. The central panel of the Marian hanging shows a vine with a sickle and is inscribed VIRESCIT VULNERE VIRTUS' (virtue flourishes by a wound); a reference to her treatment at the hands of her cousin Elizabeth I (*see p. 86*). The panels of the Oxburgh hangings, although probably remounted at a later date, are of value as some of the few surviving embroideries in which Mary is definitely known to have had a hand. Moreover they perfectly illustrate the type of furnishing embroidery undertaken by the upper class amateur.

Canvas work clearly emerged at this stage as the amateur embroidery technique *par excellence*. It was simple to learn, yet permitted the translation of pictorial devices into stitch with full subtlety of shading.

32. Fragment of a bed valance. French or Flemish, *c.* 1580.

It was hard-wearing, and became widely used from this century for furnishing embroidery, particularly for bed valances, cushions, and carpets. A large number of long, narrow bed valances survive from the last quarter of the century, worked in silk and wool in tent stitch, which have narrative subjects, both biblical and classical, told in a series of scenes along their length. Whatever the subject matter, they are essentially representations of men and women richly attired in court dress, disporting themselves in idealized formal gardens (32). They are frequently adapted from Flemish and French engravings, and the court dress shown is French in fashion. They are found in Flanders, England, Scotland and France, and it may be that they represent the output of a French professional workshop, some-times copied by professional and amateur embroiderers of the countries to which they were exported.

The canvas work table carpet is another class of item which seems clearly to have been the subject of pro-fessional production although not beyond the skill of a patient amateur to copy. Imported Turkish carpets had been a desirable luxury in European homes for some hundred years. Their value was such that they were used to cover tables and cupboards rather than floors. It was natural that native embroiderers should be called

upon to produce copies. European table carpets were sometimes made in direct imitation of Eastern carpets, and at other times took the plan of a rectangular textile with a field and borders and incorporated more familiar ornament. Such an example is the late sixteenth-century Bradford table carpet in the Victoria and Albert Museum (33), one of the largest and most magnificent English table carpets to survive. It is worked in coloured silks on linen canvas using tent stitch with about 60 stitches to 1 sq cm (400 to 1 sq in). The central field is a trellis enclosing bunches of grapes, and the borders are continuous landscapes containing buildings, animals, and figures, many of them engaged in day-to-day occupations. It has a parallel with the interest in genre subjects shown in contemporary tapestries and em-broideries of Flanders, Germany and Switzerland.

Counted thread embroidery was not only used for enormous items like carpets, but also for small objects such as the purse with matching pincushion illustrated (34). This is typical of the square, flat purses called 'sweet bags' which have survived in some number, and which are commonly mentioned in the lists of New Year gifts made to Queen Elizabeth.

The decades between 1580 and 1630 saw the height of lavishness and ingenuity in English secular embroi-

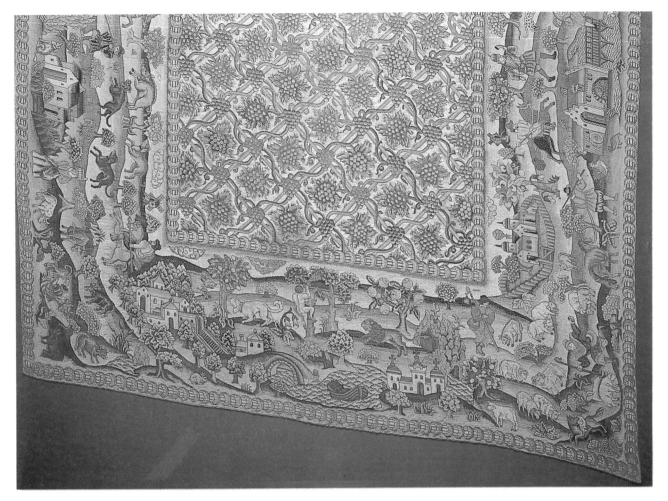

33. *(above)* Detail of the Bradford table carpet. English, late sixteenth century.

34. *(left)* Purse with matching pincushion. English, early seventeenth century.

dery. Nowhere was this more evident than in costume. The fashions of this period reached a peak of decorative extravagance which focused upon the Queen and her courtiers, and was aped by the gentry and merchants who formed part of the circle of London society. Expenditure upon dress was phenomenal, and is so frequently commented upon by contemporary writers, that their complaints cannot simply be the result of the dissatisfaction with changing times found in every century. A German visitor to London in 1592 commented that many women 'do not hesitate to wear velvet in the streets, which is common with them, whilst at home perhaps they have not a piece of dry bread'. Another observed the men's dress and their extravagant hats, ruffs, embroidered shirts, and doublets 'slashed, jagged, cut, carved, pinched and laced . . . and stuffed with four five or six pounds of bombast at the least'. The Earl of Arundel, to give an example of aristocratic expenditure, owed £1023 to forty-two mercers, silkmen, tailors, embroiderers, and other tradesmen.

THE SEVENTEENTH CENTURY

By this date embroidery might be used to decorate an entire gown, doublet and hose, quite apart from separate items such as stomachers, sleeves, partlets, gloves and ruffs. The value lay not so much in the labour, as in the materials and trimmings, particularly the gold and silver thread, spangles and braid. The predominant decorative style was the all-over scrolling stem pattern enclosing flower heads, executed either in coloured silks or black silk, and inevitably enriched with gold and silver thread. The series of early seventeenth-century portraits by William Larkin in the Suffolk Collection, Rangers House, Blackheath, well illustrate this apogee of extravagance in dress.

Richard Sackville, 3rd Earl of Dorset (*see p.* 140), painted in 1613, is wearing clothes described in an inventory of 1617:

> . . . one doublett of cloth of silver embroadered all over in slips of sattin black and gold . . . one cloake of uncutt velvett blacke laced with seaven embroadered laces of gold and blacke silke, and above the borders powdred with slipps of sattin embroadered with gold and lyned with shagg of black silver and gold . . . one pair of white silke stockings embroadered with gold, silver, and blacke silke.

The earl's gloves, which have gauntlets embroidered to match his doublet, had obviously disappeared by the date of the inventory.

Isabella Rich (**38**) is wearing a bodice embroidered in gold and coloured silks with the characteristic English floral pattern. Her petticoat is embroidered with a more formal floral design in the continental style, and this too is worked in coloured silks and gold and is bordered with gold bobbin lace edged with spangles. The table upon which she is leaning is covered with a velvet cloth embroidered and fringed with gold. Both she and the 3rd Earl wear lace cuffs and stand upon Turkey carpets.

In an embroidery such as the woman's coif (**35**) we have an actual example of the class of embroidery illustrated on Isabella Rich's bodice. Coifs were informal women's headwear in very common use at this period, judging by the number which survive, although they are rarely recorded in formal portraits. The example here is opened out flat. The embroidery on this and similar examples shows great technical distinction. The stems are worked in plaited braid stitch and the coloured silk flower heads and leaves, in a variety of detached buttonhole fillings, in which the needle only enters the fabric at the beginning and end of each row. The stitches are otherwise worked into the row above so that the embroidery creates a patch of needle-made fabric which is akin to knitting.

This range of detached filling stitches is particularly characteristic of English embroidery at this date, and continues in amateur work throughout the seventeenth century. They are not techniques in evidence before the sixteenth century, and show one of the ways in which the embroiderer's repertoire grew at this time. Detached buttonhole stitch is the basic stitch used to make needle-point lace, which developed as a professional product in North Italy in the late sixteenth century.

Whitework Embroidery

As fashion placed increasing importance upon the decoration of linen shirts and chemises which were intended to be seen at the neck and wrist, the techniques of whitework embroidery were expanded accordingly.

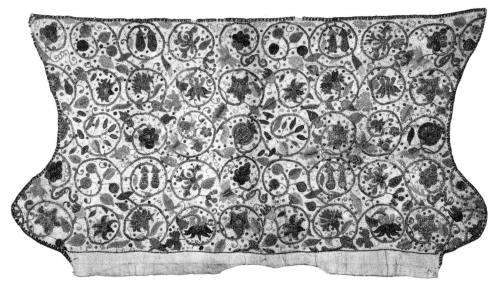

35. Coif of linen embroidered with coloured silks and silver-gilt thread. English, *c.* 1600.

36. Standing collar of cutwork. Italian, probably Venice *c.* 1610.

37. *(below)* Detail of a whitework sampler. English, mid- to late seventeenth century.

The sixteenth century saw the development of open work effects, which reached a peak at the end of the century when court dress dictated a starched, standing ruff. Threads were withdrawn from the ground linen, or sections of the fabric entirely cut away. The remaining edges were buttonholed and complex fillings were worked into the remaining spaces, again using buttonhole stitch over diagonally laid bridge threads. Tiny loops or picots were worked along the various edges, and detached buttonhole stitch was used to create free, infilling motifs in the manner described above. The fineness of the cutwork embroidery (Italian *reticella*) reached the stage where little of the original linen warp and weft remained (36). It was a technique also used for other fine linen items such as aprons and covers.

At some point professional cutwork embroiderers abandoned the use of the ground linen altogether, and

38. Portrait of Isabella Rich, by William Larkin, showing embroidered bodice and petticoat. English, 1615.

39. *(opposite)* Sampler showing nine different stitches with laid, couched and pulled work. English, mid- to late seventeenth century.

simply worked their buttonhole stitches over a grid of threads tacked over a parchment pattern. This constituted the first true needlelace. Bobbin lace had meanwhile emerged as a distinct technique at a slighter earlier date, having developed from the plaiting and weaving techniques employed in making trimming braids. Both needle and bobbin lace followed the fashionable requirement of geometric form until about 1620, so that it is often difficult to establish whether the lace worn in portraits is cutwork, needlelace or bobbin lace.

Many pattern books containing designs for cutwork were published, showing that, like lacis, it was a popular technique among amateur embroiderers. As lace designs became more organic and scrolling, cutwork, tied to the geometric base of its woven ground, was abandoned for costume items. However, it remained in use for decorating domestic linen for much longer and was one of the main forms of embroidery learned by young girls in the course of acquiring proficiency in needlework. It was thus still a feature of samplers in the late seventeenth century (37).

The Rise of Amateur Embroidery

The development of the sampler, and its proliferation in every European country from the sixteenth century, accompanied the rise of amateur embroidery. We may assume that a reference cloth which recorded patterns and stitches had been long in use among both professional and domestic embroiderers, but from the late fifteenth century, European documentary references tend to link them with the noble or gentlewoman embroidering for pleasure. They survive in great quantities from the seventeenth century from all over Europe, and by this date are clearly the work of young girls who frequently signed and dated them. The example illustrated (39) is a typical English sampler of the type which collected together many motifs and small blocks of all-over repeating pattern – often called spot samplers.

Such samplers show that girls were continuing to learn many of the diverse and complicated stitches of the late sixteenth century, with a similar use of gold and silver thread combined with coloured silks, and repeating patterns. This example is worked in rococo, tent, eyelet, chain, Florentine, cross, double running, raised braid and interlacing stitches with couched and pulled work. The bird, insect, and flowers are traditional subjects of sixteenth-century slips, and the central panel containing obelisks and flowers is also seen on purses around 1600. On the whole, however, these patterns were ceasing to have practical application for

costume and furnishing embroidery; they had greater connection with the small novelties – pictures, book cushions, boxes and mirror frames – which the seventeenth-century English amateur embroiderer seems to have produced in such great quantity.

Embroidery as Illustration

The embroidered picture meant, like a painted picture, to be framed for hanging, emerged as an object in its own right in the seventeenth century. This followed to a certain extent the international vogue for panel embroideries, often for devotional purposes, by professional embroiderers after contemporary paintings. Three surviving English examples of these, dated 1637, were worked by Edmund Harrison, embroiderer to James I, Charles I, and later Charles II, and are worked in the *or nué* technique described above (41).

But the popularity of embroidered pictures among amateurs also no doubt reflected the fact that embroidery was of less importance for dress in the middle decades of the seventeenth century. Needlework was firmly established as an element of female education and accomplishment, and had therefore to be directed towards some end. Amateur embroidered pictures from this century exist in great numbers, and many are virtually identical. Some continue the tradition of grouping individual motifs from herbals and bestiaries into a picture with no defined horizon. The panel illustrated (44) is composed of small tent stitch motifs applied to cream satin and is very reminiscent of Elizabethan cushions. The central figure represents the sense of smell, one of the five allegorical senses which were often themes for embroidery. The same figure is used in the centre of the beadwork panel of about the same date (43). Here the embroiderer has introduced a landscape of hummocks, although her slips still float in the air. Beads of coloured glass were one of the many ancillary materials introduced into embroidery at this date, emphasizing its 'novelty' character.

Other pictures were entirely in tent stitch or, from about 1650, in raised work (42, 45). This technique, later named stumpwork, enjoyed extraordinary popularity in England for some thirty years. Some influence from Flemish, German, and Central European high-relief church embroidery may have been involved, and amateur raised work is found on the continent at this period. In England the techniques used grew directly out of the detached buttonhole range of stitches seen in late Elizabethan and Jacobean embroidery. The nature of these enabled petals and insect wings to be worked up freely from the surface, and permitted individual motifs to be padded. These features can already be seen in use very early in the seventeenth century, and become more pronounced until the almost complete three-dimensionality of the raised work pictures is reached.

Detached buttonhole stitch was worked over thread padding and sometimes over wooden forms, the folds of costume were literally reproduced with needlemade fabric, and lace edgings to garments made with minute needlelace stitches. Bullion knots and metal purl were used for hair and the foliage of trees. Beads, pearls, and mica were introduced, and even paint was employed over the laid metal purls. The embroiderers displayed endless ingenuity in these pictures, which evidently took many months to make. Although we see the same stories and motifs used time and time again, each picture is in some way uniquely delightful and repays long and close study.

The subjects of these pictures, and of the scenes used on the caskets and mirror frames in the same style, were frequently taken from contemporary engravings illustrating classical or biblical stories. Of the latter, Old Testament themes were preferred: illustrations of New Testament subjects smacked of Roman Catholicism. Particularly popular stories were the Judgment of Solomon, Solomon and the Queen of Sheba, the Finding of Moses, Esther and Ahasuerus, and David and Bathsheba. Among classical subjects the Judgment of Paris, and scenes from Ovid's *Metamorphoses* were common. Another class of picture had central, oval portraits of Charles I, or of female personifications, set within a raised work frame.

In recent years the discovery of an inscription of the name of a Covent Garden dealer on the edge of one of these pictures has enabled historians to confirm what had long been assumed; that many of these pictures were sold ready drawn by pattern drawers who also dealt in the materials for their making, and in other trifles and novelties. There was obviously a flourishing trade in supplying this market, and this explains the great similarities of style and subject among embroideries produced miles and years apart.

Crewelwork

If embroidery was less evident in costume during the middle part of the seventeenth century, it continued in importance for wall and bed hangings, now a common feature in middle-class households. While major houses such as Knole in Kent, or Ham House in Surrey – which still contain seventeenth-century furnishing textiles – might continue to make much use of imported woven

40. Part of a crewel-
work bed curtain.
English, *c.* 1650.

41. *(left)* Panel, 'Adoration of the Shepherds', signed by Edmund Harrison. English, 1637.

42. *(above)* Raised work picture, 'The Judgment of Paris'. English *c.* 1660–80.

43. *(below)* Picture with coloured glass beads. English, *c.* 1670.

44. *(above)* Picture with tent stitch motifs on cream satin. English, *c.* 1670.

45. *(right)* Detail of the front of a casket. English, *c.* 1660–80.

46. Detail of a crewelwork bed valance worked in red wool in a style imitative of a woodcut. English, *c.* 1650–75.

silks, the majority of smaller, but comfortable homes contained hangings of linen and cotton twill embroidered with crewel wool. The use of this material, a long-staple, worsted yarn, seems to have become popular around 1600 and is soon seen in use for hangings and women's informal jackets. Early crewel embroidery was inevitably monochromatic (often using red wool) and extended Elizabethan scrolling flower designs into much larger patterns under the influence of imported Baroque silks (**40**). A wide range of surface stitches were used; the example illustrated is worked in stem, herringbone, back, running and speckling stitch.

Crewel embroidery was produced both professionally and at home. Town dwellers were quite accustomed by this time to buy ready-made fashionable furnishings, and while many crewelwork hangings are known to have been made by particular amateurs, such as the famous set signed by Abigail Pett in the Victoria and Albert Museum, others are of a scale and repetitiveness of technique which suggests that they were done for profit rather than pleasure. A large valance worked in red wool now in the Embroiderers' Guild collection (**46**) shows a series of biblical scenes and slip motifs executed in stem, back, straight and speckling stitches. The embroidery would seem to be directly imitative of woodcut illustration. There is a similar panel in the Museum of London's collection, and it has been suggested that both were the product of a London workshop.

A Blend of East and West

In the later part of the century the leaf and flower-head patterning of crewelwork became bolder, polychrome, and more exuberant. To the influence of Baroque floral patterning was added elements derived from eastern textiles. Both Dutch and English East India Companies were exploiting the superior qualities of the Indian-painted and resist-dyed cottons known as chintzes, by supplying colonial craftsmen with designs suitable for their home markets. Many of those supplied were already subject to the taste for Chinese ornament which had been cultivated through imported Chinese textiles, porcelain and laquerwork.

The average European probably did not have a very clear perception of the cultural and decorative distinctions between India, the East Indies and China: he was simply avid for goods which represented the exotic East in any form. The resultant blend of European, Chinese, and Indian elements in the hangings imported from India was suitably exotic, yet assimilable within European decorative tradition.

In embroidery, and particularly in crewelwork, it became apparent in the introduction of fantastic growing trees reflecting Eastern 'tree of life' designs; in small hillocky rock formations, holed like gorgonzola cheese with Chinese-looking caves, and in the appearance of exotic birds and figures among the foliage. The latter was sometimes opulently Baroque, or had characteristic Eastern stylized floral ornament. From this period to the middle of the eighteenth century, geometric patterning within naturalistic plant forms became a noticeable feature of the designs of woven silks, lace, and embroidery.

An early eighteenth-century crewelwork hanging in the Embroiderers' Guild Collection (**48**) is probably professional embroidery, and shows marvellous pattern and shading effects achieved with a wide range of stitches: long and short, stem, chain Cretan, detached chain, laid fillings and basket stitch, with French and bullion knots. The hard, and almost glossy quality of the crewel wool permits the texture of particular stitches to be exploited to the full. What is called crewel wool today is much too soft and fluffy to achieve these effects.

By the end of the seventeenth century canvas work was confirmed as a most important embroidery technique for furnishing textiles. Chairs were by now inevitably upholstered, and this most hard-wearing form of needlework was highly suitable for this purpose (**47**). Canvas work chair covers, together with wall hangings and stretched wall panels, such as those found in a house in Hatton Garden, London, and now in the

47. Canvas work chairback. French, late seventeenth century.

Victoria and Albert Museum, mark the beginnings of the enormous popularity which the technique would enjoy in the eighteenth century.

Some illustration of the proliferation of embroidery and other patterned textiles in the late seventeenth-century English home is given by the diarist Celia Fiennes in her description from one room of a house in Epsom, Surrey:

> You enter one roome hung with crosstitch in silks . . . window curtains white satin callicoe printed flowers, the chairs crosstitch, the two stooles of yellow mohaire with crosstitch true lovers knotts in straps along and across, an elbow chaire tent stitch . . . many fine pictures under glasses of tentstitch, satinstitch, gumm and strawwork also Indian flowers and birds.

THE EIGHTEENTH CENTURY

During this century the principal sources for embroidery designs were derived from those produced by specialist textile designers for woven silks, tapestries and lace. France now dominated the production of these luxury textiles and took the lead in matters of fashion much as

48. *(opposite)* Detail of a hanging. The original ground had rotted and the crewel wool embroidery was remounted, probably around 1900, on a new ground. English, *c.* 1700.

49. *(right)* Thirty years later the 'tree of life', with its stylized plants, exotic birds and variety of animals, still remained a popular subject. Canvas work panel with background work in diaper stitch. English, *c.* 1730.

Italy had done two centuries before. The designers who worked within the major silk weaving industry at Lyons produced designs yearly, and the idea of annual, or even seasonal, fashion in dress and dress fabrics dates from this period. A large-scale professional embroidery industry also developed at Lyons, producing work to commission for the court, and luxury furnishing embroideries for the great houses of France and the rest of Europe. The embroidery designs were naturally closely related to current silk patterns, and in turn influenced the professional production of embroideries elsewhere. Amateur embroiderers were ultimately affected by these trends but also preserved their own idiosyncratic tastes and traditions.

By this stage England had its own silk weaving industry at Spitalfields in London, but this depended heavily upon the French lead in design. Despite much resentment, exemplified by such groups as the Anti-

Gallican Society, at the country's dependence upon the old enemy, French taste and French luxuries dominated fashionable life:

> We import Wine, Brandy, Silks of various sorts, Cambricks, Laces of Thread, and of Gold and Silver, Paper, Cards, and an inumerable quantity of trifling Jewels and Toys, for all of which we pay an annual Ballance of One Million and a Half. In reckonging up the Imports from France, I should have mantioned Pride, Vanity, Luxury and Corruption, but as I could make no Estimate by the Custom House Books of the Quantity of these Goods entered, I chose to leave them out*.

The textile designs of the late seventeenth century had been dominated by heavy Baroque floral motifs, These became lighter and more naturalistic during the first years of the new century. Eastern influence, particularly as manifested by chinoiserie, remained important in every sphere of decorative art. To this was added a new pastoralism, giving rise to a love of landscape vignettes, and representations of idealized gardens. Greater botanical realism was evident in floral ornament. Alongside the fantastic growing plant forms of Eastern inspiration, flowers were as frequently depicted as cut bouquets in urns or baskets. Dutch still-life painting played a role here, as did the general interest in horticulture and the cultivation of new hybrid species. Floral ornament was frequently combined with scrollwork, shell motifs, cartouches and architectural detail, reflecting elements in chinoiserie, and a revival of the 'grotesque' style under such French designers as Bérain and Marot.

In the middle years of the century ornament became even lighter and more widely spaced upon its ground under the influence of French rococo design. Asymmetry and serpentine line were features of this style: in embroidery the latter was noticeably manifested in intertwining ribbon designs incorporating small flower sprays.

The great neo-classical revival which swept Europe in the last years of the century resulted in a radical reduction of pattern scale so that ornament was increasingly confined to borders of geometric form, with fields decorated simply in stripes or tiny sprigs. The possibilities for practical decoration using embroidery were accordingly much wider at the beginning of the century than at the end, and this factor naturally affected popular techniques and the type of textile to which they were applied.

By 1700 embroidery was well established among women of the class which Defoe described as 'the middle sort who live well', and such social refinements were no longer restricted to a London upper class. Travelling conditions were much improved, and fashionable intelligence also reached provincial towns through the rapid increase in newspaper circulation. Even the wives and daughters of tenant farmers now took tea and sewed in the parlour.

Professional Embroidery

The professional embroiderer still excelled in fine, realistically shaded silk work using the painterly stitches such as long and short stitch, and in the various

50. Saddle: blue velvet embroidered with metal threads. French, 1760s.

*R. Campbell, *The London Tradesman*, 1747.

51. Embroiderer's workroom from *L'Art du Brodeur* by Charles de St Aubin, 1770.

techniques of metal thread embroidery. A superb example of such work is the French Régence chasuble of the 1720s (**52**) with its elegant scrollwork and luxuriant blooms. It is a church vestment entirely reflecting secular taste. The detail shows skilful and confident workmanship in what must have been a commission of great importance. The ground fabric is cloth-of-silver, although most of the silver strip woven into the fabric has now rubbed away. The scrollwork is composed of gold thread laid over cut vellum shapes, and the fillings of some of the cartouches are padded into relief pattern using cording. A matt crinkled gold thread is laid within the cartouches to provide contrast with the scrollwork, and points of glitter are created with gold strip. The flowers are delicately shaded long and short stitch in coloured silks; the tips of the petals in silver thread.

An embroidery of this kind would have been the work of many hands. Charles de St Aubin, French embroidery designer, whose book *L'Art du Brodeur* of 1770 provides the best description of eighteenth-century professional embroidery practice, lists the main classes of embroidery and indicates a clear division of labour, not only between design and execution, but within the techniques themselves. The embroideresses had to provide their own needles, scissors, and thimbles,

and were overseen by the workshop manager. In the plate from his book which shows an embroidery workroom (**51**), two embroiderers can be seen seated at one frame – one is right-handed, the other left-handed.

The English mantua skirt (**57**) shows techniques described by St Aubin: laid and couched metal thread, partly raised, and fine naturalistic flower embroidery in silks. In *The London Tradesman* of 1747 Campbell comments upon English professional embroidery:

It is chiefly performed by Women; is an ingenious Art, requires a nice taste in Drawing, a bold Fancy to invent new Patterns, and a clean Hand to save their Work from tarnishing. Few of the workers at present can draw, they have their Patterns from the Pattern-Drawer, who must likewise draw the work itself, which they only fill up with Gold and Silver or Worsteds, according to its Use and Nature. We are far from excelling in this Branch of Business in England: the Nuns in Foreign Countries far exceed anything we can perform. We make some good Work, but fall short of the bold Fancy in French and Italian Embroidery. This I take to be chiefly owing to a want of Taste for Drawing in the Performers they may go on in a dull Tract, or servily imitate Foreign Pattern, but know not how to Advance the Beauty of the Old or strike out any new Invention worth Notice.

One feels that Campbell is very hard on the embroiderers: like those of France they were dependent upon the designers for patterns, and not necessarily responsible for initiating designs themselves. Embroidery of the quality of the mantua shown is hardly a case of simply 'filling up the pattern.' No doubt his sneer was as much directed at French styles of ornament as against English craftsmanship.

Embroidery on Costume

In the eighteenth century embroidery for costume assumed new importance, particularly for formal dress. Women's court mantuas, supported by side hoops, grew to staggering proportions by the 1740s, providing a rectangular expanse of petticoat which was the subject of lavish professional embroidery. A spectacular example in the Victoria and Albert Museum bears enormous stylized flowers and leaves growing from a central trunk, over scrollwork cartouches filled with geometric patterning. It is worked entirely in silver thread, strip, cord, and purl on red silk. Mrs Delany, an eminent eighteenth-century craftswoman and embroiderer, enthusiastically described a petticoat worn at a reception in 1740 as of

> . . . white satin embroidered: the bottom of the petticoat brown with hills covered with all sorts of weeds, and every breadth had an old stump of a tree that ran almost up to the top, broken and ragged, and worked with brown chenille, round which were twined nasturtiums, ivy, honeysuckles, periwinkles, convolvulus, and all sorts of twining flowers which spread and covered it.

This rampant naturalism was obviously not simply confined to silk embroidery: a rather similar American example seems to be described in an advertisement in the *Boston Gazette* in 1749, which requests information regarding a stolen crewelwork petticoat 'with large work'd Embroider'd Border, being Deer, Sheep, Houses, Forest ect.'.

Men's court dress was usually equally gorgeous with coat, waistcoat and breeches embroidered '*en suite*', either with metal or silk threads or a combination of both. Such dress embroidery was professional work embroidered to shape and purchased for making up by one's own tailor.

The informal day dress of both sexes, however, made greater use of plain silks, velvets, and wool cloths, with embroidery confined, in the case of men, to the waistcoat or perhaps to some gold or silver embroidery around the borders of the coat, and in women to the apron, linen accessories, or the stomacher and robings of the dress. As in the Elizabethan and Jacobean periods,

52. Detail of chasuble: a superb example of metal thread embroidery. French, *c.* 1720–30.

53. Muslin apron embroidered
with linen thread and edged
with Flemish bobbin lace.
English, early eighteenth
century.

54. (left) Woman's linen
waistcoat. English, 1690s.

a greater diversity of embroidered costume is indicated by surviving items than is documented in contemporary portrait paintings. This is a reflection both of the informality of many of the garments which survive, and their making and use by a much wider section of the population than commonly sat to portraitists.

The embroidered apron is a good example of this. Short embroidered dress aprons are very common in costume collections but are rarely seen in paintings. They are generally of silk taffeta embroidered with coloured silks and metal thread. Long aprons of the new fashion fabric, Indian muslin, have also survived in quantity and are usually decorated with white embroidery. The early eighteenth-century short, muslin apron (53) is embroidered with a delightful chinoiserie fantasy with craggy rocks and fishermen.

Embroidery in silks and crewelwork was also much used upon pockets, which at this stage were detachable accessories which tied around the waist under the skirts of the robe. These are usually typically amateur products. Shoes, gloves, and neck handkerchiefs were also at times the subject of polychrome floral embroidery.

Quilting and Whitework

A rise in the popularity of decorative quilting in the late seventeenth century owed much to Eastern textiles. Quilting, as we have seen, was an established European technique, but interest was re-awakened in its decorative possibilities by the importation of Chinese, Persian, and Indian quilted covers in which monochrome quilted patterning provided a subdued foil to polychrome embroidery. The Satgaon quilts imported into Europe from Bengal by the Portuguese were usually worked in undyed tussor (wild silk), which ranged in colour from straw yellow to honey, on white cotton grounds. Since yellow was also a colour associated in the European mind with China (it was the Imperial colour), yellow silk on white linen was most frequently used for English quilting in the Eastern style. It was quilting without wadding – called flat or false quilting – worked simply through two layers of linen using back stitch. Some bed hangings, covers and pillow shams were worked entirely in geometric or vermicular patterns of this flat quilting, but it was also a most common ground for polychrome floral embroidery from 1690 to 1750.

The woman's waistcoat of the 1690s (54) shows a diagonal trellis of flat quilting behind growing floral trees and exotic birds. Back stitch is used for the quilting and chain stitch for the motifs. The palampores and piece goods embroidered in Gujarat for the Western

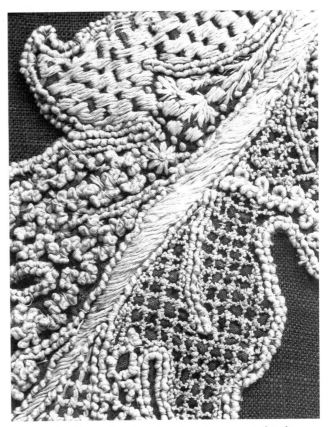

55. Detail of knotted motifs, from hangings reputed to have been worked by three women, the Duchess of Newasch, Lady Chichester and Princess Amalie, or Emily, daughter of George II. English, mid-eighteenth century.

market were worked in an exceptionally fine chain stitch used to fill motifs in concentric rows, and often in stripes of colour. They looked almost painted from a distance, a feat which no doubt led European embroiderers to emulate the technique. Certainly chain stitch is much in evidence in the first half of the eighteenth century, not having been noticeably exploited before.

This waistcoat is also of great interest in bearing upon the lining an ink inscription of the name of the pattern drawer: 'John Stilwell, Drawear at ye Flaming Soord in Russell Street, Cov.' Stilwell's shop was in Covent Garden; as we have already noted, a centre of the novelty and luxury trade, where many pattern drawers would be found. It was a trade which continued in importance throughout most of the century, until changing fashions in embroidery and the appearance of ladies' magazines containing printed patterns rendered their services no longer necessary.

The fringing on this waistcoat is made of knotted linen, couched down in loops to make a shag. The technique of knotting had been used in the seventeenth century, not only for fringing, but also for couched patterns upon upholstery and hangings. Knotting was taken up enthusiastically as a popular pastime in the early eighteenth century. It had the advantage to the

56. *(opposite)* Detail of a bedcover showing the influence of Indo-Persian design. English, *c.* 1720.

57. *(right)* Detail of silk embroidered court mantua. English, mid-eighteenth century.

amateur of being easy to take out when visiting: the little boat-shaped shuttle on which the thread was wound, and the completed knotting, were carried in flat knotting bags which were to be the precursors of ladies' handbags. It was remarked of Queen Mary II that 'when she rides in coach abroad [she] is always knotting threads'. The detail of the knotted work shown (**55**) uses two weights of linen thread, knotted and couched down, together with surface embroidery in the same thread. Mrs Delany makes several references to knotting in her letters, and a white linen knotted bed-cover made by her as a gift in 1765 still survives.

The bedcover of which the central detail is illustrated (**56**) is the product of an English professional workshop, and shows strongly the influence of Indo-Persian design in its central cusped motif, and borders with quarters extending into the field. The growing flower sprays around the sides are particularly Mughal in inspiration. Here the all-over flat quilted ground is based upon a pattern of overlapping circles. A pillow cover with very similar embroidery now in the Royal Ontario Museum, Canada, may have originally been part of a set with this cover, or is at least a product of the same workshop. The design was inked onto the linen before working, often quite casually, so that ink blots appear from behind the stitches – a curious lapse in what would otherwise appear to be a relatively expensive product.

Wadded quilting was still regularly used for warm bedcovers, but these utilitarian textiles have rarely survived from the first half of the century. The technique was used decoratively for costume, however; particularly for women's petticoats. The plain taffeta quilted petticoat wadded with raw wool and backed with linen or glazed wool was an essential item of informal dress for the first three-quarters of the century. It was worn unfashionably by older women, and by working women, well into the nineteenth century. The patterns on these petticoats and other wadded-quilting costume items, such as informal jackets and babies' long christening coats, are usually worked in running stitch. They are very similar to those seen on nineteenth-century provincial quilts: geometric patterns created from a few simple templates – scallops, feather scrolls and simplified flower heads (**58**).

Another form of quilting was employed for white embroidery on linen using thick cord to raise elements of the design. It is seen on surviving children's caps, pillow shams and pockets. The man's waistcoat (**59**) is entirely executed in this technique known as corded or

58. Detail of a quilted petticoat hem. English, 1700–50.

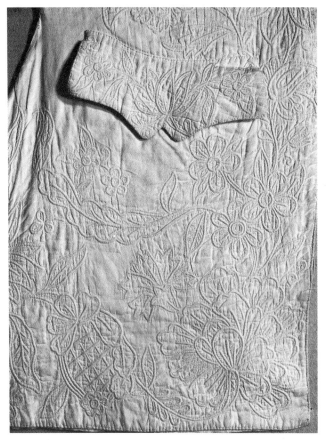

Italian quilting. The stitching is worked through two layers: the upper of a fine close-weave linen, and the lower of a looser-weave linen or cotton. The lines of the design are followed with two parallel rows of back stitch in linen thread and the cord is afterwards run into the channels from the back using a bodkin.

Cord quilting was also incorporated into highly elaborate whitework embroidery in which the surface was entirely worked with a combination of cording, pulled work, and surface stitches such as blocked satin stitch and French knots used as fillings (**60**). It is frequently seen used upon men's white linen waistcoats of the middle decades of the century, and seems to have been an international class of work. St Aubin describes it as 'Marseilles quilting' although this town was probably only one centre of its production.

59. *(left)* Detail of man's linen waistcoat showing corded quilting. English, mid-eighteenth century.

60. *(below)* Detail of a linen twill cover which combines corded quilting with other techniques. English, second quarter of eighteenth century.

Whitework Embroidery

A most important class of whitework embroidery was executed on muslin in imitation of lace. India muslins were of a fineness and transparency which, in the early years of the century, enabled them temporarily to oust lace for dress accessories. Plain muslin neckcloths, cravats, sleeve ruffles, caps and lappets became all the rage. In order to combat this competition, continental lace makers created laces of dense cloth-like patterning, yet with a filmy transparency which vied with muslin. The bobbin laces of Flanders achieved extraordinary fineness at this period, and were by 1720 again essential to fashionable dress. Lace was among the most expensive of all professionally made textiles, and in a country like England whose thread laces did not approach the quality and design of those of France and Flanders, the continental products were highly desirable yet heavily taxed. A solution for the less wealthy was to imitate them in embroidery, and this was done all over northern Europe.

The finest work of this kind is almost indistinguishable from the real thing (61). It is only upon close study that one can see that what appears to be the mesh fillings of lace are in fact pulled work embroidery. Muslin was particularly suitable for this type of embroidery as it was so loosely woven that the threads could easily be pulled this way and that by the stitches. The great professional centre of production was Dresden in Saxony, and the embroidery became known as Dresden work even when practised by amateurs. Pulled work on muslin became one of the standard techniques learned by young girls in Europe and North America, and was frequently advertised in the curricula of boarding schools.

There was one class of whitework which seems to have been uniquely English: the making of a form of

61. Woman's sleeve ruffle of Dresden work in imitation of lace. Saxony, mid-eighteenth century.

needlelace called Hollie point. This technique was related to detached buttonhole stitch and like needle lace was worked freely over parchment. It created a needle lace fabric in which the design appeared as tiny holes. It was only used to create very small pieces which were used as insertions in linen baby clothes such as the cap illustrated (62).

62. Linen baby's cap with Hollie point insert. English, eighteenth century.

63. Canvas work settee. English *c.* 1710.

64. *(left)* Pair of chairs in the style of Robert Adam. English 1770s.

Eighteenth-century Canvas Work

While crewel embroidery continued in importance well into the eighteenth century for hangings and for costume, it was canvas work which became the most popular technique for furnishing embroidery: used for wall hangings, carpets, upholstery (63), firescreens, and even card tables. The designs for these, particularly in the case of professional production, were often closely derivative of French tapestries, and indeed tapestries remained the most desired form of wall covering for those who could afford them.

French workshops such as St Cyr and St Joseph produced quantities of canvas work embroidery, usually as stretched wall panels and chair covers, which reflected the excellence of French design. Chinoiserie and revived 'grotesque' ornament was combined with flourishes of leaves and flowers both realistic and stylized, to produce designs in the spirit of contemporary Bizarre silks. An early eighteenth-century wall panel in the Victoria and Albert Museum has a dense and vigorous scheme which incorporates classical statuary, Chinese vases, cherubs and genre vignettes surrounded by spiralling trails of ragged leaves, and totally abstract ornament of Oriental origin. The embroidery itself is no less rich, being executed in wool, silk and chenille threads using tent, satin and Hungarian stitches on a ground of laid gilt thread. French canvas work upholstery often showed finely detailed and shaded tent stitch scenes of exotic figure subjects with scrollwork frames of cross stitch. All the work shows a characteristic brilliance of palette and is frequently on bright blue, white or black grounds.

The fashion for canvas work upholstery reached a peak in the eighteenth century. Exotic themes were only one element in the range of designs used. Chair seats

65. Set of Queen Anne chairs with canvas work upholstery, made for Canons Ashby House, Northamptonshire.

and carpets were often entirely decorated with floral ornament with large, brightly coloured flowers and leaves closely set against plain grounds. Single urns overflowing with blooms, very similar to Dutch still-life paintings (65), or large bouquets tied with a ribbon, were frequently the single motif used for a chair back or chair seat (64).

Classical and biblical scenes continued to be of great importance; subsumed within the general popularity for vignettes which were essentially figures in a landscape. Francis Cleyn's seventeenth-century illustrations to Virgil's *Aeneid*, *Eclogues* and *Georgics* were popular sources for classical subjects. The last were used for the

66. Canvas work picture worked by Sarah Warren. Boston, 1748.

well-known set of canvas work screens at Wallington Hall, in Northumberland, executed by Lady Julia Calverley and completed in 1727 (*see p.* 105). These typify the new pastoralism which distinguished eighteenth-century embroidered landscapes from those of the century before. Nature is more realistically portrayed, but in the manner in which leisured society would wish to find it: transformed into a perpetual Arcadia occupied by aristocratic shepherds and shepherdesses. The amateur embroiderer reflected the pre-occupation of the land-owner with laying out new formal gardens and, later in the century, with landscaping the parkland beyond. Two of the enormous Stoke Edith hangings, now at Montacute House, Somerset, are tent stitch illustrations of typical formal gardens of the first half of the century, with parterres, fountains, clipped yews, statuary and orange trees in tubs (*see p.* 108–9).

A great number of canvas work pictures survive from the first half of the century which embrace all these themes in miniature. They are generally worked in tent stitch in wools and silks, but contrast is often provided by working some parts of the design in cross, rococo or Hungarian stitch. They range from simple bouquets of flowers in baskets to classical, biblical or theatrical subjects, or even depictions of the embroiderer's house and family.

American Embroidery

More comfortable living standards and social imitation were by now also features of urban American society, which by this century was sufficiently well-established to be a ready market for fashionable textiles. In the nature of things, it was English, rather than French, goods which supplied the demand. In the first half of the century North America represented the largest market for English silks outside London itself. All imported luxuries were nevertheless expensive and could be afforded only by the wealthiest merchant families. The colonial tradition, established through necessity, of home-made and home-decorated textiles and of careful re-use of imported fabrics, continued even in the middle class urban context, although recognizing current European fashionable design.

Domestic needlework was a mark of leisured refinement in America as in Europe, but its deployment was sharpened by scarcity of bought alternatives. This was particularly true of furnishing textiles. As we have noted in other contexts, the high cost of imported decorative textiles could be a great stimulus to native embroidery, and thus American crewelwork hangings, canvas work upholstery, and quilted bedcovers achieved

67. Detail of crewelwork bedcover worked by Mary Breed in wool on linen. Boston, Mass., 1770.

a characteristic style and excellence which usually equalled, and often excelled, their English counterparts.

Canvas work pictures were just as popular as in England. On both sides of the Atlantic private schools for young ladies taught embroidery as part of a kind of 'finishing' process and many such pictures were produced under these circumstances. Even if they had no purpose they were decorative, and indicated that young women were being trained to occupy themselves in a genteel and feminine manner. A school in Boston was probably responsible for initiating some thirty-six canvas work pictures which survive, all showing variants of a landscape with a lady fishing as one of the central features (66). They are otherwise difficult to distinguish from similar English 'pictures' of the period.

Flame stitch or Florentine stitch (also called Bargello work and Hungarian point) was a class of counted thread embroidery which produced geometric designs in horizontal, chevron bands of colour. It had been popular in Europe since the seventeenth century and continued to be used, particularly for upholstery, well into the eighteenth century. American canvas workers made especially good use of this style producing endless variants of pattern in jewel colours. Fine examples of its use in upholstery survive (*see p.* 116) but it was also much used to make hand screens, and small folding pocket books, often signed and dated by the embroiderer.

The popularity of crewelwork declined in England during the second half of the century, but in America, particularly in in New England, the tradition continued much longer. A detail of one of the cherry trees on the cover made by nineteen-year-old Mary Breed in 1770 (**67**) shows that American crewelwork did not slavishly repeat earlier English motifs but had devised its own vocabulary of design. The motifs are widely spaced and have a fresh crispness of line. Romanian, stem, herring-bone, buttonhole and darning are the most common stitches used.

The indigo plant was introduced into South Carolina from the West Indies, and by the 1740s this blue dye was a major colonial product. Its cheap availability made blue a favourite colour in American embroidery and much early crewelwork is entirely worked in indigo-dyed wools on white linen.

New England also gave rise to a characteristic form of bedcover known as a bed rug. The name grew from the fact that many early examples were worked in a looped pile technique known as Turkey work, also used for carpets, and imitative of oriental woven pile carpets. The use of this technique for bedcovers developed, like the making of quilts, out of the need to provide warm bedding in the earliest colonial period. The bed rugs are usually rounded at one end, and were worked in other embroidery techniques, like the fine example by Mary Foot (**70**) which has stylized flower and leaves of wool pattern-darning.

Late Eighteenth-century Embroidery

By the third quarter of the century embroidery designs were becoming altogether lighter and more spaced, incorporating the ribbon trails and serpentine lines of the French rococo style (**68**). Flowers were much smaller; either highly naturalistic essays in silk painting of the type at which Mrs Delany excelled, or increasingly tending towards the all-over sprigged patterns which were to be common by 1800.

Tambour embroidery was introduced from the east around 1760, according to St Aubin and immediately became popular in both professional and amateur embroidery. It was chain stitch worked with a hook instead of a needle, and took its name from the circular, drumlike, frame on which the fabric was stretched. The thread was held behind the fabric and the hook used to pull a loop through to the front. The second loop was

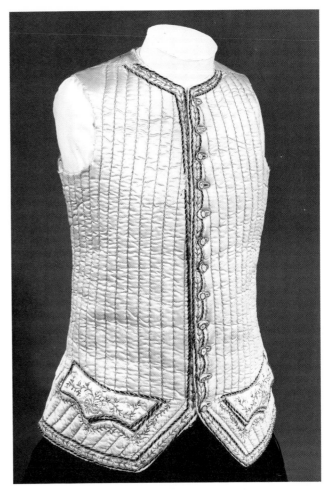

68. Padded satin waistcoat. English, *c.* 1775–85.

69. Detail from a panel for a court petticoat; silk embroidered with coloured twisted silk. French, *c.* 1770.

70. Bed rug, with leaves of wool pattern-darning, signed by Mary Foot. Connecticut, 1778.

pulled through the first and so on and the stitch produced was identical to that of early chain-stitch hand sewing machines. Tambour-worked chain stitch is always distinguishable from needleworked, since a continuous line of stitches is produced on the back of the work, as opposed to the slightly broken line produced by the latter. France produced large quantities of professional tambour embroidery in the second half of the century; usually worked in polychrome silks on pale shades of satin. The panel illustrated (69) is part of an un-made dress piece in the style of the great designer Philip de la Salle (1723–1805). Similar work was produced for chair covers and firescreens.

The influence of the revived neo-classical style which made itself felt across Europe was stimulated by the archaeological finds at Herculaneum and Pompeii. It was cool and severe by comparison with former classicism, resulting in minimal ornament in a limited colour range. Although English architects such as Robert Adam (1728–1792) were working in this style in the third quarter of the century, it resulted in little furnishing embroidery in the same mode. Adam himself designed a set of wall hangings for Newiston House in Scotland, and the hangings of the state bed at Osterley House in London (*see p. 152*), as a part of neo-classical redecorative schemes, but they are lonely exceptions. Plain fabrics and woven silks with subdued design were increasingly used for furnishing textiles in the late eighteenth century.

A similar reduction of ornament occurred in costume, where neo-classicism went hand-in-hand with a liking for 'natural' dress which expressed a rustic simplicity. England set the mode for dark suits, and male styles of dress which reflected the sporting life of the countryside. Women turned to simple printed cottons, white muslin and plain silk gauzes. Embroidery, where it was used, was on a miniature scale: narrow Greek key and scrolling borders, small flower slips and sprigging.

By this period a muslin weaving industry had been established in Scotland in response to the great demand for this fashionable fabric. It was now frequently ornamented with embroidery in the piece. In 1782 an Italian, Luigi Ruffini, set up a workroom in Edinburgh to produce 'flowered' muslin using the tambour method.

It was soon followed by similar workrooms all over Scotland and England, which employed girls, some as young as eight or nine, at this repetitive task. This industrial production was at the opposite extreme to the pleasures of embroidery as practised by the leisured classes. At the trial of a London tambour workshop master for cruelty in 1801, conditions among tambour apprentices were described as 'disgraceful to any civilized state'. Sprigged muslin continued to be an important professional product into the 1820s, when the expertise was directed towards different types of whitework embroidery.

Since the amateur embroiderer found herself with little to do in the way of furnishing and costume embroidery in the last quarter of the century, her efforts were primarily directed into sampler-making and picture-making. By this stage the sampler was a shadow of its seventeenth-century intricacy — generally a set of verses surrounded by stylized motifs occasionally enlivened by representations of natural flowers or the worker's house. They were still an essential part of the training in needlework given by young ladies' schools, and were diversified by fashions for pattern-darning samplers and embroidered maps and almanacs (71).

Adult embroiderers abandoned their canvas work pictures in favour of silk pictures using the painterly technique of long and short stitch. The notion of needle painting went hand-in-hand with the popularity of watercolour drawing as a female pastime. The majority of pictures were sentimental and romantic depictions of young men and women in fashionable rural dress mourning at tombs, strewing flowers, or generally playing at agricultural tasks. The lovesick 'shepherd' (72) is inscribing his sweetheart's name upon a tree. Many were taken from engravings and mezzotints after such artists as Nicolas Poussin, Francesco Zuccarelli, Francesco Bartolozzi, Francis Wheatley and Angelica Kauffmann. As if to confirm their association with water-colours, the faces, hands and skies of these pictures were frequently painted onto the silk ground, with the draperies and landscapes embroidered in silks. One class of picture was called 'printwork' and executed entirely in black silk or horse hair. This fashion for silk pictures lasted well into the 1820s.

Certain embroiderers made a name for themselves by copying famous paintings in wool embroidery. Mary Knowles (1733–1807) was commissioned by Queen Charlotte to copy Zoffany's portrait of George III. The famous Mary Linwood (1756–1845) produced well over a hundred copies of paintings ranging from Rubens and Raphael to Stubbs and Gainsborough. One lost painting by Gainsborough is only known through her

71. Three-dimensional terrestrial globe made by Ruth Wright. Westtown School, Pennsylvania, 1815.

72. Silk picture of shepherd inscribing the name 'Julia' on a tree. English, late eighteenth century.

copy. She exhibited in London, Edinburgh and Dublin, and a permanent London exhibition of her work became one of the visitor attractions of the capital. She herself was received by royalty. The pictures were worked in crewel wools which she had specially dyed to provide the fullest range of shades, and imitated the painter's brushstrokes with long and short stitches.

Her output, and those of the other amateur copyists of paintings, did not add anything to the aesthetic impact of the works they reproduced, and cannot be particularly admired from a technical point of view despite one enthusiastic reviewer's comment that 'there cannot be a more excellent school for the study of all ladies who are desirous of attaining proficiency in this wonderful art of needlework'. They were the result of a craft having become a social imperative for women, yet one of which no particular practical purpose was required. This was deadening to craftsmanship and its end was bad art.

THE NINETEENTH CENTURY

In this century, more than any other, an account of embroidery is largely a description of amateur work, its changing techniques and enthusiasms. Embroidery was not as essential for the decoration of the home or of costume as it had been at certain times in the past. Patterned fabrics, both printed and woven, could be had in plenty and at a relatively much lower cost. Trimmings of all kinds were more generally available. By the 1840s one might buy machine embroidery and machine lace. Even professionally embroidered costume items were inexpensive, due to mass production and the low wages paid to sweated workers. Many of the types of embroidery produced by various professional industries were also techniques copied by the amateur.

Britain was the first industrialized country, and changed during this century from a nation where four-fifths of the population lived in the country to one where four-fifths lived in towns. The numbers of the middle classes were larger than in any other country, and most middle class women embroidered. Apart from supervision of the domestics, needlework was one of the few approved activities open to them; reading novels was an idle occupation. Plain sewing of household and personal linen was one way of contributing to the domestic economy or, like embroidery, might be devoted to charitable purposes by sewing for the parish baby basket or embroidering for the bazaar. Even if embroidery was purely devoted towards the superfluous ornamentation of the home it at least contributed to women's appearance and feeling of usefulness.

A great industry grew up to stimulate and supply the needs of a million needlewomen. Throughout the century there was a tendency for novelty to follow upon novelty, the pace quickening after the 1840s. The growing range of women's magazines aimed at the same middle class market, devoted a great deal of space to patterns find instructions for embroidery, and too for crochet, knitting, tatting, netting and every kind of fancy work. Since so many of the techniques and designs stemmed from a commercial origin, they were often internationally popular. America experienced many of the same embroidery fashions as Britain, with only a slight time delay. It soon had its own range of publications aimed at the amateur needlewoman.

A reaction against fancy work, and the most popular commercial embroidery of all, Berlin woolwork, was formulated in several sectors, but generally sought to elevate embroidery from what was perceived as a mire of tastelessness, and to endow it with a new artistic justification. Faced with industrial art and machine duplication, the arts and crafts required re-definition. Much of this process involved looking back to a pre-industrial age.

Berlin Woolwork

Since canvas work had long been established as a technique which anyone could master with practice, it was not surprising that it should occur to some enterprising printer to print patterns for this work. It was only odd that no one had thought of it before. Eighteenth-century embroiderers had had to draw out their own canvases in copying published engravings, unless of course they paid someone else to do it for them.

Patterns which first appeared in Berlin in 1804 were printed on squared paper with the colours hand-painted, square by square. All the embroiderer had to do was to take each square of the paper as a square of the canvas, select the correct colour of thread, and make her stitch. The patterns very shortly enjoyed great popularity on the continent, and by the 1820s were becoming better known in England. Early designs were fairly small in scale, being repeating borders and little bouquets of flowers, which are seen worked in silks or wools using tent stitch, on objects such as hand screens and babies' pincushions.

In 1831, Wilks Warehouse, a major needlework shop in Regent Street, began importing the patterns in large quantities, together with the specially dyed German wools for working them. In 1844 Wilks advertised his shop as having the 'largest and best assorted stock [of Berlin patterns and wools] in the Kingdom'. From the

73. Berlin woolwork picture in shades of grey (grisaille) with an embroidered frame. English, 1840s.

1840s the patterns were also widely produced by printers in England and America. The designs were now much bolder in scale and colouring, and were being used to reproduce pictures by the popular artists of the day. The prevailing, but heavily romanticized, Medievalism found expression in such subjects as 'Bolton Abbey in the Olden Time' and illustrations to the novels of Sir Walter Scott. Biblical subjects, as ever, were highly appropriate as household pictures, and these too were usually taken from well-known paintings. Even Leonardo da Vinci's 'The Last Supper' made its appearance in Berlin wools. Landseer's animal studies were also fruitful sources, particularly his paintings of royal pets.

Berlin work was not simply framed as pictures, but was adapted to cover every possible household object: footstools, chair seats, carpets, table mats, bell pulls and cushions. Many types and sizes of canvas were available

and were sold under such names as 'Berlin', 'French', 'German' and 'Penelope'. Berlin silk canvas was the finest and permitted the canvas to be left plain around a worked motif. Heraldic devices in silk tent stitch were often worked upon firescreen panels in this manner. The cotton canvas known as German had every tenth thread coloured yellow to facilitate counting stitches.

The Byronic young man in Turkish dress (**73**) shows a typical design of the 1840s. The portrait is in shades of grey (grisaille) and is surrounded by an embroidered frame. The turban is decorated with blued steel beads. A similar *trompe-l'œil* effect was produced by borders which imitated black lace, the finer meshes worked in black silk using straight stitches, and the *toile* in black wool or black glass beads.

Beadwork was widely introduced into Berlin woolwork from the 1850s. It was as easy to use the patterns in this way as for cross stitch; one simply placed a bead for every square instead of a stitch. Grisaille motifs were worked in black, grey and white beads against a plain ground of a single, strong colour. Cut steel, blued steel and brass beads were used alongside coloured glass. Beadwork was used for footstools, teapot stands, slippers, curtain ties, purses and bags. The bas-reliefs of 'Morning' and 'Evening' by the Danish sculptor Thorvaldsen were frequently reproduced as shield-shaped firescreen panels in beadwork. The Embroiderers' Guild owns an enormous padded tea-cosy with grisaille beadwork roses in urns on either side, on a bright red ground, the ruched fabric around the top decorated with pom-poms.

In the late 1850s aniline dyestuffs produced a new range of bright colours: magentas, pinks, purples, limy greens and a dense black. Aniline-dyed English wools, which were thicker and stronger, increasingly replaced the German wools from this date. Floral designs became extravagant, featuring full-blown roses and exotic lilies, drawn much larger than life. One critic referred to 'fuchsia as big as hand-bells'. The startling presence of these blooms was sometimes accentuated by relief embroidery called plushwork. Worked in special plush wools using a loop stitch like Turkey work, the loops were subsequently cut and brushed up before being clipped into contours. It was much used to work exotic birds such as parrots, toucans and macaws, inspired by the beautiful colour plates of bird books by Audubon, Gould and Lear.

Not even costume items were exempt from the Berlin woolworkers' attentions. In the 1840s and 1850s men's waistcoats were worked in all-over geometric patterns, often combining silks and wool, and sometimes even gilt beads and laid metal thread. Slipper patterns were published in hundreds and were typical of the kind of design that magazines included as a pull-out supplement. A popular example of these was a disembodied fox's head, face-forward on the toe, surrounded by foliage which trailed around the sides of the foot to the heel. In the 1860s many small flat square ladies' purses were produced; generally of geometric design, sometimes with lace work borders, and trimmed with thick silk chenille tassels.

Many long narrow Berlin woolwork samplers survive made by adult needlewomen as a record of patterns and stitches collected from friends and from magazines. These temporarily revived the original use of the sampler. Some are thought to have been produced by professional needlewomen for use in Berlin woolwork repositories as worked examples of patterns for the guidance of customers. Certainly many of them contain a much wider range of canvas work stitches, more

creatively used, than is always seen on the embroideries themselves.

The designs of the 1860s were to some extent toned down in the 1870s, as quieter colouring and a greater use of geometric pattern succeeded the bold floral and animal motifs of the 1860s. Berlin woolwork was finally ousted as the most popular form of embroidery in the 1880s with the advent of Art Needlework.

Traditional Crafts

These techniques of appliqué, patchwork and quilting, particularly as used for bedcovers, were practised both as traditional, functional crafts in provincial areas, and as part of the urban amateur's repertoire. Wadded quilting and patchwork had both been used for bedcovers in Britain and America throughout the eighteenth century, but relatively few examples survive due to wear in use: most of these date from the last quarter of the century. An interesting cover in the Embroiderers' Guild collection is said to date from this period. It is made of alternate pieced white linen squares and stars made from printed cottons. Each linen square is embroidered with a small spray of crewelwork flowers, and the central panel has a large bouquet of flowers tied with a ribbon. It is not wadded, but quilted with running stitch in widely spaced chevron lines across its whole width.

In America, the continued westward expansion over the continent made the production of warm bedding essential, and the scarcity value of all kinds of fabric had naturally encouraged the saving of every scrap of material for piecing together into new textiles. The pleasure of devising patterns for quilt tops was, one can imagine, one of the few restful and self-expressive occupations for pioneer women in an otherwise hard life. Most American bedcovers were quilted, whether their tops were plain, patchwork, or appliqué.

After the introduction of machine processing for cotton in the 1790s cotton wool rather than raw wool was commonly used for wadding. As materials, particularly printed cottons, began to become more plentiful, so the utilitarian reasons for piecing fabrics together were less pressing and fabrics could be chosen with designs in view. The use of appliqué followed on from this; it was a decorative rather than a functional technique.

In the first thirty years of the nineteenth century covers were often made using motifs cut from printed furnishing chintzes with large scale designs. These might be combined with pieced work and quilting to provide a very rich effect. A typical early design was a large central motif, such as a star made of diamond patches radiating from the centre, with smaller motifs between the points and a wide patterned border. In the second quarter of the century the block method of piecing a quilt became common. The whole top was made of perhaps twenty-five squares worked individually which were joined, either edge to edge or point to point, to form the quilt top. They were more convenient to work than quilts entirely worked in one piece on a large frame, and the approach to designing based upon a number of repeating units gave rise to some of the most beautiful examples of the American quilt.

Quilting had also come to have an important social role. It was expected that a girl should have as many as twelve quilts to her dowry, one of which, the Bride's Quilt, had the most time and attention devoted to its design and making. The custom grew of holding quilting parties when women gathered to work at a neighbour's quilt. This was particularly helpful in the repetitive task of quilting the completed top to its wadding and backing. Among hard-working family communities, these meetings provided a welcome opportunity for women to meet together and talk.

A tradition which grew out of communal quilt making was the Album quilt or Autograph quilt, in which each block was sewn and signed by one individual, and joined to form a cover intended as a gift. The example illustrated (75) was made by the ladies of the United Presbyterian Church of West Alexander in Pennsylvania, as a gift for the Reverend and Mrs Chauncey Murch in 1857. It is entirely of cotton, both printed and plain, and is pieced, appliquéd and quilted.

North America also produced a class of white quilt of stuffed quilting (trapunto) in which motifs were raised with wadding inserted through the lining to produce much higher relief than in straightforward wadded quilting. Very fine examples in this technique date from around 1800. Candlewick bedcovers were white cotton, embroidered with a soft, bulky cotton yarn like the wick of a candle. Such stitches as chain, whip, French knots, and tufting were used to produce white relief embroidery not dissimilar to early Mountmellick work (79). In the 1840s machine-woven candlewick covers became readily available and the use of the hand technique declined.

Appliqué using printed motifs cut from chintz was also very popular in England during the first thirty years of the century, but covers decorated in this manner were rarely quilted. Patchwork utilizing printed cottons remained constantly popular, but after the middle of the century there was a much greater use of silks, both figured and plain, and velvets. English patchwork covers were most commonly all-over pieced work of geometric shapes – hexagons, diamonds and squares – without the bold designs seen on American examples. Log Cabin patchwork, which arranged narrow strips of fabric, or ribbons, concentrically around an initial square, was introduced from America in the 1860s. Heavy, plain felted fabrics, such as the facecloth used for uniforms, were used in the 1850s and 1860s to make covers featuring many pictorial motifs. For some reason these seem to have been frequently the work of men – tailors or ex-servicemen. In the last half of the century patchwork covers used much richer fabrics, and stronger colours combined with a more prevalent use of black. The Tumbling Block pattern, which uses triangular and square pieces to create the effect of three-dimensional cubes, is commonly seen on covers made in the 1880s and 1890s.

'Crazy' patchwork was popular in both Britain and America during the same period. It used randomly shaped pieces of every kind of fabric which were joined and embroidered across the seams in various threads. Embroidered motifs were then worked on the patches themselves. It was also known as Japanese patchwork, having some supposed resemblance to the abstract blocks of pattern seen in Japanese decoration which was then enjoying a general vogue. The perceived connection between this type of work and the Japan beloved of the Aesthetic Movement is amusingly drawn in a description of the 'Oscar Crazy quilts' made in 1882 by sewing circles which Oscar Wilde addressed during his American lecture tour:

> On a piece of cambric half-yard square there is basted in the centre a sunflower made either of yellow broadcloth, silk or velvet, or else a lily, daisy or pansy. The square is then filled in with bits of silk or velvet of all colours, the edges turned in and the pieces sewed down firmly with a chain stitch of old gold colour, alternating with cardinal sewing silk.

What Wilde thought of these efforts is not recorded.

An English fireplace mantle hanging of crazy patchwork is illustrated (74), in which the random silks and velvets have been overlaid with tinsel thread, glass beads and sequins. The Embroiderers' Guild owns a large crazy patchwork cover of very elaborate workmanship made by a young German girl in 1886, which makes the point that by this period most amateur needlework fashions were international.

The making of traditional wadded quilts was concentrated in Wales, the West Country and the north of England. It was a rural craft which had been transplanted to mining and industrial communities by

74. Crazy patchwork mantle hanging (1880s) and a Berlin woolwork sampler (1857), backed by a cover of 'Anglo-Indian' embroidery (1880s). English.

migration to the towns in the early nineteenth century. Although quilting was a family activity, there were also professional and itinerant quilters, both men and women. The designs used for quilting were not greatly different from those seen on American quilts, being of feather, fan, star, cable, shell and geometric patterns, but there were regional differences in the way they were combined. Welsh, West Country and Yorkshire quilts more often had patchwork tops, while those of Durham and Northumberland were usually plain. Traditional quiltmaking was unaffected by the vagaries of fashionable needlework and continued to be made into this century. It was organized on a commercial basis under the aegis of the Rural Industries Bureau in the 1930s and as such enjoyed some success until the outbreak of the Second World War.

Fashionable Whitework

White embroidery on linen or cotton remained important throughout the century, particularly for costume accessories and baby clothes. It was the basis of a variety of professional industries, and continued in popularity among amateur needlewomen, retaining a high standard of technical proficiency in the face of more repetitive forms of embroidery.

White muslin and lawn remained highly fashionable for women's dress in the first twenty years of the century. Sewed muslin with tiny all-over sprigs worked either in tambouring or in satin and trailing stitches was available by the yard. In the 1820s the character of whitework changed under the influence of French styles and techniques. Designs incorporated tiny openwork holes which were often filled with needle-made fillings, and which were combined with more elaborate floral ornament worked in padded satin and buttonhole stitches.

75. Album quilt, made for the Reverend and Mrs Chauncey Murch. Pennsylvania, 1857.

76. *(below)* Detail of a dress hem showing puffs of muslin gathered into holes cut in the fabric. English, 1820s.

The popularity of raised and three-dimensional effects upon the hems and bodices of dresses of the 1820s is reflected in the detail shown (76). Puffs of muslin have been gathered into holes cut into the ground fabric. The vandyked edge is typical of this period, and shows openwork white embroidery in which small holes have been cut out and the edges finished with oversewing.

The Scottish sewed muslin industry turned from tambour work to white embroidery in the French style and soon the name of Ayrshire work was applied to all white embroidery of this type in Britain. The Scottish workers became famed for their delicate needlemade fillings in cut work surrounded by intricate floral patterns worked in padded satin and trailing stitches. It was outwork; the printed patterns were supplied by agents to cottage workers, and the completed embroideries were taken back to the factories to be made up. The wages were not high, and many pairs of eyes were ruined in attempts to meet deadlines by candlelight.

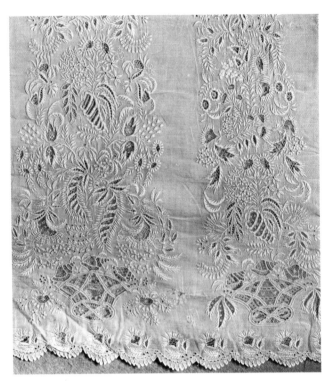

77. Detail of skirt panel of a baby robe. Ayrshire, Scotland, 1840s.

78. Woman's undersleeve: lawn embroidered with linen thread (*broderie anglaise*). English or French, *c*. 1860.

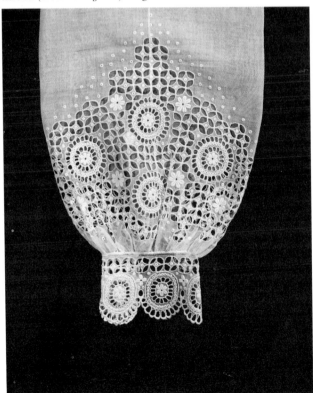

Although called Ayrshire work the industry also provided employment for many thousands of Irish workers: one Glasgow firm employed 20–30,000 embroiderers.

It was used to decorate collars, particularly the wide pelerines of the 1830s, children's and babies' clothes, caps, and handkerchiefs. Elaborate babies' robes were a most typical vehicle for the work; the central panels of the bodice and of the long skirts were densely worked, and scalloped-edge borders of embroidery ran around the robings, sleeves and hem. The detail of an 1840s robe (77) shows the needle-made fillings which were such a feature of the best professional work.

It was a type of embroidery also widely practised by amateur embroiderers in both Europe and America. Many manuscript pattern books survive from the 1820s and 1830s filled with designs for borders and babies' cap crowns. America was an important market for Ayrshire work and the cessation of imports at the outbreak of the Civil War did much finally to kill an industry which was already suffering from having to compete with the advent of automatic machine embroidery.

Fashions in whitework also changed in the 1850s. Ayrshire work was increasingly abandoned in favour of a bolder, geometric openwork known as *broderie anglaise*. It was somewhat quicker and easier to work than the surface embroidery and needle fillings, and was much undertaken by amateurs (78). By the 1860s the Swiss machine embroidery manufacturers had solved the problems involved with reproducing this type of openwork embroidery, and could even imitate the buttonholed, scalloped edges of hand work. Although ready-holed borders cut by machine became available to assist the amateur *broderie anglaise* worker, the necessity to spend hours labouring at such a task seemed pointless. Most babies' robes made after 1870 are decorated with Swiss machine embroidery, and the same applies to women's undergarments which by this period were the other main items decorated with this class of whitework.

In the 1870s, however, white cutwork was extended into much more openwork techniques based upon the *guipure* principle: large sections of the ground were removed so that the design appeared to be motifs held together by worked bars. It often imitated the large scale needlelaces of the seventeenth century, a connection reflected in the name of one of the more popular forms, Richelieu work.

Embroidery on net was much used for accessories such as pelerine collars, scarves, and bonnet veils in the first half of the century. A machine-made net became available from 1808 and was soon being used to imitate lace with tambouring, darning and needle-running. It formed the basis of many small local industries; one such was at Coggeshall in Essex, and workers from this industry were said to have trained workers at Limerick, in Ireland, to make the embroidered lace which was most commonly known by this name by the end of the century. Carrickmacross lace was the product of another Irish industry based upon machine net, but in this case muslin motifs were applied to the net and connected by surface embroidery. It was a popular embroidered lace in the second half of the century, and was also made as a guipure. Both techniques were copied by amateur embroiderers and commercial patterns were widely available by 1900.

Mountmellick work, another type of Irish whitework, was said to have been introduced into the town of that name in the 1820s. It was surface embroidery in a variety of raised stitches executed in thick white cotton, and was used to decorate household articles such as bedcovers and toilet mats. The designs featured naturalistic plants such as oak leaves, acorns and blackberries. The industry was in decline in the 1880s but was briefly revived as a philanthropic organization, like so many others at this time. Later Mountmellick work is generally on soft cotton with a satin face, and the items are finished with a knitted cotton fringe (**79**). It too was promoted by magazines aimed at the amateur so that it is often difficult to distinguish amateur from professional work at the end of the century.

Smocking

It has sometimes been said that English smocks represent one of the few claims the country has to a peasant dress. The highly decorated smock was, however, a relatively brief phenomenon whose duration, curiously, coincided with the period of the country's most rapid industrialization. It seems to have developed as a garment in the late eighteenth century and was at its most elaborate in the first half of the nineteenth, declining in quality towards the end when the home-made smock was increasingly supplanted by commercially made garments produced at centres like Newark-on-Trent.

The technique of embroidering over pleats to draw in the fullness of a garment constructed of square and rectangular pattern pieces can be noted in the peasant dress of other European countries, but in these instances the embroidery tends to hold the pleats in a rigid position. English smocking is characterized by its flexibility; essential where it occupied a major portion of a working garment.

79. Detail of a toilet cover in Mountmellick work (or amateur copy). Irish, late nineteenth century.

80. John Turvey wears a dark glazed linen smock as his Sunday best. Swanbourne, Buckinghamshire, 1910.

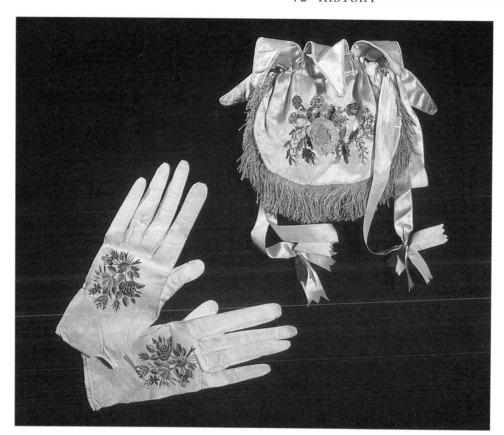

81. Woman's bag and gloves. French, 1830s.

Smocks seem to have been confined to the English South and Midlands. There were regional variations in shape: some had a front opening, while others were 'round frocks' which were the same back and front. The smocking itself was confined to a panel at chest level, back and front, and to two panels on the sleeve to gather it into the cuff. The collar, cuffs, shoulder sections and the 'boxes' on either side of the smocking were embroidered with mainly geometric patterns using such stitches as feather, herringbone, chain and stem stitches (80). The notion that motifs were an indication of the wearer's occupation has been proved romantic.

Smocking became popular for fashionably 'artistic' dress at the end of the century and was executed on fine silks for tea gowns and children's dresses. Liberty's Mab smock for children was one of the shop's most popular lines in the early years of this century.

Fancy Work

The Victorian middle classes seem to have exhibited a general enthusiasm for the imitation of one material by another, and a regrettable curiosity in exploring just how many uses one material could be put to. This was as true of embroidery as anything else, and was an approach much evident in the new techniques and designs promoted by magazines and manufacturers.

The term 'fancy work' was actually used from the 1840s, and embraced every conceivable technique applied in innumerable domestic items both useful and decorative. Some of the effects were not unpleasant, such as the embroidery in ribbons and aerophanes (coloured gauzes) popular in the 1830s (81) and revived in the 1880s under the name of rococo embroidery. This was carried out in very narrow China ribbon, usually shade-dyed across its width, and was used for toilet sachets, bags and screen panels on cream and black satin. The designs were reminiscent of French rococo ornament with swags, ribbon motifs and delicate rose and forget-me-not sprays.

Braidwork of all kinds was enormously popular in the second half of the century and had many kinds of applications, from narrow white braid used on cotton piqué for children's clothes, and toilet articles, to Russian silk braid and woollen braid used upon adult costume and furnishing items. It was usually couched down in scrolling designs.

Fish-scale embroidery involved scraping the scales from fish and cleaning and soaking them so that they could be pierced with a hole. They were then dried, and incorporated into embroidery as the petals of flowers. Iridescent beetle wings from India were also used in embroidery. They were popular in the 1820s and 1830s for the decoration of muslin evening dresses.

Anglo-Indian embroidery was worked on cheap, brightly coloured cotton covers and bandanas printed with designs based upon Indian shawl patterns. Its popularity in the 1880s grew out of a class of Art

Needlework of much greater sophistication which used printed Art silks as the basis for embroidery. Anglo-Indian work was generally brash and fussy; the printed designs embroidered with every colour of silk, and further embellished with metal threads, glass beads and imitation jewels.

To describe every one of the brief crazes which came under the general umbrella of fancy work would take up a great deal of time and space. The fact was that many of the directives for the amateur needlewoman in books and magazines combined many materials and techniques in the making of a single item. These might not simply involve embroidery, but fringing, knitting, crochet, beading, painting and gluing. The general effect of useless and inappropriate ornament, ill-chosen colours, and conflicting materials and pattern, must have made many homes an aesthete's nightmare. The technical expertise of generations had largely been lost, since the main object of the various prescriptions provided by the amateur needlework industry was that they should produce an effect with ease. It was the corollary of social conditions which required women to possess certain skills and undertake certain kinds of activity, yet which provided no practical or economic necessity for these to be employed. It was craft for craft's sake.

Reaction and Revival

While the fashion for Berlin patterns and fancy work flourished until the 1880s, the seeds of a counter-revolution had been sewn many years earlier. The major changes in nineteenth-century decorative art were brought about not so much by general changes in fashion or by the assimilation of foreign influences as in the past, as by the almost crusading spirit of individual designers and artists for whom the integrity of design and workmanship constituted part of a much wider set of philosophical ideas.

The giant who bestrode this movement was William Morris (1834–1896). As an undergraduate he had been greatly influenced by John Ruskin's strictures for the craftsman:

1. Never encourage the manufacture of any article not absolutely necessary, in the production of which Invention has no share.
2. Never demand an exact finish for its own sake, but only for some practical or noble end.
3. Never encourage imitation or copying of any kind except for the sake of preserving records of great works.*

*The Stones of Venice, 1851.

Morris initially trained as an architect in the office of the Gothic enthusiast George Street (1824–1881), and then devoted a period to painting as a member of the Pre-Raphaelite Brotherhood, but he was becoming increasingly concerned with the whole spectrum of craftsmanship: and with the notion that he could entirely recreate domestic interiors to reflect his ideas of beauty. He was strongly influenced by medieval design and craftsmanship, but his designs were never medieval pastiche. He believed that the medieval craftsman's close involvement with design had led, through the intimate knowledge of his materials, to a much higher level of achievement than the nineteenth-century machine age could produce. 'It is the pleasure of understanding the capabilities of the special material, and using it for suggesting (not imitating) natural beauty and incident, that gives the *raison d'être* for decorative art.'

He first put many of his ideas into practice in decorating his first marital home, The Red House at Bexleyheath, to which he moved with his wife Jane in 1860. He designed embroidered curtains and hangings which were worked by Jane and her friends, and which included a number of panels based upon Chaucer's *The Legend of Good Women*. In 1861 Morris joined with other colleagues to create the firm of Morris, Marshall, Faulkner and Co. and their stand at the International Exhibition held only one year later showed stained glass, furniture, tableware, tiles and embroideries. The firm undertook the design and production of hangings, portières and church furnishings, designs being supplied by Morris, Edward Burne-Jones and Philip Webb, and the execution undertaken by Jane and by other relatives and friends.

Morris had earlier experimented with appropriate stitches and materials for his designs, even unpicking old embroideries in order to understand how they were made. He favoured straight stitches such as darning, running, long and short and satin, since they permitted the most freedom of interpretation and were not distracting in themselves. The serges and silks used as the basis for the work were specially dyed, as were the silk and wool threads, since Morris abhorred the colours produced by aniline dyes.

He was a pattern maker *par excellence*, transforming familiar flowers and plants into surface ornament in a way that is still recognized as uniquely his. The portière (82) shows his extraordinary ability to produce designs of real depth and movement by simply using line, and without overstepping the constraints of a flat plane.

By the 1880s, when the firm had become Morris and Co., his Chief Assistant, J. H. Dearle, and his daughter

82. Portière 'The Vine' designed by William Morris in 1878, embroidered by Mary Morris at a later date.

May, ran the embroidery section and were largely responsible for initiating design. They produced work which was very much in Morris's own spirit, so that it is difficult in some cases to say whether Morris or Dearle was responsible for a design. By this stage, besides making embroideries for sale or to commission, the firm was also supplying the amateur embroideress with ready-drawn designs and specially dyed threads. Many pieces were sold with a corner of the design already worked to show the amateur how it should be completed. The enormous popularity of these embroideries among the upper middle class intelligentsia made them a major component of the fashion for art needlework.

Church Embroidery

The revival of interest in Church embroidery had its roots even further back, in the 1830s, and had the positive effect of involving leading architects and designers in the design of embroidery. The Catholic

Emancipation Act of 1829 led to the building of many new churches which from the beginning were planned to be richly furnished in the manner which the Roman church had always preferred. The major architect associated with this development was the Catholic, Augustus Welby Pugin (1812–1852), who advocated a return to the Christian purity of the Gothic style for church architecture and furnishings. A call for the re-introduction of more elaborate liturgy and church ornament simultaneously occurred in the Anglican Church, led by the supporters of the Oxford Movement.

From the 1840s there was widespread interest and discussion as to the most suitable forms and designs for church art. The Cambridge Camden Society's magazine *The Ecclesiologist*, published from 1841, was an important vehicle for this debate. It showed new designs for all manner of church furnishings, including embroidery, and held up the medieval Gothic church as the example to be followed in all things. In 1848 the Society published a volume entitled *Ecclesiastical Embroidery* which provided needlewomen with flower patterns drawn directly from medieval church embroideries.

Pugin himself designed many embroideries at this period, and he made it clear to amateur workers for the church that 'the only hope of reviving the perfect style is by strictly adhering to *ancient authorities*: illuminated manuscripts, stained glass, and especially brasses, will furnish excellent examples, and many of them easy of imitation'.

The architect George Street was influential in the Anglican High Church movement. Like Pugin he concerned himself with the design of church furnishings as much as with the building itself, and he too drew upon medieval embroideries for his essays in this medium.

Pugin had commented in 1843 that 'we cannot yet hope to revive the expression and finish of the old work'. Indeed the technical skills represented were far beyond the abilities of most contemporary embroiderers and were no longer common currency. In an attempt to correct this a number of organizations grew up which attempted to reinstate older techniques for church work. The first was The Ladies' Ecclesiastical Embroidery Society formed in 1854 by Street's sister and Miss Agnes Blencowe. Vestments and church furnishings were produced based upon old designs, and upon designs provided by Street and other leading architects such as George Bodley (1827–1907).

The ecclesiastical textiles of the 1840s and 1850s tended to be geometric in style, and based upon formal Gothic ornament, but in the 1860s rather romanticized figures were introduced, and more elaborate foliage ornament. A much higher standard of work in older techniques was realized through the efforts of the ecclesiastical work societies and the participation of professional firms of church furnishers. From the 1870s techniques were not simply confined to the silk split stitch and laid goldwork of medieval embroidery; all forms of appliqué were widely used, and there was a freer use of stitching in silks and wools reflecting the influence of Morris and the secular Art Needlework movement.

This was particularly true of embroideries produced by the Leek Embroidery Society founded in 1879 by Elizabeth Wardle, wife of Thomas Wardle, silk-dyer and printer, and friend of Morris. The Society is best remembered for silk embroideries worked over the printed designs of Wardle's silks, used for domestic furnishings, but during the 1880s and 1890s it was responsible for the execution of many fine church embroideries and banners by notable designers.

The Art Needlework Movement

The Dictionary of Needlework published by Caulfield and Saward in 1882 defined Art Needlework as 'a name recently introduced as a general term for all descriptions of needlework that spring from the application of a knowledge of a design and colouring, with skill in fitting and execution. It is either executed by the worker from his or her designs or the patterns are drawn by a skilled artist.'

It is clear that the teachings of Morris and his fellow designers were having some effect at a popular level. The 1870s had seen the emergence of a number of societies and organizations concerned with promoting better design and technique in embroidery. The first, and historically the most important of these, was the Royal School of Art Needlework founded in 1872 under the Presidency of H.R.H. the Princess Christian of Schleswig-Holstein, Queen Victoria's third daughter. It included many titled women upon its organizing committee and one of its aims, apart from the elevation of embroidery to an art, was to provide suitable employment for poor gentlewomen. By 1875 the School was established in premises in South Kensington, and employed over 100 women who worked on embroideries designed by some of the leading designers of the day, including Morris, Burne-Jones, Bodley, and Walter Crane (1845–1915). Old embroideries were also repaired. Besides the artistic embroideries in silks and crewel wools in the form of hangings, screens and portières, the School also rapidly set the highest standards of design in metal thread embroidery and appliqué work used for church furnishings and ceremonial work. An enormously successful stand at the Philadelphia Centennial Exhibition in 1876 cost the School some

83. Four-fold screen, designed by Selwyn Image and embroidered by the Royal School of Needlework. English, late nineteenth century.

£2000 to mount, which was more than repaid by the enthusiastic response which it engendered among American needlewomen and prospective customers. It led indirectly to the formation of the first Decorative Art Society in New York City, whose founders included the glass designer Louis Tiffany (1848–1933) and the embroiderer Candace Wheeler (1828–1923). The Royal School of Art Needlework soon had agencies in Philadelphia and in Boston, and teachers were sent out from England to instruct pupils in the art of 'Kensington embroidery'. By the 1880s the School also had a branch school and showrooms in Glasgow, and agencies in all the major British cities. It became the most important exponent of art needlework, which increasingly became associated with a style of design, rather than a philosophy. It was the first large institution to offer a complete training in fine needlework techniques, and as such had a foremost place in the revival of the craft (83).

A number of other craft organizations were also set up in the 1880s which had an impact upon embroidery: The New Century Guild (1882), The Art Workers Guild (1884), The Guild and School of Handicraft (1888), and The Arts and Crafts Exhibition Society (1888). All these organizations were concerned with reinstating the crafts to their 'rightful place alongside painting and sculpture', and with the notion of the artist-craftsman. The proponents recognized the split that had taken place between these two fields during the Renaissance. Morris had borrowed from the medieval tradition in an attempt to get back to first

84. Detail of a tablecloth, Fisherton-de-la-Mere Industries. English, early twentieth century.

principles: the Arts and Crafts movement also took great interest in peasant industries in its search for simplicity of design and traditional use of materials.

A number of embroidery industries sought to recreate styles of work which were inspired by peasant textiles, and which, in their organization, reflected simpler modes of production. Many of these were philanthropic cottage industries. The Fisherton-de-la-Mere Industry in Whiltshire, founded by Mrs Arthur Newall in the 1890s, employed many housebound workers whom Mrs Newall trained in the techniques of cut-and-drawn work based upon sixteenth- and seventeenth-century linen embroidery and upon Italian peasant embroidery. The industry continued until the

85. Hanging, 'The Spies', designed by Godfrey Blount. Haslemere Peasant Industry, c. 1900.

1920s and produced beautiful work in traditional techniques, although not often of novel design (**84**). Haslemere Peasant Industries was founded in 1896 by Godfrey Blount in order to enable village embroiderers to earn money by producing work of simple technique but excellent design. Hand-woven and hand-dyed linen was the basis of the appliqué work, for which Blount provided designs; mainly for hangings and portières. The hanging (**85**) is typical. It uses soft shades of linen, applied to the ground and outlined with satin stitch in hand-dyed silks.

The Langdale Linen Industry was set up by Alfred Fleming in 1893 with the support and patronage of John Ruskin. It too produced hand-woven linen, and this was used for embroidery based, like some Fisherton work, on sixteenth-century cutwork or reticella embroidery. It was promoted as Ruskin work to emphasize its arts and crafts image.

At a popular amateur level, the arguments advanced by Morris, and later by the leaders of the Arts and Crafts movement, were not always understood. Art Needlework was enthusiastically taken up by many because it was perceived as a new form of interior decoration fashionable with the upper classes, and also because institutions like the Royal School received the highest aristocratic patronage. The simple stitches promoted by Morris & Co.'s embroideries were as easy to learn as those of canvas work, and it was thought by many that it was only necessary to obtain designs of the new floral range – sunflowers, daisies, irises and lilies – and to work them in 'art' silks or wools. One critic complained in 1880 that:

> Many people think that no more is needed than to work crewels on crash instead of as formerly in Berlin wool on canvas. Others think that if the work be 'dowdy' in colour it may pass under the sacred name of Art. Others again show a blind and touching faith in South Kensington and maintain that 'Art Needlework' is only to be had there . . . All would say that it is a modern invention, much in fashion just now and therefore they must by no means neglect it.

Crewel embroidery enjoyed an enormous revival among amateur workers under the aegis of art needlework. Patterns were closely based upon late seventeenth-century originals, and were worked using wools, or even silks, upon crash or linen for hangings, curtains and portières. There was also a general enthusiasm for any designs based upon historic originals, particularly those in the collections of the Kensington Museum (Victoria and Albert). Renaissance putti, dolphins and grotesque ornament were seen alongside patterns drawn from Persian and Turkish embroidery. Commercial pattern printers and magazines were no less assiduous in promoting Art Needlework than they had been with Berlin woolwork. In the last ten years of the century designers were still imploring needlewomen to initiate their own designs and to work from nature.

In America crewelwork also enjoyed a revival under the Deerfield Blue and White Industry, at Deerfield, Massachusetts, which was started in 1896 by two painters, Margaret Whiting and Ellen Miller. This was particularly concerned with a revival of eighteenth-century New England crewelwork done in indigo-dyed wools, which in its day had exhibited quite a different character from English crewel embroidery. The revived work, however, was executed in dyed blue linen on white linen crash, and the designs consisted of simple flower and leaf sprays, sometimes in vases, and like the older work was fresh and delicate.

The Glasgow School

An entirely new direction was taken by embroideries produced from the 1890s under the influence of the internationally important Glasgow School. Led by the architect Charles Rennie Mackintosh, a group of students at the School of Art produced furniture, metalwork, and embroidery in a completely novel style. Although it had some roots in the Arts and Crafts movement, it was more closely related to the continental Art Nouveau style, and was received abroad with much

86. Cushion cover, designed and worked in crewel wools by Jessie Newbery. Glasgow, 1890s.

87. Cushion cover decorated with pink glass beads, designed and worked by Ann Macbeth. Glasgow, early twentieth century.

greater enthusiasm in Britain. One student, Jessie Rowat, married the director of the school and, as Jessie Newbery, founded an embroidery class in 1894 which was open to both students and non-students.

Her own work naturally reflected the prevailing style of the School – sinuous line contrasted with strong vertical and horizontal lines, plant motifs, and colour schemes which were predominantly black and white with a range of pale pastels – but her approach to embroidery was entirely new. She encouraged individuality in design and completely rejected copying. The design of embroidery was to grow out of the materials and stitches used. These could be of the simplest and still be effective, as long as they were appropriate to the materials being used and the object being decorated.

She made wide use of appliqué and of needleweaving: a technique used in peasant embroideries of the Near East, in which threads were withdrawn from the ground fabric and the remaining warp or weft threads whipped together with silks. Her designs were bold and simple, and frequently featured inscriptions in the characteristic lettering style of the Glasgow school. She stated that she was as interested in the spaces of a design as in the components which made it up. These

features can be seen in the cushion cover (**86**), with its formalized sweet pea pattern worked in crewel wools using satin, long and short and stem stitches. The border is needleweaving.

Many of Mrs Newbery's students became important embroidery designers and workers in their own right, but one in particular, Ann Macbeth, continued her teacher's philosophy and practice (**87**). She succeeded Jessie Newbery as Head of the Embroidery Department on her retirement in 1908. Under Ann Macbeth the programme of training of primary and secondary school teachers was expanded. She was a talented embroiderer and a gifted teacher, and was particularly interested in the possibilities of the new approach to embroidery, believing that if children could learn to experiment with stitches at an early age, under the guidance of a good teacher, then they would naturally grow into the habits of good design and execution. This was one method of improving the general quality of embroidery which the other reformers had not tackled.

Ann Macbeth, and her assistants Margaret Swanson and Anne Knox-Arthur, became internationally noted for their teachings in the field of needlework education, especially after the publication of their book *Educational*

Needlecraft in 1913; the first of some ten books which they produced between them. Even when the particular style of the Glasgow school had passed out of fashion, their ideas continued to exert great influence, and still form the basis of teaching creative needlework.

THE TWENTIETH CENTURY

The nearer we come to our own day the more surviving examples of embroidery proliferate: we have more information about the embroiderers and embroideries of the last eighty years than of any other period. Nevertheless it is still difficult to chart a clear course through lines of development. We are still too near to be able usefully to sum up eighty years of embroidery produced under an unusually wide variety of circumstances: by the amateur still following commercial patterns; by the semi-trained amateur working within organizations and groups; by highly skilled professionals following traditional techniques; and by art school-trained artist-craftsmen.

Machine Embroidery

Machine embroidery was firmly established by 1900. The multi-needle automatic machines developed by the Swiss were capable not only of producing whitework borders, but of decorating whole widths of fabric in shaded, silk flowers that looked like hand embroidery until one examined the reverse. There were also a range of single-needle hand machines: the Domestic machine, and the Irish and Cornelly, which were trade machines. All of these were used for embroidery.

The Singer Sewing Machine Company had for some time promoted the use of its hand machines for embroidery to the extent of employing expert machinists to teach the techniques in the firm's workrooms. Most of the effects of hand stitching could be imitated, even to cutwork and needlelace fillings. The Edwardian fanleaf shown (**88**) probably emanated from the Singer workrooms. It is worked on shade-dyed silk gauze using silk threads. The only hand stitching on it is that used to sew on the picot edging.

Singers continued to take the lead in training embroiderers to use the machine up to the 1950s. Dorothy Benson was head of the workroom during the 1930s and 1940s, and was a notable technician who trained many well-known embroiderers, including Rebecca Crompton (*see page* 84). Since the 1960s however, although machine embroidery has greatly increased in importance, it is rarely used to imitate the effects of hand embroidery, but is exploited for its own effects.

Much beautiful embroidery and beading for costume was produced by professional embroidery houses in the first thirty years of the century (**89**). Paris led the field in this respect, particularly in the all-over beading used for tea and evening dresses in the 1920s. This type of work is now largely restricted to haute couture, although some women in Britain still work at home beading for 'rag trade' evening dresses at very low wages.

Theories and Debates

There has been more written about the theory and practice of embroidery in the last eighty years than in the previous 1000 years, yet there is still no consensus of opinion as to what constitutes good embroidery. The subject is still excitingly fraught with polemic.

The ideas of the Arts and Crafts movement have continued to play an important role in attitudes to the craft. The personal satisfaction which the individual can derive from 'understanding the capabilities of the special material' has, as Morris predicted, provided a *raison d'être* for the pursuit of such a craft for its own sake. It had appeared in the nineteenth century that the relentless march of the machine would remove the necessity for the practice of craft, or that, without direction, it would die in a welter of fancy work.

Yet many of the other desiderata posed by Morris and the Arts and Crafts movement have been implicitly questioned. Morris had feared the machine and the consequences of its monotonous duplication. He therefore advocated the total involvement of the artist from start to finish in the production of craft. This notion has been strongly current throughout this century among leading embroidery teachers. The need for embroiderers to learn how to draw and to design has been reiterated in every decade, and is still urged in embroidery classes every week. Morris's and Newbery's themes of fitness of materials, design and technique to purpose are also still current, although embroiderers now have a potentially enormous range of materials to choose from.

Yet other views have been posed. Lewis Day (1845–1910) was an industrial artist of great influence, who designed for embroidery among other crafts, and published a book entitled *Art and Needlework* in 1900. Day firmly believed in the division of labour, and in the future of the machine. He took a less idealized view than Morris of an individual embroiderer's technical skill always being equal to his or her ability to produce good designs. Either a good design would be spoiled by poor workmanship or great technical skill be wasted on bad design. Most of the great embroideries of the past had involved collaboration between artist and embroiderer.

88. Fanleaf: domestic machine embroidery on dyed silk gauze, probably from the Singer workrooms, *c.* 1900–10.

89. *(above)* Detail of embroidery on the hem of an evening coat. French, *c.* 1920.

90. *(right)* Banner, designed by Joan Drew and executed by Women's Institute members. English, 1915–20.

Throughout this century the debate has continued. Avant-garde critics have condemned, often rightly, the repetitious copying of historical embroideries and the amateur's constant clamour for patterns and transfers. Marion Stoll, a keen exponent of modern embroidery, made a bitter attack on contemporary British embroidery in 1925:

> It seems very likely that the ban laid upon modern needlework arises from several, though closely related sources. Of these, perhaps the chief is the incredibly powerful inhibition set up in the English mind by the omni-present Jacobean work and the mass of imitations. We are continually told by those who are themselves the victims of tradition, that the fourteenth-century Elizabethan and Jacobean work, not to mention the Near Eastern atrocities of a later date, are the be-all and end-all of our art . . . Could an Englishwoman of adult age be found who had never seen nor heard of Jacobean embroidery, and could she be faced with an example without comment, she would say that it was as clumsy and ugly as anything she had ever seen.

To a great extent this passionate interest in historic embroideries had stemmed from the same set of ideas which produced artist-craftsman like Marion Stoll. There had in any case been a general enthusiasm for antique collecting from the late nineteenth century, and public appetite for historical embroideries had been whetted by several major exhibitions in the early years of the century. Amateur embroiderers were obviously not always able to see past the embroideries themselves to the wider principles they had to teach.

Group Projects

Day's belief that everything would come right if embroiderers were provided with good designs has not always come to pass. Few major artists and designers in this century have chosen to design for the craft, unless of course they were embroiderers themselves. The exception of the Omega Workshop, for which Vanessa Bell, Duncan Grant and Roger Fry designed embroideries between 1913 and 1919 is one of the few exceptions that proves the rule.

On the other hand, many fine pieces of embroidery have been produced in situations where embroiderers skilled as designers have produced a design and supervised its working by a group of technically competent embroiderers. This has happened so often in this century that it must be one of the characteristic features of our age. The banner (90) is one of several designed by Joan Drew (1875–1961), and worked under her supervision by Women's Institute members. The main technique is linen appliqué, recalling Blount's Haslemere pieces, but it also uses laid Japanese gold thread for the apples.

Many ecclesiastical and civic embroideries have been undertaken in this fashion. A seminal project was the working of the kneelers and choir hangings for Winchester cathedral between 1931 and 1936. The designs for these were prepared by Louisa Pesel and Sybil Blount. Stitches and colours were worked out in advance, and samplers prepared for the embroiderers to work from. They were entirely carried out by local women known as the Winchester Broderers.

Miss Pesel was a student of Lewis Day, and had been head of the Royal Hellenic School of Lace and Embroidery in Athens before the First World War. In 1920 she became first President of the Embroiderers' Guild when it was re-formed after the war. A similar kneeler scheme was shortly afterwards carried out at Guildford cathedral, and many other kneeler projects have been since completed, or are in process of working.

The embroiderer Beryl Dean, whose great contribution to twentieth-century church embroidery was recognized by the award of an M.B.E. in 1975, has supervised many such group projects for the church. Perhaps the best-known and best-loved is the cope for the Diocese of London, made to mark the Queen's Silver Jubilee in 1977 (*see* p. 249). Miss Dean designed the cope and supervised its working by thirty-six of her students from the Stanhope Institute of Adult Education. All the churches of the Diocese are represented, each worked separately on silk organza and applied to a wool ground; gold thread and purl are used to highlight the design.

The best ecclesiastical work in this century has been produced by embroiderers with a proper training in art and design. Beryl Dean trained at Bromley School of Art and the Royal College of Art. She also had the benefit of the excellent technical training provided by the Royal School of Needlework, which enables her to excel in such classic techniques as *or nué*. Among other artist-embroiderers who have produced work for the church in recent years one might single out Pat Russell, whose frontals and vestments are colourful essays in

machine appliqué; Ann Butler Morrell, now Head of the Embroidery Department at Manchester Polytechnic, for her magnificent patchwork and appliqué dossal curtain in a modern Methodist church in Timperley, Cheshire (1974); and Hannah Frew Paterson now in Jessie Newbery's shoes at Glasgow, and whose pulpit fall for Gorbals Parish Church, also in patchwork and appliqué of silks and gold kid, shows her to be within the finest tradition of Scottish embroidery.

Sadly for every good frontal, cope and set of kneelers, there are many more amateur pieces of poor design which in no way contribute to the heritage of art which each century has successively added to the parish churches and cathedrals of Britain. It is comforting to believe that they will one day be quietly removed.

Schools and Techniques

The various nineteenth-century moves to improve knowledge and practice of embroidery techniques resulted in a veritable Renaissance of technical skill in the early years of this century. While Morris showed little interest in the wide range of stitches and techniques available to be learned, this subject was taken up with great seriousness by others. In this century the Royal School of Needlework has played a central role in technical training, and this has been built upon by many Schools of Art. A notable exponent of the stitch was Mrs Grace Christie (1872–1938), who taught at the Royal College of Art from 1907. She was an

91. The central motif of a cushion cover uses Elizabethan blackwork patterns in a floral design reminiscent of early eighteenth-century embroideries. English, *c*. 1920.

92. Sampler of ecclesiastical techniques worked by Katherine Powell for a City and Guilds examination. English, *c.* 1910.

authority on historical needlework and published the first major account of English medieval embroidery in 1938. Her students had to follow a rigorous training in stitch techniques, as is shown by many examples of work produced at the Royal College up to 1920. Her book *Samplers and Stitches* (1920) is still a classic.

93. Velvet cushion embroidered with silks. English, *c.* 1920.

The ecclesiastical sampler (92), worked in about 1910 for a City and Guilds of London Institute examination, gives some indication of the range of techniques which a student might be expected to master at this period. It was worked by Katherine Powell (1890–1977) who was born with only one hand.

Due to the efforts of embroidery historians such as Mrs Christie, an enormous range of stitches had been identified upon historical and foreign embroideries by the second decade of the century. Many of them acquired their present names during this interesting archaeological period, since they either had not been used in living memory, or had not been used in English embroidery before. In about 1912 Louisa Pesel worked enormous samplers of all the known stitches, from which she published three sets of stitch cards: 'Historic English Embroideries', 'Stitches from Western Embroideries' and 'Stitches from Eastern Embroideries'. These are still set up in the textile study gallery at the Victoria and Albert Museum.

The predominant design styles of the art colleges still reflected the influence of art needlework well into the early 1920s. There was much meticulous re-creation of the historic forms of embroidery, albeit adapted to new designs (91). The prevailing mood of historicism combined with sub-Morris floral ornament was somewhat allieviated in the 1920s with a general enthusiasm for all forms of peasant embroidery. But the exciting themes reflected in foreign textiles and embroidery—

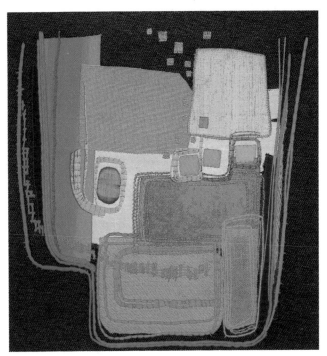

94. 'My Mother', by Elizabeth Grace Thomson. English, 1930s.

95. Wall hanging, 'Fire on the Mountain'. Julia Caprara, member of the 62 Group of embroiderers. English, 1983–4.

96. 'Fire Glow' by Constance Howard using felt in appliqué, embroidered with wool and silk. English, late 1960s.

97. Chancellor's Purse, showing the royal coat-of-arms, made by the Royal School of Needlework. English, 1984.

98. Cot cover designed by Winsome Douglas for the Needlework Development Scheme. English, 1950s.

Cubism, Fauvism, Art Deco and the influence of the Bauhaus school – seem to have largely passed Britain by, apart from a few individuals such as Mary Hogarth, Marion Stoll, Madeleine Clifton and Rebecca Crompton. European influence made itself more felt in the 1930s. Continental embroideries were shown in exhibitions, and through work bought for the 1934 Needlework Development Scheme. This project, sponsored by thread manufacturers J. & P. Coats, began in Scotland with the aim of providing the four main art institutions with a collection of contemporary European embroideries. This not only included work by artist embroiderers from Britain and abroad, but also many copies of European peasant embroideries.

The circulation scheme was temporarily closed down during the war, but after 1945 it was revived and expanded to cover art colleges and schools all over Britain. Many new pieces by the leading embroiderers of the day were added in the late 1940s and early 1950s. These were often simple designs which concentrated upon the effect produced by the stitches (**98**). The scheme had a great influence on several genera-

tions of young embroiderers, enabling them to see a wide range of work. It was felt that it had fulfilled its purpose by 1961; it was closed, and the embroideries distributed to various art colleges and museums.

There were one or two art schools in every decade which tended to take an innovative lead, largely due to particular teachers. Croydon School of Art enjoyed a reputation for exciting work in the early 1920s, under the directorship of Rebecca Crompton (1895–1947), a dynamic personality committed to experiment, who revolutionized approaches to the craft. Her designs were partly figurative but filled with abstract shape and pattern. She combined every type of fabric, thread and stitch, often deliberately leaving raw edges. She set down her views in a book, *Modern Design in Embroidery*.

Her pupil and associate Elizabeth Grace Thomson (1895–1983) worked much in her style (**94**) and went on to become head of fashion and crafts at Bromley and Sidcup Schools of Art. Under her leadership, Bromley came to have a name in the 1930s for fashion and embroidery, particularly machine embroidery.

The embroidery of the post-war period has firmly stated its claims as art by being predominently panels and wall hangings, although some amateur embroiderers have continued to favour practical items such as tablecloths, pincushions and boxes. The making of bed quilts and patchwork has never gone out of fashion and some extremely fine and original work is being done. The best work of the 1950s and 1960s is now beginning to be appreciated, after the passing of its immediately unfashionable phase. The work of such British embroiderers as Constance Howard, Margaret Kaye, Kath Whyte and Alison Lilley shows the qualities of good design and skilful use of materials and techniques which are the timeless essentials (**96**).

Since the 1970s much embroidery has been completely abstract in design. In some ways it has continued to derive its ideas at second hand from painters, and in other cases has worked over well-worn tracks, but this tendency has been diminished by the breaking down of barriers between embroidery and a whole range of other media. The foremost embroiderers of the 1980s are perhaps more precisely termed 'textile artists', although there are few for whom the manipulation of threads and fabric with a needle is not of prime importance.

The ancient techniques are in no danger of dying out. Every new generation of embroiderers discovers them with pleasure and experiments with their methods in order to make them their own. They are currently learning to tambour, to experiment with amusing twentieth-century versions of 'stumpwork', to quilt with cords, and to use tufted stitches in canvas work. Julia Caprara's 'Fire on the Mountain' (**95**) uses many traditional techniques, yet is completely original in the way it employs them. Who could fail to enjoy this vibrant textile? In the same year that it was made, professional embroidery of the highest traditional excellence was also produced (**97**). We seem to have the best of both worlds.

————— BIBLIOGRAPHY—————

Antal, F. *Florentine Painting and its Social Background, XIV and Early XV Centuries*, London 1948

Arthur, E., and F. Macfarlane *Glasgow School of Art Embroidery, 1894–1920.* Exhibition catalogue, Glasgow Museum 1980

Art Institute, Chicago *Raiment for the Lord's Service.* Exhibition catalogue 1975

Arts Council of Great Britain *Opus Anglicanum.* Exhibition catalogue, Victoria and Albert Museum, London 1963

—*English Romanesque Art, 1066–1200.* Exhibition catalogue, Hayward Gallery, London 1984

Bath, V. C. *Needlework in America*, New York 1979; London 1980

Beck, T. *Embroidered Gardens*, London 1972; New York 1979

Brett, K. B. *English Embroidery in the Royal Ontario Museum, Sixteenth to Eighteenth Century*, Toronto, Ont., 1972

Bridgeman, H., and E. Drury (eds) *Needlework: An Illustrated History*, London 1978

British Museum *The Golden Age of Anglo-Saxon Art.* Exhibition catalogue, London 1984

Buck, A. 'The Countryman's Smock', *Folk Life* 1963

Burnett, J. *A History of the Cost of Living*, London 1969

Campbell, R. *The London Tradesman* (1747), repr. London 1969

Cennini, Cennino *Libro dell'arte*
Various translations, including:
Herringham, Lady C. J. *The Book of the Art*, London 1899
Thompson, D. V. *The Craftsman's Handbook*, 1960

Christie, A. G. I. *Samplers and Stitches*, 3rd edn, London 1934

—*English Medieval Embroidery*, Oxford 1938

Clabburn, P. *The Needleworker's Dictionary*, New York 1976

Colby, A. *Patchwork*, London 1958; Newton Centre, Mass., 1976

—*Quilting*, London 1972; Newton Centre, Mass., 1976

Crompton, R. *Modern Design in Embroidery*, London 1936

Edwards, J. *Crewel Embroidery in England*, London 1973

Embroiderers' Guild *Embroideries in the Permanent Collection*, London 1971

Fitzrandolph, M. *Traditional Quilting*, London 1954

Freeman, J. *Quilting, Patchwork and Appliqué, 1700–1982: Sewing as a Woman's Art.* Exhibition catalogue, Colchester, Essex, 1982

Geijer, Agnes *A History of Textile Art*, London 1979

Hackenbrock, Y. *English and Other Needlework, Tapestries and Textiles in the Irwin Untermeyer Collection*, London 1960

Hall, M. *Smocks*, Shire Album No. 46, Princes Risborough, Buckinghamshire, 1972; Cincinnati, Ohio, 1984

Hayden, R. *Mrs Delany: Her Life and Her Flowers*, London 1980

Howard, C. *Twentieth-century Embroidery in Great Britain*, 3 vols (to 1939; 1940–1963; 1964–1977), London 1983–4; Newton Centre, Mass., 1984

Howe, M. B. *Early American Embroideries in Deerfield, Massachusetts*, 1963

Hughes, T. *English Domestic Needlework, 1660–1860*, London 1961

Irwin, J. 'Origins of Oriental Style in English Decorative Art', *Burlington Magazine*, Vol. 96 (1955), pp. 106–114

Kendrick, A. F. *English Needlework*, 2nd edn, London 1967

King, D. *Samplers*, London 1960

Levey, S. *Discovering Embroidery of the Nineteenth Century*, Princes Risborough, Buckinghamshire, 1971

—*Lace: A History*, Leeds, W. Yorkshire, 1983

Lucie-Smith, E. *The Story of Craft*, Ithaca, N.Y., and Oxford 1981

Marshall, B. *Smocks and Smocking*, Sherborne, Dorset, 1980

Morris, B. *Victorian Embroidery*, London 1962

Nevinson, J. L. *Catalogue of English Domestic Needlework of the Sixteenth and Seventeenth Century*, Victoria and Albert Museum, London 1938

—'John Nelham, Embroiderer', *The Bulletin of the Needle and Bobbin Club*, New York 1982

Oddy, R. *Catalogue of Embroideries Given to the Museum by the Needlework Development Scheme*, Royal Scottish Museum, Edinburgh 1965

Parker, R. *The Subversive Stitch*, London 1984

Parry, L. (series ed.) *How to Make Historic Embroideries*, London 1986

Saint-Aubin, C. G. de *L'Art du Brodeur*, Paris 1770

Santangelo, A. *The Development of Italian Textile Design from the Twelfth to Eighteenth Centuries*, trans. P. Craig, London 1964

Schuette, M. and S. Müller-Christensen *The Art of Embroidery*, trans. D. King, London 1964

Seligman, G., and T. Hughes *Domestic Needlework*, London 1926

Stenton, Sir F. (ed.) *The Bayeux Tapestry: A Comprehensive Survey*, 2nd edn, London 1965

Strong, Sir R. *Artists of the Tudor Court.* Exhibition catalogue, Victoria and Albert Museum, London 1983

Swain, M. *The Flowerers*, London and Edinburgh 1955

—*The Needlework of Mary Queen of Scots*, New York and Wokingham, Berkshire, 1973

—'Mrs Newbery's Dress', *Costume No. 12* (1978), pp. 64–73

—'John Nelham's Needlework Panel', *The Bulletin of the Needle and Bobbin Club*, New York 1982

Swan, S. B. *Plain and Fancy: American Women and Their Needlework, 1700–1850*, New York 1977

Swanson, M., and A. Macbeth *Educational Needlecraft*, London 1913

Synge, L. *Antique Needlework*, Poole, Dorset, 1982

Tarrant, N. *Smocks in the Buckinghamshire County Museum*, Aylesbury, Buckinghamshire, 1976

Victoria and Albert Museum *Rococo: Art and Design in Hogarth's England.* Exhibition catalogue, London 1984

Wardle, P. *Guide to English Embroidery*, London 1970

Wingfield-Digby, G. F. *Elizabethan Embroidery*, London 1963

CANVAS WORK

CAROL HUMPHREY

Canvas work would seem a simple enough description for embroidery on an evenly woven foundation fabric, often of a lattice-like construction, usually of linen or cotton. But, such a simple expression is frequently confused with less accurate terms. For instance, needlepoint is widely used in the United States for all types of counted-thread embroidery, particularly canvas work. Curiously the earliest inventories of mid-seventeenth century American households refer to canvas work and not needlepoint. Until the nineteenth century needlepoint was the common term for needle-made lace, distinguishing it from bobbin lace. The decline of the former and the dominance of bobbin and machine lace contributed to the loss of its original meaning and its regeneration as an alternative name for canvas embroidery. Another descriptive term in general use is tapestry work – despite canvas work being a form of embroidery, and tapestry one of the most important types of decorative weaving. An historical justification for the term is often cited, this being that the needlewomen from the sixteenth to the eighteenth centuries sought to imitate tapestry when making household hangings, covers and upholstery and thus the two terms became interchangeable.

1. *(opposite)* Detail of the Marian panel from the Oxburgh Hangings, attributed partly to Mary Queen of Scots, c. 1570.

2. *(above)* Detail from an unused border showing a double-twist design, Traquair House. Scottish, seventeenth century.

However, it should not be forgotten that such early needlework was the work of a very privileged class. Relatively few were blessed with the leisure and wealth that enabled them to devote themselves almost solely to the production of embroidery. It was no small expense to maintain the ladies of a large household, their attendants and servants and to supply them with fine quality canvas, wools, silks and metal threads, and possibly to pay for the work of resident or itinerant journeyman embroiderers to design and participate in the work. Where such wealth existed both tapestries and needlework were afforded and often regarded as complementary to each other. Perhaps the tapestries tended to be in the more formal, public areas of the house and the needlework in the more intimate, private rooms. Both were expensive and could be used for similar purposes but technically they are distinct. Tapestry should not be used to describe any embroidery whether the Bayeux Tapestry, historical canvas work, or even today's misnamed tapestry embroidery kits.

Two further muddling misnomers occur when canvas work is called *petit point* or *gros point*. The implication is that the first is a small stitch on a fine gauge canvas and the second a larger stitch on a coarse canvas. In fact *petit point* should be synonymous with tent stitch, one of the most commonly used counted-thread stitches, worked on the slope, over a single thread. Consequently its size is regulated by that of the canvas mesh and can range from the tiny, dense stitching of sixteenth- and seventeenth-century table carpets and bed valances, often at about 90 stitches to 1 sq cm (600 per sq in), to thick wool and a large mesh with perhaps less than 9 stitches to 1 sq cm (60 per sq in). Not surprisingly *gros point* does not mean a large tent stitch but cross stitch, its size similarly depending on the gauge of the canvas. As it has to be worked over at least two horizontal threads it is unsuitable for extremely fine work, but it is a robust stitch creating a durable textile, and the many variations of cross stitch are also useful for creating surface interest. So, if the simple term canvas work is used, many misunderstandings are removed.

Basic Materials and Stitches

The canvas is usually of cotton or linen, the embroidery generally worked with woollen threads, often highlighted with silks and occasionally worked in silk. The two most popular stitches, tent and cross, give an end product that is strong, durable but rather inflexible. Variations in canvas mesh allow for the finest find the coarsest stitching, suitable for anything from a minutely detailed picture to large-scale upholstery.

Compared to many forms of embroidery, such as whitework or metal thread work, canvas work using the basic stitches is not technically difficult. Rather than great dexterity it requires time and patience, an ideal craft for the leisured amateur. Although professional workshops have been in existence for the last 400 years much historical canvas work is a domestic product. Perhaps it is worth emphasizing at this point that it was mainly the stitching that was done by the home embroiderer. It is very much a late nineteenth- and early twentieth-century concept that a competent needlewoman should also be an able and creative designer and draughtsman; an idea that many may agree has hardly brought about an improvement in artistic standards or in technical competence. Previously it was common practice for a professional embroiderer to be at hand in the great houses. There were, too, itinerant journeymen, and professional workshops who could execute or simply design to order. Designs were often derived from pattern books featuring illustrations from biblical and classical stories, herbals, bestiaries or popular engravings – all were adapted and transferred directly onto the canvas.

It was not until the early nineteenth century that the first coloured designs on squared paper were published, so that each printed square could be reproduced as a stitch on the canvas, thus eliminating the need for drawing. Previous to this, various methods had been used to transfer designs from paper to fabric. At what might be called the luxury end of the trade the commission was drawn directly onto the canvas by the designer. If the canvas was very fine the 'prick and pounce' method would be used by either workshop apprentices or competent ladies of a household. A very large object to be worked would possibly have a strongly outlined drawing put behind the mounted canvas, which would then be held against a good light, allowing the design to be traced and finally painted. If professional help was not available the embroiderer still sought the inspiration of increasingly varied printed matter, often pricking and pouncing through sheets of patterns or illustrated books – this practice helps explain the rarity of complete early pattern books.

From the sixteenth century onwards, relatively accessible embroidery materials and an increasingly prosperous upper strata of society contributed to the great flowering of secular needlework, canvas work being an important part of the output. Popularity is usually linked to fashion, and for canvas work, a technique unsuitable for costume, the fashions in furnishings and interior decoration have been the prevailing influences. Quality and quantity rarely go together, well illustrated by the vast production of Berlin woolwork of dubious merit in the nineteenth century. But apart from the intrinsic qualities of this embroidery technique it is important to consider how canvas work fits into a social context. It has always been closely associated with household furnishings and decorations and it is instructive to try to consider the artifacts in contemporary settings. Many museums and houses open to the public have examples of canvas work on display, but it requires imagination and knowledge to transpose them to a more suitable visual background. Where contemporary room settings have been created, or more rarely where a house retains its original furniture and fittings, then reality takes over from imagination and canvas work can be seen as part of a total domestic scene and not as a lone and isolated exhibit.

Hardwick Hall

One of the best starting points for the study of early canvas work in its original setting is that found in Hardwick Hall, Derbyshire, built between 1591 and 1597 by Bess of Hardwick whose second of four financially advantageous marriages was to Sir William Chatsworth. He bought and then built on the nearby Chatsworth estate and after Bess's death in 1608 the descendants of the Cavendish line, the Earls and Dukes

3. The bed in the Blue Room at Hardwick Hall, Derbyshire with applied canvas embroidery. English, c. 1620.

4. A piece of the original blue bed valance, Hardwick Hall. English, seventeenth century.

of Devonshire, took Chatsworth as their main family seat. Hardwick fell from favour and was little altered or restored over the following centuries. Many of the original contents, their cost and their makers' names are still there, the information surviving in Bess's accounts and the 1601 inventory. Externally the overwhelming architectural feature is the great glass windows, which could only have exacerbated the perennial problem of making life tolerable before efficient forms of domestic heating. The problem must have been greatest in the large ceremonial rooms of the house, perhaps less insuperable in the smaller withdrawing rooms and bed chambers — the latter's function was similar to today's bed-sitting room.

In the sixteenth century upholstered furniture was non-existent or very rare, and by far the most important object was the bed with its hangings and valances. Seating was provided by stools, benches and window seats, made more comfortable with cushions. Further comfort and decoration was supplied by tapestry or needlework wall hangings. These soft furnishings were essential for warmth and repose and they were a perfect vehicle for canvas embroidery. Some of the different approaches are well illustrated by the treatment of bed hangings or curtains and their valances. To remain flexible the hangings most usually had applied canvas work, but the flat, taut valances were more suitable for quite complex, large-scale pictorial canvas embroidery. At Hardwick two beds display applied work. In the inaccurately named Queen of Scots Room a much-restored bed has been hung with nineteenth-century black velvet on which are mounted sixteenth-century canvas work motifs, possibly the ones recorded in the 1601 inventory where the original hangings are described as 'imbrodered with nedleworke flowers'. The second bed (3), in the room originally called the Pearl Bedchamber after a richly hung bed that no longer exists, is hung with nineteenth-century blue damask decorated with applied canvas work of the 1620s of a typical Renaissance twist design. Some of the original blue damask and embroidery is displayed in an adjoining corridor and shows a richer style of applying canvas work (4), with outlining in couched silk cord and a speckling of cream silk French knots. The beds are in rooms decorated with tapestries, elaborate plaster work, panelling and chimney pieces, so it was essential that the embroidery was visually strong. The very survival of this canvas work also proves its physical strength; the greatest signs of wear are generally found on the areas of silk highlighting rather than among the predominant woollen threads. Often detailing and small-scale designs were worked in tent stitch and the background worked in cross stitch; where disintegration has occurred it is possible to see the distortion of the canvas created by the combination of stitches. At first glance the canvas can appear double-threaded (a type not manufactured until the nineteenth century); in fact the double appearance is caused by the threads being pulled together in the cross-stitch area.

Canvas Embroidery Furnishings

Similar hangings can be found on beds throughout Britain as far apart as Knole in Kent, Cotehele in Cornwall and Scone Palace in Scotland. All the floral motifs or 'slips' are probably based on illustrations in early herbals. The motifs on the remnants of the hangings at Scone are smaller in scale than those of Hardwick but of similar design and are bordered with yet more of the Renaissance twist pattern. Very close in design to these well-worn canvas work motifs is a recently discovered collection of unused slips and borders in pristine condition from Traquair House in the Scottish border country. The linen canvas panels are uncut (**2**), some are complete, some partially worked, but all have their original

vibrant colouring. They are believed to have been worked in the early seventeenth century by ancestors of the present family. For some reason they were put away and forgotten; protected from the destructive qualities of bright light, dirt and extreme temperature changes, they have retained their brilliant colours. The fruits and flowers, birds, beasts and insects depicted on them were almost certainly copied from one of the popular sixteenth-century books illustrated with both native and exotic wild life.

The incomplete panels show clearly that the slips were first of all drawn onto the canvas, then outlined in black cross stitch and worked in tent stitch; many are of silk though the larger ones tend to be wool. The yards and yards of border pattern have been similarly produced. The quality of the soft and loosely woven canvas suggests that there was a practical as well as an aesthetic reason for outlining applied motifs, as seen at Hardwick, with a couched silk cord. In this way frayed edges would be hidden, for fraying must have occurred

5. Two armchairs from the large suite in the High Great Chamber at Hardwick Hall. English, 1635.

even though such work was usually stabilized by a sealing coat of flour and water paste on the back.

Applied canvas work of similar style has also been used to decorate a rare suite of early upholstered stools, farthingale chairs and two armchairs (5) in the High Great Chamber at Hardwick. The frames and brown velvet upholstery of the chairs are nineteenth-century reproductions of those originally made in 1635: it is the embroidery that is original. Such a large set of chairs was evidence in itself of a wealthy, almost regal life style and the lavishly applied embroidery using wool, silk and metal threads in tent, cross and satin stitch with some couching, further emphasizes this point. But the actual designs are traditional, not dissimilar to those on the bed hangings and the Traquair panels. The exceptions are the two complex scenes mounted on the backs of the armchairs, one of hunting, the other of a coach and horses, both including a considerable amount of metal-thread work. In the then Duchess of Devonshire's account book payment was made to a 'George Savage the Imbroyderer' for seven weeks' work on the 'purple Imbroydered Suite'. As, at this date, 'Imbroyderer' also meant upholsterer, it seems more likely that George Savage was employed to arrange and mount the embroidery (which looks amateur rather than professional) rather than to work it himself.

It is worth noting that the purple suite of the seventeenth century must have faded to a dull brown over the ensuing 200 years, hence the dull brown of the nineteenth-century replacements. But even today, with its deep, polychrome plaster frieze, its original Brussels tapestries, decorated panelling, great glass windows and the exuberantly embroidered chairs, the chamber remains an historic room rich in colour and pattern.

In strong contrast to such amateur domestic work are the sets of bed valances made in professional workshops; their pictorial character and even standard of work is closer to the table carpets and cupboard covers

6. Bed valance, from one of the few complete sets remaining, showing the arms and initials of Sir Colin Campbell of Glenorchy and his wife Katherine. Scottish, sixteenth century.

of a similar date. Typically they are worked on fine linen canvas in tent stitch, mainly in wool with some silk highlights. The subject matter was invariably based on classical or biblical stories although the figures often appear dressed in contemporary French costume. Curiously the setting often appears to be a formal Elizabethan garden. It is sometimes tentatively suggested that such valances are of Scottish origin, hence the strong links with French fashion.

Certainly this could be true of one of the few complete sets of valances remaining together. Now in the Burrell Collection in Glasgow, they probably date from the mid-sixteenth century (6). They carry the arms and initials of Sir Colin Campbell of Glenorchy (d.1585) and his wife Katherine, daughter of Lord Ruthven. Another fine panel, hanging in the Lady Lever Art Gallery, is assumed to be from a set of valances as it measures approximately 1·9 m × 0·5 m (6 ft 2 in × 1 ft 8 in) and depicts the history of King Jehosh. The figures are characteristically dressed in the French fashions of the late sixteenth century and are made particularly eyecatching by silk highlights and additional surface stitching. The similarity of the valances, especially in the attitudes and dress of the figures, hints at a common design source though none has yet been found. Only among a suite of valances and coverlet or table carpet at the Victoria and Albert Museum has a definite attribution been possible. The table carpet from this set (7), which came from Compton Verney, Warwickshire, has a central pictorial panel whose figures have been adapted from an engraving of 'Lucretia's Banquet', published by Philippe Galle, a Netherlander who lived between 1537 and 1612. Contrasting to the French style of the figures, the borders of the cover and valances are English in character with fruits and flowers enclosed by a strap-

work pattern. Much less sophisticated in design and execution is a single valance at Hardwick Hall; it tells the story of the Prodigal Son and is also probably based on an engraving or illustration in a contemporary Bible.

Small-scale Canvas Work

Cushions covered by canvas embroidery were common at a time when little furniture was upholstered; sometimes done professionally, their smaller scale made them a very popular field for the amateur. Some good examples of both still exist in their original home, Hardwick Hall, though most are now hung in frames, which does make comparison easier. Two cushion covers displayed in the Hall were originally in the Long Gallery according to the 1601 inventory. The subjects are the Sacrifice of Isaac and the Judgment of Solomon, both popular Old Testament stories.

The quality of the work and the French costumes indicate a similar workshop to that producing the valances already discussed, and presumably similar

design sources. A group of three other cushion covers, although worked in tent stitch in wool, silk and a little metal thread, are crude compared to the professional products. They are boldly initialled ES, for Bess of Hardwick. However, all three are based on the woodcuts of Bernard Salomon, even if their adaptation for canvas work has destroyed the elegance of the original composition. The embroidered scenes (8) are 'The Death of Actaeon', 'The Fall of Phaeton' and 'Europa and the Bull', illustrated in the edition of Ovid's *Metamorphosis*, published in Lyons in 1557 by Jean de Tournes. Four years earlier he had published a book of biblical illustrations, also by Salomon. Both books were reprinted several times, pirated by other publishers and used for decades as sources for embroidery designs. In complete contrast to such pictorial and narrative compositions there is a charming small cushion cover at Hardwick worked with rows of alternately placed oak leaves (9). Each leaf is in tent stitch but varies slightly in outline and shading, and they stand out well on the dark red ground worked in the less usual long-armed cross

7. Table carpet or hanging adapted from an engraving of 'Lucretia's Banquet'. English, late sixteenth century.

8. *(below)* Cushion cover worked in tent stitch by Bess of Hardwick showing 'The Death of Actaeon'. English, late sixteenth century.

stitch. The simple, almost abstract character of the pattern has a timeless quality far removed from the busy intricacies of much sixteenth- and seventeenth-century work, and more satisfying than the consciously attempted abstract designs of much twentieth-century canvas work.

Wall Hangings

Very different from the restrained leaf pattern is the complex work found on some of the large wall hangings, perhaps the most famous being the Oxburgh Hangings, at Oxburgh Hall, Norfolk. A family heirloom of the Bedinfelds, they were undisputably made by Bess of Hardwick and Mary Queen of Scots (when the latter was imprisoned at Hardwick Hall) though not for Oxburgh Hall. Over the centuries they have been cut up and fragmented – parts are at the Victoria and Albert Museum and Hardwick – but the three reconstructed hangings are now at Oxburgh. The background fabric is green velvet onto which have been applied canvas work panels. Each of the three hangings has a large central panel (I), one signed by Mary, the others by Bess. Disposed around them are embroidered octagons containing emblems with Latin tags, mottos or initials.

Smaller cruciform panels (II) are filled with delightfully naive renderings of the creatures of the land, sea and air. Many of these have been copied from a famous illustrated book of Natural History, Konrad von Gesner's *Historia Animalium* (10), a second edition of which was

9. Detail of a cushion cover from Hardwick Hall, Derbyshire. The leaves are worked in tent stitch, but the dark red background is in long-armed cross stitch. English, late sixteenth century.

printed in Zurich in 1560. The panels are worked in silk tent and cross stitch, not particularly elegantly, their subject matter being more interesting than the actual needlework. Bess of Hardwick, who had risen from yeoman stock, was probably most interested in completing the work to add to her scheme of household furnishing. It was certainly Mary, educated at the French court, who found pleasure in embroidering the panels containing the mysterious witticisms of contemporary emblematic literature, giving her some intellectual amusement sorely lacking in her imprisonment.

Similar in date but very different in composition and construction are the two sets of hangings now in the Hall and the Chapel staircase at Hardwick. Probably made in the 1570s they are amazing examples of different needlework techniques. Basically they are applied work using velvets, silks and cloth of gold, some cut from vestments. Much of the design is outlined in cord and many details are made up of applied canvas work. The five most striking hangings are of the Virtues; they are 3·7 m (12 ft) deep and made to alternate with tapestries – further evidence that needlework was considered equal in decorative worth to tapestries. The strength and balance of their composition suggest that

they were professionally designed. An acrimonious correspondence between Bess and her husband, the Earl of Shrewsbury, makes it plain that wages were paid to professional embroiderers but that much of the actual work was done by Bess, her ladies, grooms and boys; certainly the canvas motifs were domestic work. The remaining hangings from the second set of Virtues and Vices, though as large in size, do not have the visual impact of the others and were perhaps of wholly amateur design and execution. In contrast another large

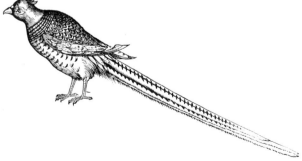

10. *(above)* Woodcut of a pheasant from K. von Gesner's *Historia Animalium.* Zurich, 1551–8 (2nd edition 1560).

11. *(opposite)* A detail from the Oxburgh Hangings showing a pheasant based on the reproduction above. *c.* 1570.

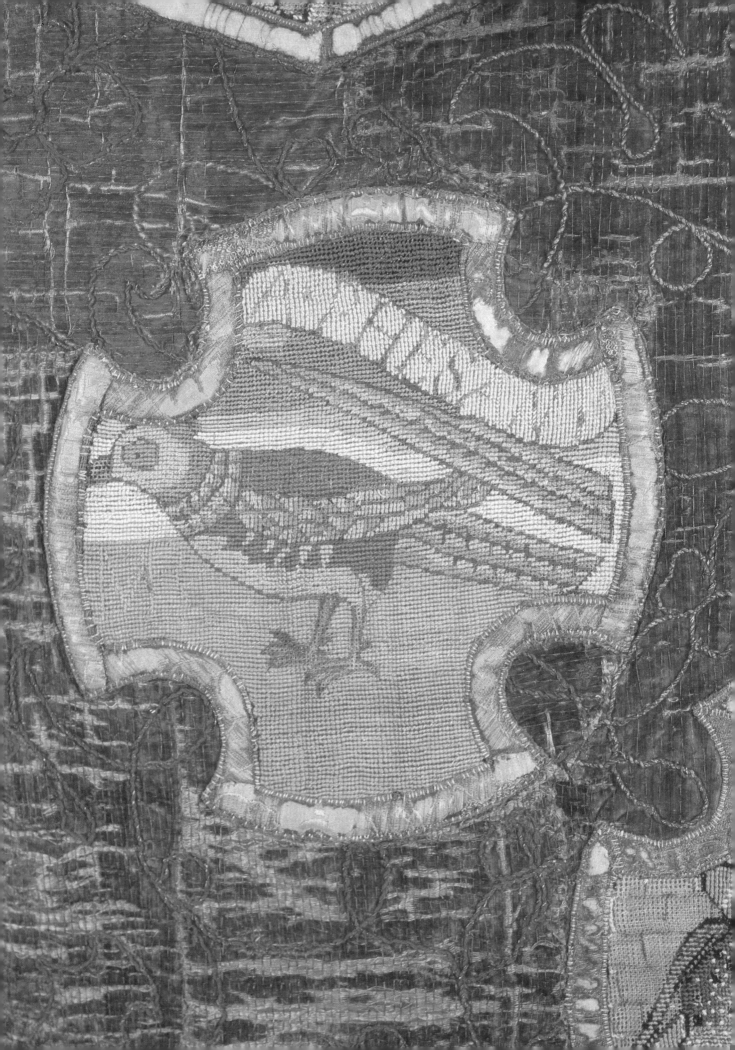

hanging, now at Scone Palace, almost 3·5 m × 1·5 m (11 ft 6 in × 5 ft), is completely worked in fine tent stitch using wool and silk on a linen canvas (12).

It too has been attributed to Mary Queen of Scots, but the quality of the work and the complexity of the subject matter, a combination of classical and biblical stories, point to it coming from a very competent workshop. The design is based on an allegorical engraving published in Antwerp by Hieronymus Wierix, in about 1574, from a drawing by Martin de Vos. The subject is 'Righteousness and Peace Embracing', but biblical scenes ('Moses receiving the Ten Commandments' and 'The Crucifixion') have been added in the embroidery and the original Latin text replaced by a verse from Psalm 85.

Table Carpets

In the sixteenth and seventeenth centuries floor covering other than rush or matting was rare. Oriental carpets were imported and so prized that they were more usually spread on tables or cupboards. They were a sign of wealth and for a designer a source of new, exotic patterns and motifs. Needlework carpets were often a blend of traditional and oriental influences, well illustrated by the Gifford carpet in the Victoria and Albert Museum. Probably dating from the mid-sixteenth century, it is worked in woollen tent stitch on linen canvas, a central medallion enclosed by a floral wreath carries the family arms but the border pattern is based on cufic lettering derived from Caucasian imports. Its size, 5·5 m × 1·4 m (18 ft × 4 ft 9 in) and its even texture indicate the work of professional embroiderers. Another, much smaller table carpet at Hardwick, dated 1574, also carries the family coat-of-arms worked as part of a fruit and floral frame for the central cartouche of the Judgement of Paris. The pictorial scene is not very well drawn but the embroidery is extremely fine and it is difficult to conclude whether it was made on the premises or in a workshop.

The characteristics of canvas embroidery, its simplicity of execution and its robust strength made it an ideal means of providing decorative furnishings well into the seventeenth century. After this time, the taste in interior decoration changed and gradually affected the role of canvas work. Wooden panelling for walls became a fashionable alternative to textile hangings and simple oak furniture gradually gave way to walnut pieces with their own decorative graining and inlay work. The general standard of all embroidery underwent a gradual decline from the heights of Elizabethan work through the seventeenth century and, during the latter part of the century, canvas work had a new rival in the decoration of bed hangings and covers.

Crewel embroidery became the vogue with designs owing much to imported oriental textiles and perhaps a little to Flemish verdure tapestries. The large trees and coiling plants, exotic animals and birds were embroidered in worsted wools on a plain twill cloth; canvas work was relegated for use on more frivolous items. Embroidered pictures to hang on newly panelled walls, caskets and work boxes, looking-glass frames and book bindings, all became the province of the needlewoman. Much was done in silk threads on a satin ground, but canvas work persisted as a popular alternative. Three-dimensional raised work is typical of the second half of the seventeenth century and canvas embroidery could be said to provide a soothing alternative to its luxurious extremes.

Classical and Biblical Scenes

Despite a prolific output of pictorial work the subject matter of all techniques rarely left the confines of familiar biblical and classical scenes. Adaptations of the engravings from the 1585 *Thesaurus Sacrarum Historiarum Veteris Testamenti* published in Antwerp by Gerard de Jode were among the most popular. A superb example based on the engraving of the story of David and Bathsheba is in the Burrell Collection, Glasgow (13). The picture, dated *c.* 1650, is worked in silk and metal thread on a very fine canvas. The basic tent stitch is enhanced by brick, satin and rococo stitches to give textural interest. Unable to resist the temptations of the fashion for raised work the embroideress has added details in purl, laid threads, mica and needlelace and has discreetly padded the creatures that crowd in on the main figures. The same subject is treated in a less lavish manner in a canvas work picture in the Irwin Untermeyer Collection at the Metropolitan Museum, New York. The date may be a little later and the canvas is worked simply in silk tent stitch.

A dramatic rendering of the same subject can also be found on the top of a mid-seventeenth-century cabinet in the Fitzwilliam Museum, Cambridge, embroidered in various canvas work stitches, tent, rococo and back with some couching. The sides and back are of the same technique but the topic changes from the biblical to

12. (*opposite above*) Allegorical panel 'Righteousness and Peace Embracing', Scone Palace. English, late sixteenth century.

13. (*opposite below*) Silk and metal thread picture on fine canvas of 'David and Bathsheba', based on an engraving by Gerard de Jode. *c.* 1650.

interpretations of the Five Senses. Inside there are equally disparate subjects – Orpheus, the Elements, a hunting scene – worked in silk on silk with some slight raised work.

In the Fitzwilliam Museum there is another picture where the drama of another biblical story, the Judgment of Solomon, has been quite successfully translated into canvas embroidery (**15**). Wool and silk is used for tent, rococo and gobelin hitch, the last worked over four vertical and one horizontal thread. The figures come from an engraving (**14**) by Boetius A. van Bolswert (1580–1633) after the painting by Rubens, now in Copenhagen. It was not one included by de Jode but it was among a similar collection published by Visscher in Amsterdam in 1660. Surely based on another engraving from such a publication is the interpretation of 'The Sacrifice of Isaac' worked on one side of a book binding. Boldly dated 1613 and signed E.I., simply worked in fine tent stitch, the bookbinding is a good example of a popular seventeenth-century fashion that was more often executed in raised work on silk or laid and applied work on velvet.

By way of contrast to such well-established Old Testament stories are the rare embroideries based on secular subjects. One celebrated print by Samuel Ward published in Amsterdam in 1621 commemorated the defeat of the Armada in 1588 and the failure of the Gunpowder Plot in 1605. Despite its complicated design it obviously appealed to the patriotic needlewoman and

a charmingly naive example of it as an embroidered picture in silk tent stitch hangs in the Lady Lever Art Gallery, Port Sunlight, Merseyside.

Pattern Books and Publishers

Whether the subject matter was relatively unusual or particularly popular few compositions were unique and most were found in a variety of embroidery techniques – canvas work, raised work, silk on silk etc. The inevitable conclusion must be that designs were supplied, ready-

14. (*above*) Engraving showing the Judgment of Solomon by Boetius Bolswert (after the painting by Rubens) published in 1660.

15. (*left*) A successful translation of the engraving above into canvas work using wool and silk thread.

drawn, from specialist shops or studios. The rising middle classes were unlikely to employ a resident embroiderer as in the aristocratic households of the previous centuries, but they could buy from designers and draughtsmen who had access to a great deal of popular printed material. Not only were there the old favourites such as Gesner, Salomon and the volumes of biblical and classical illustrations largely originating from the continent, there were also contemporary English pattern books. Richard Shorleyker's *The Schole House for the Needle* was first published in 1624 and contained patterns and designs derived from many sources. Seven years later James Boler's *The Needle's Excellency* appeared with an even more encyclopedic approach which included the names of stitches and references to other publications. Records show that print sellers in the City of London published books of designs which could be used not just by the embroiderer but by anyone involved in the decorative arts; a typical example is Peter Stent (16) of Giltspur Street who was trading between 1640 and 1662 specializing in patterns for all the crafts. The great wealth of material available during the seventeenth century was not, however, reflected by variety in interpretation. The same design was repeated over and over again, so presumably the most popular subjects were reproduced by the designers for the equivalent of the 'mass market'. It was then up to the 'consumer' to choose the technique and materials and thus give the finished product its individuality.

Much of the canvas work of the seventeenth century was small in scale and frivolous rather than useful in intent. However, the richer textures sometimes produced by a variety of stitches on small objects was not unknown on a grander scale. The Hatton Garden Hangings (17) from the Victoria and Albert Museum are exceptional large-scale canvas embroideries of *c.* 1690. There are six of them in all, each measuring approximately 2·4 m × 1·2 m (7 ft 9 in × 4 ft) and only discovered accidentally when work was being done on an old house in Hatton Gardens in 1896. The stitches include not only tent and cross but also rococos, satin,

16. Engraving by John Dunstall, typical of those used by embroiderers, printed and sold by John Overton (1640–1708?).

17. One of the Hatton Garden Hangings showing the influence of textiles from the Far East. English, *c.* 1690.

brick, rice, eye and Florentine with some detailing in French knots. They all demonstrate that canvas work stitching is more limited by the imagination of the worker than by its inherent qualities. These hangings, having languished behind layers of wallpaper for two hundred years, also remind us forcibly of the strong colours that were used. The brilliant colours on a dark ground, the confidence of the composition and shading and the boldness of the stitching suggest professional work. The design of each panel is similar. Pillars and columns linked by arches entwined with exotic flowers and foliage, rest on a base of hillocks scattered with a great variety of creatures. The influence of the textiles of India and the Far East is obvious.

Florentine Work

More usually large-scale hangings, and especially bed hangings with fashionable adaptations of the Tree of Life and other exotic motifs, were embroidered in crewel work. But canvas work persisted even for bed hangings. Florentine stitch was often used on these large projects, although it is occasionally found on smaller items. An early fragment in the Bowes Museum, County Durham, is probably mid-seventeenth century, and of course the four seventeenth-century chairs in the Bargello Museum, Florence have given the stitch

18. The Onslow state bed at Clandon Park, Surrey. English, c. 1700.

one of its alternative names. Their covers are worked in silk in shades of green, yellow, cream and blue in a complex repeating wave pattern. Technically Florentine work is made up of simple straight stitches, its total effect depending on the variations of length combined with the calculated shading of the pattern bands.

At its simplest it is quick to work and was popular throughout the eighteenth century for furniture upholstery. Stunning seventeenth-century examples of Florentine stitch can be seen on bed hangings at Parham Park, in Sussex, and on a breathtaking ensemble (18), c. 1700, of bed hangings and matching chairs at Clandon Park, Surrey. The linear quality of the stitching is broken up by stylized floral motifs all worked in pink, yellow and cream silks giving an almost luminious quality to the work. Their luxuriousness is apparent and their highly professional work must have cost many hundreds of times more than the wooden frames of the bed and chairs.

With the vogue for the oriental strengthening during the latter years of the seventeenth century and into the eighteenth century, stitch variety and the more abstract Florentine patterns were far less prevalent than the traditional mixture of tent and cross stitch for pictorial and floral compositions. The dating of early needlework is made difficult not only by the continuing use of popular designs over several decades, whether from European or Eastern sources, but also by the understandable practice of remounting valued work onto later furniture and frames. There is, however, a certain amount of truth in the generalization that designs from the early part of the eighteenth century tended to be quite bold in scale and colour, and became gradually more refined as the decades passed. The increasingly important fashion for matched sets of chairs may have contributed to both restraint in design and to an increase in the production of canvas upholstery. The quality and quantity of furniture from this period well illustrates the pervading climate of domestic prosperity and stability.

Canvas Work Upholstery

Sets of chairs, or even just a substantial wing chair, provided continuing scope for the narrative and pictorial themes previously popular on valances and coverings as well as for the lush floral designs so beloved of the English woman. Many houses and museums contain examples of eighteenth-century wing chairs covered with canvas embroidery. Two fine examples from the early part of the century can be found at Clandon Park, Surrey. One has a mixture of flowers,

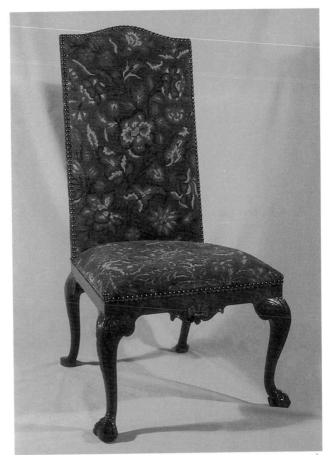

19. *(above left)* A wing chair from Clandon Park by Rebeck Hornblower. English, 1738.

20. *(above right)* A chair from a set of eight chairs and a settee. English, *c.* 1720.

21. *(below)* The Long Gallery or Saloon at Temple Newsam House, Leeds, W. Yorkshire, showing some of the gilded suite of furniture, comprising twenty chairs, four settees and a day bed.

22. *(right)* One of the chairs in the Long Gallery or Saloon, Temple Newsam House. English, mid-eighteenth century.

indigenous and exotic, worked in a rather indiscriminate manner on a dark ground. Another possibly later example has a variety of ground colours – blue, red and a strong yellow for the back (this was a favourite choice when there was an oriental influence, the yellow aping the imperial yellow of the Chinese court). In addition to the exotically shaded and highlighted flowers and foliage there are little grotesque masks on top of the wings providing an unexpected but not so unusual mixture of oriental and classical influences. Less usual is the signed and dated canvas work upholstery (**19**) of 'Rebeck Hornblower 1738', rare among a largely anonymous heritage. Now at Aston Hall, Birmingham, the complete needlework has been mounted on a modern frame. The colours are still strong and again the ground has been worked in contrasting hues, blue for the back and wings and red for the seat cushions. Predominantly covered by flowers and foliage, there is also a pictorial element, this time biblical, portraying the prophet Jonah. The woollen needlework of the wing chairs was necessarily robust and a more delicate treatment of similar floral designs can be seen on four superb early eighteenth-century marquetry armchairs, also at Clandon. The flowers and the yellow ground are all worked in silk in quite a fine tent stitch. Only on chairs not intended for heavy domestic use could silk be used exclusively; generally it was limited to details on figures or highlighting on flowers but even here the seats of these armchairs are very worn.

Although some examples of canvas work with surface textures created by stitch variety have been discussed it seems that most work depended on the colour, pattern and pictorial quality for interest, and that speed of execution and consequent simplicity of stitching was often paramount. During the eighteenth century there was an increasing feeling for complementary furnishings with common design elements. The unifying upholstery on sets of chairs was typical of this new feeling and a good example is a set of eight chairs and a settee dating from about 1720, now in the Bowes Museum. The upholstery (**20**), the nailing and even the plain dark woollen fabric lining the backs is original (time was not wasted embroidering the less visible parts and the fashion was for chairs to be arranged against the walls not placed informally about the room as today). Woollen cross stitch is used for the dark blue-green ground and for the design of flowers and foliage in reds and creams. Emphasis is given to the pattern by dark outlining and the use of two-coloured cross stitch for some of the details, for example, the flower centres.

Comparable in intent but using a more formal design are four chairs of about 1730–40 now at Temple Newsam House, Leeds, but formerly at Braban Castle, Scotland, where the complete suite was six chairs and a settee. Wool and cross stitch are used for a pale grey ground with a formal pattern worked in reds, creams and beiges that is reminiscent of the luxurious woven damasks and velvets of the period. Even these patterns had long been influenced by the Near and Far East and it is interesting to see an English embroidery reflecting the style of woven European textiles that in turn owed much to the Orient.

About twenty years later a superb suite of gilded furniture was upholstered in woollen canvas embroidery of amazingly vibrant colours in a flowing over-life size, naturalistic floral design. This seating furniture was made for the Long Gallery (**21**) or Saloon at Temple Newsam House, recently almost completely restored to its eighteenth-century state; only the walls have to be changed from the present red to the original green. In 1736 the 7th Viscount Irwin decided to modernize the old gallery and to install a gilded suite of furniture comprising twenty chairs, four settees and a couch or day bed. The frames were supplied by James Pascall, probably a French immigrant, whose bill exists today, dated 9 August 1746. Less is known about the provenance of the needlework, nonetheless what is probably the finest suite of rococo furniture in the country is upholstered with canvas work (**22**), not a woven fabric. It can only have been commissioned from a very high-class workshop to produce such a quantity of such consistently even quality. It seems unlikely that needlework was chosen for reasons of economy: the fine woollen tent stitch with ground and pattern worked in opposing directions must have occupied many working hours; the subtlety of shading and colouring is the work of highly skilled professionals.

The Pictorial Tradition

Alongside and often combined with the interpretations of flowers and foliage the pictorial tradition continued. Particularly popular were rather romantic pastoral scenes as well as those taken from printed sources. A typical example of the former is a wing chair (**23**) long owned by the same family at Arniston, Midlothian, with haywain and harvesters, and a red-brick farm house worked on the back. Sometimes the needlework composition was further removed from rural reality and was closer to a mythical rustic idyll; beautifully dressed shepherds and shepherdesses or scenes of country dancing were frequent themes. On chairs they were

23. Detail of the front of an embroidered wing chair from Arniston House, Lothian. Scottish, mid-eighteenth century.

24. Armchair at Temple Newsam House, Leeds, showing Jacob wrestling with the Angel. English, *c.* 1755–60.

quite often combined with totally unrelated subjects as on some of a set of five mid-eighteenth-century mahogany armchairs at Saltram House, Devon. The canvas work of woollen cross and tent stitch with silk highlights is believed to be the original upholstery and the choice of subject matter surprisingly eclectic. On the back of one are some very regal figures with a couple indulging in energetic country dancing on the seat (25). On another the back carries three Roman soldiers and the seat a conventional flower design. Slightly different again is a back with a king and attendants with a distinctly oriental cast of features. The fashion for chinoiserie and all things oriental is evident in much eighteenth-century embroidery and canvas work was no exception. The motifs were not only adopted direct from imported textiles and artifacts, they were copied from influential publications. Foremost among these was Stalker and Parker's *A Treatise of Japenning and Varnishing* published in 1688 and intended for those attempting to imitate Japanese lacquer. In fact it seemed to have a greater influence on silversmiths, potters and embroiderers who reproduced the European interpretation of oriental motifs in a great variety of media.

Many embroidered compositions on furniture can be attributed to quite specific sources. A popular folio of biblical engravings was published by Visscher in Amsterdam *c.* 1660; called the *Biblia Sacra Veteris et Novi Testamenti*, it contained many engravings originally published by de Jode in 1585 but also included two after paintings by Rubens, the Visitation and the Judgment of Solomon. A set of eight chairs at The Lady Lever Art Gallery, Port Sunlight, are embroidered with biblical scenes based on Visscher's publication, the canvas work probably dating from the middle of the century. From the same folio comes the rendering of Jacob wrestling with the Angel (24) worked on one back of a pair of armchairs now at Temple Newsam House. The embroidery is contemporary though not original to the chairs, dating from about 1755–60. The back of the second chair tells the story of Hagar and Ishmael in the Wilderness. Typically the pictures are framed by naturalistic flowers on a dark blue ground and the seats are covered by landscapes with various animals. Tent stitch is used for both the wool and the silk highlights.

Naturalistic Interpretations

With much eighteenth-century canvas work it is quite difficult to differentiate between domestic and workshop production. Pictorial designs were probably nearly

always directly commissioned or bought from the stock of a specialist shop. But even sizeable canvas work projects were undertaken by the needlewomen at home, for the embroidery skills of the leisured female were highly regarded. Floral design continued in popularity but gradually changed from a stylized to a more naturalistic interpretation, influenced no doubt by a flood of publications containing decorative floral illustrations. Typical was Robert Furber's *The Flower Garden* of 1734 and a little later Heckell's *Select Collection . . . for the Improvement of Ladies in Drawing or Needlework*. Both ran into several editions and in addition the latter part of the century saw the growth of several magazines, *The Ladies Magazine* from 1770, *The New Ladies Magazine* from 1785 and a year later *The Fashionable Magazine*. All included designs suitable for the needlewoman. Less usual was the exceptional woman who both designed and executed her own embroidery, the most famous probably being Mrs Delany who wrote to her sister in 1759 that she worked her patterns 'first as they come into my head'. Perhaps the set of eight chairs (**26**) and

25. *(left)* Armchair from the set of five at Saltram House, Devon. English, mid-eighteenth century.

26. One of a set of chairs by Elizabeth Newdigate at Arbury Hall, Warwickshire. First half of the eighteenth century.

27. Portrait of George Baillie, 1828, showing the wing chair *c.* 1770 still in the library at Mellerstain, Borders.

settee at Arbury Hall, Warwickshire were designed as well as worked by another of the century's most prolific needlewoman, Elizabeth Twisden (wife of Sir Richard Newdigate), a forebear of the present owners. They show embroidered bouquets of garden and hedgerow flowers, gracefully shaded and detailed in a naturalistic style on a dark green ground, all in tent stitch. Interestingly the suite remains in its original setting, the room being one of the finest examples of eighteenth-century Gothic Revival decoration, Arbury Hall having been 'Gothicized' by Elizabeth Twisden's son. She was widowed in 1727 but survived until 1765, and her traditional floral canvas work is mounted on chair frames in the Gothic style, not an entirely satisfactory combination.

Another canvas work upholstery still in its intended home is a substantial Scottish wing chair (27) of about 1770 in a library at Mellerstain, Borders. Neither floral nor pictorial, it is a good example of the restrained geometric patterns that came into fashion towards the end of the century. The colours are limited to pink, green, cream and black, and the work is in woollen cross stitch. Apart from a modern fringe its appearance has little changed for it can be seen in a life-size painting done in 1828 of George Baillie, the present owner's great-great-grandfather. Few pieces of needlework have had such a settled and recorded history.

Large Embroidered Items

Despite the popularity of wood or plaster panelling and the use of wallpapers, wall hangings and screens did not entirely disappear. Surprisingly such large items were often produced domestically; particularly fine examples exist at Wallington Hall, Northumberland, and Aston Hall, Birmingham, all worked by the ladies of the occupying families. At Wallington there is the famous screen and the wall panels embroidered by Lady Julia Calverley and her attendants. Incidentally the other

28. *(left)* 'The Swarming of the Bees', by Francis Cleyn, one of the mid-seventeenth century engravings used as patterns for the Calverley screen.

29. *(right)* Detail showing a panel from the Lady Julia Calverley screen, Wallington Hall, Northumberland. English, 1727.

canvas work in the house is mainly nineteenth-century Berlin woolwork: the proximity of the two styles provides a convenient means of comparing the balance and individuality of the early work with the somewhat stereotyped output of the later era. Julia Calverley (1686–1736) was the mother of Sir Walter Calverley Blackett who inherited Wallington in 1728, selling the original family seat of Esholt Hall, near Bradford, in 1755. Among the fittings he considered important enough for removal were the ten panels of canvas work in the drawing room of Esholt. They were remounted in fashionable rococo frames and taken to Wallington. One of the panels is dated 1717 and Lady Julia's husband noted that she had 'finished the sowed work in the drawing-room, it having been three years and a half in doing. The greatest part has been done with her own hands.' No comment is made about the *en suite* chairs but it seems likely that they were made by Lady Julia, her daughter and ladies of the household. All the work is tent stitch, mainly wool with silk highlights. The large scale of the panels has allowed a bold design of sinuous climbing plants reminiscent of painted palampores from India which were more usually interpreted in crewelwork embroidery. The chairs are covered with chinoiserie motifs, birds on the seat backs, vases and bouquets on the seats.

In the same house and by the same hand is a large six-fold screen (**29**), signed and dated 1727, also in woollen tent stitch. At first glance it may look a charmingly haphazard arrangement of pastoral scenes and rural pursuits. In fact Lady Julia's pattern drawer was not relying on his own imagination but based many of the scenes on mid-seventeenth-century engravings. The engravings used illustrated a new translation of Virgil's *Aeneid*, *Georgics* (largely poetry about country life) and *Eclogues*, published by John Ogilby in 1641. A man of many talents and discriminating taste Ogilby chose excellent artists to illustrate his books among whom was Francis Cleyn, best known as the artistic director of the Mortlake tapestry factory, and also the engraver Wenceslas Hollar. As just two examples from the many adaptations of their work to be found on the screen there is the Swarming of the Bees (**28**) from Book IV of the *Georgics* and The Making of Agricultural Instruments from Book II.

In addition to such designs are conventional scenes of the hunt, a shepherd and shepherdess, country houses and cottages, all drawn with little regard for scale and set in landscape background which includes surprisingly exotic motifs such as palm trees and a phoenix. Among one group of figures there is a prancing Harlequin; he appears in other contemporary needle-work and has been copied from a late seventeenth-century engraving published in Paris by Nicolas Bonnart.

Two other huge canvas work hangings which were made at home are now happily back on the walls they were intended for, in the state (or best) bedroom at Aston Hall, Birmingham. There is a description by a Colonel Byng in his journal of 1793 of '. . . two rooms, adorned by tapestry – the workings of former family ladies containing a view of the house; (what ladies do this now and foolishly devote their lives to such follies; instead of dancing, and flirting in London. How would my daughters turn up their noses, at such employ, and such trumpery!) . . .' Colonel Byng's ironic assessment of the younger generation is amusing but his use of the word tapestry an error; an inventory of 1771 correctly describes them as 'the Needlework hangings in the Best Room. . .'

But Colonel Byng was right in that they were made by the family, the Holtes, particularly Mary Holte (1684–1759) who inscribed on one of them:

> God be the Guide
> And the Work Will Abide
> Mary Holte Spinster Aged LX
> Anno Dom. MDCCXLIV

That Mary Holte was sixty on their completion in 1744 perhaps explains their rather old-fashioned style, more akin to the years around the turn of the century. Both hangings have central cartouches, one enclosing Aston Hall (**30**), the other Brereton Hall, inherited by the family in 1724. There is an overall background design of flowers, flower baskets, masks, putti etc. and the borders are decorated with armorial and pictorial medallions.

By way of contrast are three hangings from professional workshops, all now at Montacute House, Somerset. One is based on the illustrations by Francis Cleyn for Ogilby's *Aeneid* already mentioned in connection with Wallington, but they are used in a more complete and much bolder manner, and in this case the effect is much closer to that of true tapestry. The embroidery (**31**) is over 9 ft (2·7 m) square and the main subject matter is Aeneas with his companion Achates meeting his mother outside the walls of Carthage. Worked in tent stitch, the colours of the woods, rocks and especially the water are so delicately shaded that a feeling of flowing movement is produced, an unusual effect for this rather angular form of stitching. Above this scene, in coiling puffs of clouds, is the 'Dispute of the Gods' from the opening of Book V. Because of its likeness to tapestry the panel has often

30. (above) The Mary Holte hanging showing Aston Hall, Birmingham. English, completed 1744.

31. Hanging now at Montacute House, Somerset, based on illustrations by Francis Cleyn. Probably English.

been given a Flemish provenance, but it seems just as likely to have come from an English workshop, possibly associated with Cleyn and the Mortlake factory.

This hanging, as well as the two other large pieces at Montacute, originally came from Stoke Edith in Hereford, built for Paul Foley in the seventeenth century and destroyed by fire in 1927. The complementary pair of hangings measure 3·2 m × 6·3 m (10 ft 6 in × 20 ft 8 in) and 3·0 m × 3·7 m (10 ft × 12 ft 3 in) and though drawn on a large scale are worked in fine tent stitch in light glowing colours. They depict with grace and humour the fashionable formal garden of the early eighteenth century peopled by ladies and gentlemen, their children, servants, musicians, dogs and even pet monkey, parrot and macaw (32). The figures are disposed among flower beds and clipped hedges, alcoved walls and an orangery, fountains and statues, and orange trees in large Chinese porcelain pots – then the height of decorative fashion. The orange trees and containers have been applied to the main work, the pots, leaves, fruits and branches worked in chain stitch on linen. Despite their size the hangings could not be mistaken for tapestries and although tradition has it that they were worked by the five successive wives of one of the Foley family who died in 1749, it seems more reasonable to assume that they were made in a professional workshop.

A Contrast of Carpet Designs

If hangings were decreasing in importance during the eighteenth century, floor carpets were becoming more usual by the latter decades. At Aston Hall several carpets are recorded in the 1770s, one of which is described as being embroidered. It was commissioned by Sir Lister Holte, Mary Holte's nephew, for the best drawing room probably in the 1760s. The beautifully balanced and shaded floral composition has the family's coat-of-arms prominently displayed in the centre and is a sophisticated contrast to the business of Mary Holte's needlework. Another fine example of professional work is the Hatfield carpet with flowers and foliage worked on an almost black ground; the border, delineated by a ribbon–pattern stripe, has a contrasting pink ground. There is rich detailing in silk with further emphasis given to the flower centres by French knots.

Not all carpets were of such lavish floral design: an unusual and very restrained composition in cross stitch can be found at Clandon Park which has a fine

32. One of three large hangings at Montacute House. English, early eighteenth century.

collection of needlework carpets. This particular one (33), probably early eighteenth century, has a border of a quite sparse waving stem design; the main field contains a centrally placed coat-of-arms surrounded by a modest floral wreath, with heraldic birds at each corner. The ground colours are a rare mustard yellow and black and the total effect rather formal and sombre. A very different effect is created by another of the carpets at Clandon which perhaps shows the influence of contemporary woven French work. It is of fine woollen tent stitch with some silk. Elegant scroll and acanthus leaf borders frame three more stepped floral bands with a central composition of an urn and a profusion of delicate flowers. The main ground colour is cream, the other predominating hues being blues, reds, pinks, beiges and greens.

Two further examples on a smaller scale will serve to illustrate the quite sharply contrasted styles of the 1720s and the 1760–70s. For the former a carpet of about 1·8 m× 1·4 m (6 ft× 4 ft 6 in) made of joined canvas strips worked in cross and tent stitch. It was probably a domestic product with a narrow diaper

33. Needlework rug from Clandon Park, Surrey. English, probably early eighteenth century.

pattern border enclosing a green ground covered by curving flowers and foliage. The later carpet is more restrained in design and colour; an all-over pattern of cruciform motifs is worked on a dark blue ground; a central medallion, four corner quarter-medallions and the borders are of a controlled trailing flower design; all are edged with a repeated narrow arrowhead design.

The greater simplicity and the use of geometric motifs is typical of the latter decades influenced by neo-classicism. This movement was less suited to interpretation in embroidery and heralded the decline in needlework furnishings. The new taste in interior decoration was promoted by such designers as Adam and Kent, and the furniture makers Chippendale and Hepplewhite. Lighter, more delicate upholstery was the vogue with figured silks and damasks replacing the more robust canvas work. Socially a richer, better educated and more mobile generation of women were produced in the heady atmosphere of this prosperous, pleasure-seeking age. They looked to more amusing pastimes than hours devoted to the embroidery of household furnishings.

Small Decorative Pieces

Before passing over the relatively barren years of the end of the eighteenth century and early nineteenth century to the great flood tide of Berlin woolwork it should be noted that not all eighteenth-century work was large-scale and much was produced of a frivolous rather than utilitarian nature. A multitude of smaller objects were made of canvas work during the years of a century when needlework of all types was enormously popular. Small decorative objects such as footstools, screens, pictures and table tops were all embroidered and naturally were stylistically similar to their larger brethren.

At Arniston, home of the wing chair embroidered with harvest scenes, there are a pair of pole screens showing a lady and a gentleman masquerading as a shepherd and shepherdess. Perhaps they are the work of the same person, pursuing the popular pastoral scenes. A larger screen of about 1700 at the Lady Lever Art Gallery is worked in a very different pictorial idiom with a classical scene, the Temple of Fame, worked in strong colours on a black ground. Two splendid pole screens illustrate the popular concept of eighteenth-century embroidery: at Saltram there is the ubiquitous flower basket (35) and at the Strangers' Hall Museum, Norwich, the equally favoured ribbon-tied bouquet. Table tops were also inset with canvas work. An octagonal tripod table, c. 1720, at Clandon Park has a

34. A picture embroidered in wool and silk showing 'Christ in the Garden with Mary Magdalene'. English, *c.* 1735.

figurative central picture surrounded by a densely worked flower and foliage border; silk tent stitch highlights the woollen tent and cross stitch.

Decorative but distracting perhaps sums up another vogue of the times, the *trompe-l'œil* embroidery on card tables. For a time they were very popular; cards, counters, even bags of coins were realistically worked in wool and silk tent stitch. Two good examples can be found at Luton Hoo, Bedfordshire, and (37) Aston Hall. Even more startling than these are the needlework panels on a cabinet (36) now at Temple Newsam House. Made about 1750, probably by Gillow of Lancaster, amazingly bright floral compositions have been embroidered in silk and cotton chenille on a black tent stitch ground and set into the front and sides.

If eighteenth-century walls were less likely to be furnished with tapestries and embroideries their plainer nature provided a background for pictures, including embroidered ones. Many were of silk on silk, but canvas work persisted and was most popular in the earlier part of the century. An early well-documented example is the Mellerstain Panel of 1706. It was worked by Grisel and Rachel Baillie with a variety of creatures and plants of unrelated scale surrounding a central framed figure

of 'Smelling' – one of the Five Senses. She, and all the other motifs, can be found in a book of bound engravings inherited by May Menzies, the girls' governess. Unlikely to have come from a printed source, but of similar date, is a rather crudely drawn but amusing picture in wool and silk tent stitch depicting a timeless pursuit; a lady and gentleman seated under a tree teaching a dog to beg. This hangs in the Lady Lever Art Gallery, as does another unusual and rather faded example of a New Testament scene of 'Christ in the Garden with Mary Magdalene' (34), probably dating from about 1735. The sense of movement in the figures perhaps hints at a printed source for the design but the actual canvas work is certainly amateur.

A more realistic idea of the strength of the original colours of historical canvas work is most usually gained by a glimpse of the reverse of an embroidery or an area that has been protected. To emphasize this point it is worth noting that there are two stools at Blickling Hall, Norfolk, whose eighteenth-century canvas embroidery had become so worn that it was decided to replace it with modern copies. On removal it was seen that the original bright colours were unfaded on the reverse of the work and the copies were worked to match them. It normally requires quite a feat of the imagination to translate the soft colours of old needlework into their original vibrant tones, but only then is it possible to get some idea of the true tastes of our forefathers, and their love of strong colours.

The Old and New World

In the preceeding pages almost 300 years of canvas embroidery in Britain have been discussed and among the influences mentioned have been books, prints and engravings originating from Europe, and the embroidered and decorated wares of India and the Far East. Until the latter part of the seventeenth century, canvas work, table carpets, panels, and cushions had much in common across Europe. In the New World of North America settlers took their possessions from their homelands and any new embroidery tended to follow the old traditions. But with the dawning of the eighteenth century the splendours of the French court dominated the fashionable taste in Europe and French needlework took on a distinct and influential character.

In North America, particularly the eastern seaboard, strong links of family and language were maintained with Britain and French fashions were of less importance. Embroidery continued with traditional patterns for a considerable time before evolving and developing a more typically American style. Though eighteenth-

35. Detail of a pole screen with typical eighteenth-century embroidery.

century work may have had certain common design sources it was a period of more distinct national characteristics than in the centuries preceeding it, or for that matter the internationalism of Berlin woolwork that followed.

The ostentation of the eighteenth-century French court, and a social structure with a small, uninfluential middle class, perhaps explains why embroidery was less an occupation for the ladies of the gentry or middle classes and more a profession depending on patronage by the court and aristocracy. Such professionalism produced work of high quality and sophisticated design. As early as 1684 Mme de Maintenon had set up a school at St Cyr for young ladies to learn embroidery and to produce work acceptable for the personal furnishings of the king. Artists such as Jean Baptiste Monnoyer (1634–99) and Jean Bérain (c. 1639–1711) supplied designs.

The highest quality materials were used and often included a good deal of metal thread. Two armchairs at Waddeston Manor, Buckinghamshire, are covered in fine French canvas work which includes metal thread and dates from about 1700. The arabesques and whimsical grotesques typical of the Bérains (father and son) were immensely popular in France and were taken up by devotees of French taste in England. An unusual English gilded settee of about 1720, now in the Lady Lever Art Gallery, is upholstered in finely worked canvas embroidery in the style of Bérain.

French Influence

Between 1710 and 1730 France was under the sway of the 'Style Régence', really the first phase of the rococo period. Furniture was built on curved lines with sculptured decoration and sometimes upholstered in a

36. Cabinet, probably made by the Gillows of Lancaster with embroidery panels, *c.* 1750.

37. *(below left)* Card table with *trompe l'œil* embroidery, Aston Hall, Birmingham. English, eighteenth century.

38. *(below right)* A Louis XV armchair in the Musée des Arts Décoratifs showing the French handling of chinoiserie motifs.

very distinctive style of canvas work. Opulent and exotic stylized flowers and fruit were embroidered in strong colours, often on a cream ground. Examples can be seen not only in the Musée des Arts Décoratifs, Paris, and many châteaux but quite frequently in English houses. Again it was a case of the fashion conscious and socially ambitious looking to France for 'style', and Régence embroidery certainly contrasted strongly with the more refined floral compositions favoured by the English needlewomen of the time. The suite of Régence furniture at Polesdon Lacey, Surrey, upholstered with contemporary canvas work, is a good example of the genre. Another contrast between French and English work is provided by their different interpretation of oriental styles and motifs. An armchair (38) in the Musée des Arts Décoratifs typifies the French use of chinoiserie motifs within the rococo style. The tent stitch canvas work is of subtle toning blues with restrained green and yellow highlights on a cream silk ground. The main motifs on back and seat are framed by garlands which follow and emphasize the lines of the wood carving, the colours of the needlework enhance the light tones of the painted wood. English canvas work of the same period, mid-eighteenth century, tended to be worked on a dark ground in quite bright colours. In general French work tends to have more elegant and lighter toned designs on a paler ground.

Even when familiar biblical, mythological or pastoral scenes were used the overall impression is of greater lightness and movement. A Louis XV chair (1760–1770) in the Louvre has canvas work upholstery depicting a musician surrounded by birds, animals and plants on the back and flowers, foliage and oriental birds on the seat. The dominant colours are greens, yellows and browns on a cream ground chosen to enhance the frame, gilded and painted green. Narrative subjects were dealt with in similarly harmonious fashion; favourite stories from La Fontaine and Aesop were often incorporated into large-scale canvas embroideries. An early example using Aesop's Fables and some classical scenes is a set of French bed hangings (39) and valances now in the Metropolitan Museum, New York. Woollen tent stitch is used for the bulk of the work with some cross stitch and details emphasized by silk threads or slight padding.

The scalloping of the curtain and valance edges, the light, bright colours and the variety of the cartouches gives a very lively and rich appearance to the whole. A later interpretation of Aesop's Fables can be found on a suite of furniture and a firescreen at the Château de Breteuil, Yvelines. The pictorial medallions are within floral frames and the carved and gilded lines of the

39. Bed hangings and valances with designs based on Aesop's Fables. French, c. 1700.

furniture are complemented by the swags and borders of the colourful embroidery worked on a cream ground.

The last quarter of the eighteenth century saw French decorative fashion revert to straight lines and ordered symmetry but canvas work continued as a popular workshop product. Designs tended to get smaller in size; swags and garlands were less richly drawn; matched and repeated symmetrical patterns came into favour. Several examples of late eighteenth-century work can be seen in the Paris museums and there are a typical pair of Louis XVI giltwood settees with contemporary canvas upholstery at Polesdon Lacey. As the eighteenth century gave way to the nineteenth, the furniture of the French Empire style increased in size and tended to be covered in woven materials, often of silk from Lyons whose weaving industry Napoleon was attempting to revitalize.

North American Canvas Work

From the 1840s North America, like Britain, France and most of Europe, was to be flooded with the ubiquitous

Berlin woolwork patterns, but its earlier canvas work was both more interesting and more individual. Specialist teachers taught all types of embroidery and often also supplied materials and patterns. Some advertised that they could provide simpler and cheaper patterns than those imported from London. They were drawn locally or on the premises. Needlework inevitably became a fashionable accomplishment, but canvas work still retained its utilitarian flavour and was popular for upholstery, and was frequently worked in Florentine or flame stitch. The virtues of this stitch were that it was quick to work and no pattern drawing was required; Also the repeated pattern lines could be as simple or as complicated in stitch length and colour as desired.

It retained its popularity throughout the eighteenth century and fine examples spanning many years can be found. Examples are a wing chair (40) of about 1725 in the Metropolitan Museum and another of about 1760 in the Museum of Fine Arts, Houston. An elegant Massachusetts side chair, also c. 1760, in the Perley Parlour of Claverton Manor, Bath, Avon (The American Museum) has a seat of Florentine stylized carnations. Closer to English contemporary embroidery are the canvas work card-table tops which enjoyed a similar vogue in the United States, often with the trompe-l'œil game of cards combined with the floral motifs and borders that owed much to oriental influences.

Needlework pictures were particularly important in a society with no heritage of paintings and prints to cover their walls. A group of canvas work pictures, probably all originating in New England, are especially interesting because of the similarity of some of their figurative content. They vary in their size from quite substantial chimneypieces, perhaps 1·5 m (5 ft) wide, to small pictures only 25 cm × 30 cm (10 in × 12 in). The main figures that they have in common are the 'fishing lady' (42) and her escort. Alongside this possibly 'home-grown' design there are two other groups that occur frequently if not consistently, one of English origin, the other of French. The hunting figures found on the chimneypiece in the Museum of Fine Art, Boston, almost certainly derived from a design by John Wootton who is perhaps best known for illustrating Gay's Fables, published in 1752. The figures on the other side of the embroidery are interpretations of some of the figures from an influential set of engravings (41), 'Les Pastorales', by Jacques Stella (1596–1657) published in Lyons by his niece in 1667. The one used for the chimneypiece was 'Le Soir' and in another canvas work picture of the period, the fourth figure from the left in the original composition – the piper – is again included.

Interestingly there is also a chair-back cushion (43) at Boston with the same three figures worked in wool and silk tent stitch. This is probably French and a little earlier in date–c. 1725. This group of canvas work embroideries not only demonstrates that figurative designs on decorative objects were well established in the New World of the eighteenth century, but also that such designs were both produced by local artists and intepreted from European illustrations and engravings.

The Effects of Industrialization

The radical change in fashionable taste that developed during the latter part of the eighteenth century with the rise of neo-classicism meant the inevitable decline in popularity of such weighty embroidery as canvas work. Light silk embroidery, whitework and a new craze, needle painting in crewel wools, were more favoured techniques. Canvas work continued to be used to some small degree for upholstery with geometric or Florentine patterns replacing the more florid styles of earlier times, but it did not regain its popular appeal until the mass production of Berlin woolwork patterns beginning in the 1830s. This resurgence occurred not only in a world where fashion had changed but where the whole of society had been altered by the advent and effects of the Industrial Revolution. One of the results was the vastly increased production of woven textiles; mechanization brought unprecedented choice to the consumer. Embroidery whether for costume or furnishings was no longer an essential means of decoration, its role had changed from an important craft to a hobby.

As early as 1814 when Jane Austen's Mansfield Park was first published there is a telling description of the leisured Lady Bertram – 'She was a woman who spent her days in sitting, nicely dressed, on a sofa, doing some long piece of needlework, of little use and no beauty. . .' This description is perhaps too sweeping a judgment but canvas work of the period did tend to be on the dull side. Such work became a means of filling the hours of fashionably enforced female idleness. No longer was leisure a privilege of the upper classes: an increasing and prosperous middle class produced women whose main role was to occupy their lives with suitably genteel pursuits, one of which was needlework.

The traditions of handing down designs from mother to daughter, of using and re-using popular engravings and illustrations, of incorporating exotic motifs from the Orient, were virtually destroyed by the advent of coloured patterns on squared paper. Originally hand-painted, the patterns were soon mass-produced by colour printing. The embroiderer no longer even selected

the colours and there was little incentive to use any stitches other than tent or cross stitch; the reproduction and repetition of designs and colours necessarily destroyed the originality and individuality typical of earlier canvas work. Even on large pictures or panels for upholstery the only chore left to the embroiderer was perhaps to draw in centre lines and possibly sketch in the main outlines of a complicated design.

Although hand-coloured designs on point or graph paper existed in the early nineteenth century it was the publishing firm of L. W. Wittich in Berlin that started to print patterns from about 1810. Their success was almost instant in Germany but it was not until the 1830s that a Mr Wilks of Regent Street, a leading needlework supplier, began to import Berlin patterns and wools into Britain. Their popularity meant that this type of canvas work became the craze to the extent that for many years 'embroidery' became synonymous with Berlin woolwork. Such success created an enormous popular demand for patterns and it was not long before the imports from Germany, and later France, were supplemented by home production.

Additionally, by the 1850s and 1860s patterns were reproduced in the mass-circulation magazines such as *The Ladies' Treasury*, *The English Woman's Domestic Magazine* and *The Young Englishwoman*. The qualities of original interpretation, individual colouring and stitch variety were certainly lost; they were replaced by sheer quantity of production. Consequently it is not difficult to find examples of Berlin woolwork in many museums, houses, antique and junk shops ranging from the competent to the atrocious.

If the initial impression is of oppressive similarity there are in fact considerable distinctions in the types of canvas and the embroidery threads used.

The most delicate of the canvases was made of silk threads wound round a cotton core and it was popular for earlier, daintily hand-painted floral designs most suitable for purely decorative articles, like small screens and pictures. Often the light silk ground mesh was left unworked. Similarly, the coloured German canvases, used for domestic items such as cushions, stool tops and bell pulls would have only the design embroidered. Ocasionally the background of even strong jute canvas was left unworked, its natural beige colour darkening with age. The most common canvas was made of cotton and produced in a large number of gauges ranging from eleven to thirty-seven threads per inch. French canvas was considered the most accurately

woven and German particularly useful when transferring large designs because every tenth thread was coloured yellow. In Britain a double or Penelope canvas became a best-seller, its paired threads making cross stitch even easier!

Threads and Dyes

Originally Berlin wool was actually dyed in the city, which had a well-established dyeing industry, producing a wide range of wools that blended with each other and lasted well. Similar embroidery wools were soon being produced in England and Scotland, and although hard-wearing lacked the sheen and subtle colouring of the Berlin wool. The discovery of synthetic or aniline dyes in the late 1850s produced a new range of colours which during the following decade were renowned for their harshness and instability. It was their novelty that made them fashionable though fortunately during the 1870s colours did improve and were less prone to fading. It is the dominating colour of the embroidery, the type of dye and the scale of the design that are perhaps the main clues when trying to date Berlin woolwork. Patterns were widely available in shops, journals and books and were reproduced time and time again over the years so that they are rarely exclusive to a particular year or decade. Even the consideration of thread and colour only gives a guide to the date. So, in general the work done prior to 1840, using hand-painted patterns, tended to have quite small-scale motifs and designs which were worked in naturally dyed threads of harmonious colour, often on a canvas that was attractive enough to have the background left unstitched.

During the 1840s and 1850s silk highlights were frequently introduced into the woolwork. The 1850s also saw an increasing interest in padding and plush stitch to produce a three-dimensional effect. This was particularly popular for working the fur or feathers of animals and birds. Plush stitch was made by a series of loops held in place by cross stitches. The loops were generally cut and trimmed for a raised, sculptural effect, hence its other name of velvet stitch.

It was the 1860s that took the full impact of the harsh synthetic dyes, their vivid colours often used on unsympathetic backgrounds of bright red, blue or black. In addition the relatively restrained decoration of garden and wild flowers was ousted by the fashion for much larger scale designs of bright overblown flowers, with native and exotic species in unhappy juxtaposition. Not surprisingly a reaction set in to such excesses of colour and decoration and by the 1870s fashionable

40. A Queen Anne-style wing chair worked in Florentine stitch. American, *c.* 1725.

41. One of a set of engravings entitled 'Les Pastorales', engraved by Claudine Bouzonnet after Jacques Stella. Published in Lyons in 1667.

42. (opposite above) A New England needlework picture showing both the 'fishing lady' and (on the right) two figures derived from the above engraving. Mid-eighteenth century. (Compare to illustration on p. 59.)

43. (opposite below) Chair-back cushion worked in wool and silk tent stitch, showing the same young couple and the piper. Probably French, c. 1725.

taste veered towards smaller scale, scrolling and geometric designs using a restricted palette of colours, mainly browns, greens, dark red and blues.

Stitches and Textures

Cross and tent stitch continued to be the basic stitches of canvas work, plush stitch has been mentioned, and there were two others that had periods of popularity. The Victorians loved imitating one material or technique by another and canvas lace stitch is a prime example. Black silk running stitch was worked over canvas work in lace patterns, and was thought most suitable for small objects such as mats or the borders of cushions. It can be found on work from the 1840s onwards. Leviathan stitch, a variation on double cross stitch, is worked over four squares of canvas and was an even quicker method of covering the ground hence its other name of railway stitch. If speed was not the main consideration a popular embellishment of much Berlin woolwork was beads. They were used to highlight details as early as the 1840s. A decade later they were sometimes used for the whole design with just the background worked in wool. Obviously the beads used for canvas embroidery had to be of very even size and matched to the gauge of the canvas. France had always

produced the best quality beads, and various sizes were imported and sold by weight, which explains a common term, 'pound beads'.

When used on screens, banners and pelmets the weight of the beads could be a definite advantage, for they helped the object to hang well. But by the later 1850s less suitable articles were fashionably decorated with beads; cushions, stool tops and even upholstered chairs were covered with bead embroidery. Visually they may have provided much needed variety in colour and texture but from a utilitarian point of view they could hardly have enhanced their comfort. As with the woollen canvas work the brilliantly coloured beads of the mid-nineteenth century gradually gave way to the calmer tones of the later years when 'grisaille' work enjoyed a vogue; in this only white, grey, black and clear beads were used.

One traditional technique that was re-adopted by the Victorians was applying or inserting canvas work panels or bands onto velvet upholstery or furnishings. Often tablecloths or curtains were bordered with panels of canvas embroidery and sometimes a technique was used whereby the canvas threads were removed on completion of the work. A splendid set of curtains (44) of about 1880 at the Bowes Museum are decorated in this manner. Tent and plush stitch have been used for a

44. Detail of an embroidered canvas panel on curtains at the Bowes Museum, County Durham. English, *c.* 1880.

large-scale floral pattern on a cream flannel ground, the embroidered panels alternating with ones of green velvet. The stitching was done through a canvas mounted on the flannel, the removal of the guiding meshes left just embroidery on the flannel ground.

Victorian Decorated Furnishings

The availability and volume of nineteenth-century canvas work means it not only is easy to find for study or to buy, but that several museums and houses have been able to create period room settings which give an authentic glimpse at the taste of the times. The curtains just discussed from the Bowes Museum are part of such a room. An even greater display of nineteenth-century canvas work can be seen in the Victorian Sitting Room at the Strangers' Hall Museum, Norwich (**45**). Profusely

45. The Victorian Sitting Room at Strangers' Hall Museum, Norwich showing the rich use of canvas work.

furnished there are examples of floral embroidery on a low sewing chair and a long stool; a smaller rectangular stool has another woollen floral design but on a ground of silvered beads. The many cushions have patterns ranging from floral bouquets and wreaths to a fine beaded example of 'grisaille' work on a green ground.

Other decorated furnishings include a tablecloth edged with canvas work borders of wool with silk highlights, and a bell pull with a typical repeating pattern of flowers, foliage and scrolls. An early firescreen (46) has an embroidered flower spray on a light, unworked canvas ground whereas a later shield-shaped screen is completely covered with woolwork and beaded highlights. More bead highlighting can be seen on circular fans edged with fringing. Another specifically Victorian chair is represented; called a 'prie-dieu' it was never made exclusively for devotional purposes although often decorated with what were considered suitably religious motifs; crosses, angels and various Gothic patterns were always popular. Sometimes a coat of arms was incorporated into the design, more often than not a fake one. A prie-dieu with a coat of arms can be found at Aston Hall, Birmingham, in its Victorian Room which, as well

46. An early Victorian firescreen at Strangers' Hall Museum, Norwich.

as objects similar to those at Strangers' Hall, has a rather impressive fourfold gilded screen with each fold containing three octagonal panels of floral canvas work. There is a similarly ornate gilded chair upholstered in red velvet and decorated with panels of canvas embroidery. A particularly appealing example of this style of upholstery can be seen on a four-sided conversation sofa at Wallington Hall, Northumberland. The four backs have different canvas work pictures, the arms have floral designs as have the seats with the embroidery panels alternating with red velvet upholstery, all rounded off by an edging of canvas work in a trailing foliage pattern.

The Subjects of Pictures

Apart from furnishings Berlin woolwork was equally popular for pictures. Not surprisingly flower compositions were frequently worked, as were birds and animals. Familiar biblical subjects were taken from both the Old and New Testaments, quite often adapted from paintings by the Old Masters rather than from engravings or book illustrations. Even 'The Descent from the Cross' by Rubens and 'The Last Supper' by Leonardo da Vinci were made into printed squared patterns. More specifically for the British market representations of members of the Royal Family past and present were produced. Sometimes set in a realistic or historically correct background they were more frequently put in imaginary scenes taken from popular historical novels. Typical is 'Mary Queen of Scots mourning over the dying Douglas at the battle of Langside' this romantic theme is taken directly from a scene in Sir Walter Scott's novel *The Abbot*. One example was known to have been exhibited at the Great Exhibition of 1851 and several are now in museums. One at Fitzwilliam Museum (47) is simply woollen tent stitch, others have silk highlights and even small beads and pearls.

Contemporary painters also had their most celebrated paintings interpreted in canvas embroidery with varying success. Sir Edwin Landseer's studies of animals and birds seem to adapt to a different medium rather better than his large oil paintings like 'The Monarch of the Glen'. Exotic birds (48) had a very strong appeal, perhaps due to the availability of bright colours of synthetically dyed wool which could be used for their unfamiliar plumage. Edward Lear's *Illustrations of the Family of Psittacidae* or *Parrots*, John Gould's *Birds of Australia* and Audubon's *Birds of America* were all sources for immensely popular printed patterns which gave scope not only for brilliant colouring but for the use of the intricate textural quality of plush stitch for the

47. Berlin woolwork picture of Mary Queen of Scots at the Battle of Langside. British, mid-nineteenth century.

feathers. Many pictures, however, were copied from anonymously produced patterns from shops and magazines with the standard varying from the acceptable to the abominable.

William Morris's revival of what was basically crewel work embroidery hastened the decline in the 1870s of the increasingly unfashionable Berlin woolwork. Crewel embroidery and the whole Art Needlework movement was promoted by such contemporary foundations as the Royal School of Art Needlework (1872), The Ladies Work Society (1875) and the Leek Embroidery Society (1879).

A further blow to not only the stereotyped Berlin woolwork but also to the traditional concept of the design and execution of embroidery being distinct crafts were the ideas propounded at the Glasgow School of Art at the end of the nineteenth and beginning of the twentieth century. Very briefly it was advocated that

design should be the natural product of the materials and techniques that were used. Designs should be built up and suggested by the stitches, threads and fabrics. No longer was a designer necessary, a needlewoman would have the freedom to choose any combination of materials and stitches and to execute the design that they suggested to her. Canvas work seemed physically unsuitable for the flowing lines of art needlework and was steeped in a tradition of hundreds of years that the finest needlework was usually inspired by a fine designer. The new idea that the needlewoman was competent both to create and to execute a design meant that conventional canvas work was reduced to near oblivion for many years. It is doubtful if many mid-Victorians questioned the merit of their Berlin woolwork; the quantity and confidence of their output is unlikely ever to be repeated, and only since the Second World War has canvas embroidery regained some of its former popularity.

However, despite the lack of interest for many years and the almost insuperable problems of time and

48. A printed design for a Berlin woolwork picture.

supplies during two world wars the demand for tradi-tional canvas work, particularly for upholstery, never completely died. Painted designs, copied or adapted from old work, were always needed for re-covering antique chairs and stools, or for use on reproduction furniture. The Cambridge Tapestry Company (1898–1940) not only repaired tapestries but supplied canvas work and designs to high society and the upper end of the antique trade. Cheaper, mass-produced canvases would still be bought 'over the counter' and by the 1920s even the Royal School of Needlework, so closely associated with crewel embroidery, started to produce painted canvases for seating furniture, cushions, screens and pictures. These were nearly all based on the historical collection in the Victoria and Albert Museum and owed little to either Art Needlework or the ideas emanating from the art schools.

Obviously canvas work of this period was neither prized nor prolific and much was done simply to replace older work. However some charming examples of small canvas work articles from the 1920s and 1930s can be found in the Embroiderers' Guild Collection at Hampton Court.

Dating from about 1920 there is a roundel (**49**) of approximately 11·7 cm (4⅝ in) diameter that was possi-bly intended to be mounted in a mirror back. It is worked in very fine silk tent stitch and shows a loosely clad female figure bending to pick a flower, the background is dark blue green and is scattered with small flower motifs.

These are not unlike the sixteenth- and seventeenth-century slips taken from herbals by earlier embroiderers and it can be assumed that this twentieth-century embroiderer was influenced by their work and reinter-preted the motifs. From a decade later but similarly worked in fine silk tent stitch is a pochette with em-broidered panels on front and back. The former is covered in a brightly coloured jungle scene and the latter has a small panel of buildings set in a wide purple and yellow frame. Equally brilliant in colour is another panel dated 1939; shield shaped, it was possibly made for a small screen and is covered in a complex design of flowers and birds. These small, carefully worked objects using good quality materials suggest that some women continued to find pleasure in such a traditional tech-nique. Very different is a canvas work table top made about 1940 using an abstract design based on stars, branches and leaf shapes. Worked in wool it includes cross, tent, Gobelin, brick and straight stitches with some French knots. Although the use of various stitches and abstract forms hint of future experiments, the dull colours are disappointing. From 1940 until well into the 1950s sewing materials were not readily available, but the booming economy of the 1960s gave the con-sumer an increasing choice of fabrics and threads and perhaps provided a stimulus for the ever increasing interest in all crafts. The revival of canvas embroidery, like the revival of any craft, inevitably means that its social context is different from that of the past and that its function has almost invariably changed.

49. A roundel, possibly intended for a mirror back, worked in very fine silk tent stitch. English, *c.* 1920.

From the sixteenth to the nineteenth century canvas work changed from being an important means of embellishing walls, beds, cushions etc, a way of upholstering seating furniture with a durable and decorative covering as well as being used for less

50. 'The Mythical Monsters' Annual Party': a picture using a large repertoire of different stitches. English, 1950s.

51. The Wisborough Green Tapestry, an embroidery commemorating the Queen's Silver Jubilee and worked by the villagers. 1977–84.

52. Bench seat cover exhibiting a variety of stitches, worked in the 1970s.

robust articles such as firescreens, table tops and pictures. By the nineteenth century canvas work had largely become an essential accomplishment for the genteel female; the Industrial Revolution and machine-made textiles had removed its utiliterian role. The second half of this century has shown little concern for female gentility and mass production has reached a stage undreamt of even by our Victorian forefathers. Canvas embroidery (as with other needle techniques) can perhaps now be divided into two streams. There are those who choose to regard it as a traditional craft which can be pursued as a satisfying hobby. Others wish to bring it into the realms of contemporary innovation and experiment with much less emphasis on embroidery techniques and much more on interpretations of form, the relationships of colours and the introduction of other materials. When these become the prevailing considerations it becomes difficult to decide whether the object should be classified as canvas work or left to the complex worlds of fibre art or mixed media work.

Canvas work is now conceived very much as a decorative, non-utilitarian product, not really for household furnishings but for pictures and panels. Without going to the extremes of mixed media compositions there has been widespread interest in surface texture created by using different stitches and threads. An early example of twentieth-century work using a large repertoire of stitches is a picture worked in the 1950s and called 'The Mythical Monsters' Annual Party', now in the Embroiderers' Guild Collection (50). The foreground is of the monsters standing on a beach of rock and sand worked almost entirely in tent stitch, but the leaves and fruit of the fantasy tree

53. 'A Castle Keep' designed and embroidered by Moyra McNeill, using different stitches and threads 1965.

which covers much of the middle and background display rococo, eye, eyelet, cross, double-cross, gobelin, Jacquard and Florentine stitches. Two decades later a similar variety of stitches (tent, rocus, star, Jacquard, Moorish, Florentine, sheaf, bullian and various crossed and couching stitches) but far fewer colours – just blue, red and yellow Paisley wool – were used for a long bench seat cover (**52**). The rather formal tracery pattern is based on a design from the collection of Lady Victoria Wemyss who founded the school of that name in Fife, Scotland, in the 1880s. The bench is now at the Fitzwilliam Museum. An example of a panel where many stitches are used as well as many types of thread (tapestry, crewel, darning, rug and knitting wool plus natural and plastic raffia, Sylko, Perle and linen thread) is 'A Castle Keep' by Moyra McNeill (**53**). She designed and embroidered the panel in 1965 and it is now at the Embroiderers' Guild complete with the piece of canvas used for experiments with stitches and threads.

For those doing canvas work as a hobby and not yet persuaded that they can design as well as embroider, the last twenty years have seen many different kits on the market, containing a printed canvas, various wools and needles. Although these have been criticized for their uninspired design and the poor quality of the materials, present-day standards could be raised if talented artists were used for the original designs. Some kits are now produced with the same design in different colour ways and it is possible to superimpose one's personal taste onto a commercially produced pattern. More expensively work can be commissioned with simply the outlines and possibly shading indicated. Many kits are also provided with instructions for the less usual canvas work stitches so again the consumer has the choice of the basic tent or cross stitch or can experiment with others.

An alternative to the individual kits is the growth of groups producing quite large-scale pictorial wall hangings, often for a local church, hospital or town hall. In some ways they are the twentieth-century equivalent of the lady of the household and her attendants who did such work in the sixteenth and seventeenth centuries. Often they are made of appliqué work, patchwork and machine embroidery, all of which produce fast results. But sometimes speed has been a lesser consideration and canvas embroidery has been used. One example (**51**) was started in 1977 by the villagers of Wisborough Green, West Sussex, to commemorate the Queen's Silver Jubilee, it was completed in 1984. The artist Pat Gierth designed it and it is made up of three panels with a total length of 3 m (10 ft), each one depicting a particular local scene or event, the central picture surrounded by smaller medallions containing buildings. The basic stitch is tent with a little couching and needle lace; wool was the main thread with some silk, linen, gilt and silver threads, sequins and beads. Over eighty people participated and the framed work hangs in the village chirch. The use of a professional artist, a group of people, simple stitching and rich colouring is reminiscent of the way work was done centuries earlier. It seems a pity that such a traditional piece of work has been misnamed the Wisborough Green Tapestry rather than the Wisborough Green Embroidery or even Hanging!

BIBLIOGRAPHY

Bath, V. C. *Needlework in America*, New York 1979; London 1980

Boston Museum, *Nancy Graves Cabot: In Memoriam. Sources of Design for Textiles and Decorative Arts*, Boston, Mass., 1973

Clabburn, P. *The Needleworker's Dictionary*, New York 1976

Fairclough, O. *The Holtes and Their Successors at Aston Hall, 1618–1864*, Birmingham, W. Midlands, 1984

Fowler, J., and J. Cornforth *English Decoration in the Eighteenth Century*, London 1974

Gilbert, C. *Furniture at Temple Newsam House and Lotherton Hall*, Leeds, W. Yorkshire, 1978

Girouard, M. *Life in the English Country House*, Newhaven, Conn., 1978; London 1980

Hackenbrock, Y. *English and Other Needlework, Tapestries and Textiles in the Irwin Untermeyer Collection*, London 1960

Hughes, T. *English Domestic Needlework, 1660–1860*, London 1961

Impey, O. *Chinoiserie*, Oxford and New York 1977

Kendrick, A. F. *English Needlework*, 2nd edn, London 1967

Mayorcas, M. J. *English Needlework Carpets*, Leigh-on-Sea, Essex, 1963

Metropolitan Museum, *Bulletin of the Needle and Bobbin Club, The*, Vol 28 (1944), Nos 1 and 2; Vol 30 (1946), Nos 1 and 2. New York

Morris, B. *Victorian Embroidery*, London 1962

Nevinson, J. L. *Catalogue of English Domestic Needlework of the Sixteenth and Seventeenth Century*, Victoria and Albert Museum, London 1938

Proctor, M. G. *Victorian Canvas Work*, London 1972

Rhodes, M. *The Batsford Book of Canvas Work*, Newton Centre, Mass., 1983; London 1983

Swain, M. *Historical Needlework*, London 1970

—*Figures on Fabric*, London 1980

Synge, L. *Chairs*, Poole, Dorset, 1978

Thornton, P. *Seventeenth-century Interior Decoration in England, France and Holland*, New Haven, Conn., and London 1978

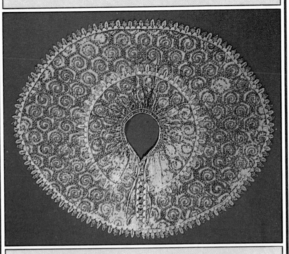

EMBROIDERY
AND
DRESS

With Feathers crown'd, with gay embroidery dress'd

The Temple of Fame by Alexander Pope

IMOGEN STEWART

Splendid dressing has always been a way of expressing a love of beauty and of grandeur; the decoration of textiles is an art form as old as textiles themselves. Unfortunately, early textiles are rare, as they tend to perish through exposure to light or rot through the accumulation of dirt, and have only been preserved in exceptional circumstances. In the first centuries of the millennium, the early Coptic Church buried its dead in the sandy soil of Egypt. The body was clad in a simple linen tunic which the sand preserved while the body rotted. A fine example of a linen tunic, which belonged to a small child, is now in the Whitworth Art Gallery, Manchester. It is decorated with applied bands of woven tapestry and purple linen in a diamond pattern. Above each cuff is a line of running stitches in a thick green thread which adds a little extra decoration of quite a different sort.

The greatest medieval embroidery was executed for the Church (3), and although some was done for secular use, very little of this remains. The main source of evidence must be through pictures, although it is not always easy to tell if the pattern depicted on the cloth is woven or embroidered.

One of the oldest pieces of decorative needlework to survive is the Bayeux Tapestry, worked with eight different coloured wools on a coarse linen. Each figure is first worked around its edge in stem and outline stitches and then filled in with laid and couched work. It was apparently executed to record the invasion of England and the Battle of Hastings, and intended to decorate the walls of a cathedral, probably that at Bayeux. The different coloured wools, all of muted tones, are embroidered on a coarse linen. Each figure is first worked around its edge in stem and outline stitches and then filled in with laid and couched work. Fragments of similar embroidery are to be found in some Scandinavian countries and it is likely that coarse embroidery of this type was applied to secular clothing. The clothes that the figures wear in the Bayeux Tapestry are generally plain although some have stripes or bands of decoration, with the priests' vestments being the most decorative.

The applying of jewels to dress is also a very old custom. In some cases jewels are gathered together to form meshes or decorative edgings. The set of tapestries 'La Dame à la Licorne', woven sometime between 1484 and 1500, depicts a series of beautiful women representing the five senses. Each is dressed in rich velvets, watered or figured silks, heavily embellished with jewels in bold patterns.

An equally rich dress is worn by Anne of Cleves in Holbein's portrait painted in the late 1530s (1). Neat bands with applied jewels edge her neckline, the ends of her sleeves, the front of her gown. Her elaborate cap is decorated with a heavy pattern made up of jewels and

1. (*opposite*) Anne of Cleves by Hans Holbein the Younger. Applied jewels edge her embroidered garments. Late 1530s.

2. (*above*) Collar embroidered with black silk thread (blackwork). English, late sixteenth century.

3. Part of a linen altar frontal with horses, hunting dogs and a unicorn. German, fourteenth century.

gold threads and covered with a fine starched linen veil, wired at the edge so that it will keep its shape. The cuffs of her linen undersleeves are also embroidered. One pattern is used against another and different textures contrast with one another. It is evident that by the sixteenth century, the embroidering of secular dress was intricate and of an excellent standard. Embroidery is used to give the dress a feeling of rich encrustation which would very definitely set the wearer apart from others. No examples remain of this splendid type of dress; once the garment began to show signs of wear, the jewels were removed and used again.

Another portrait by Holbein, this time of the third wife of Henry VIII, Jane Seymour (8), depicts embroidery taking a different form in dress. It was painted in 1536 and the Queen wears an English style of dress which is very different from the Flemish style worn by Anne of Cleves. It is simpler, and although patterns and textures are still used lavishly, the grandeur of this dress is expressed not so much through the jewels, which are none the less there, but through the plain rich cloth coupled with a sumptuous pattern. The frills of the linen undersleeves are heavily embroidered, and the square neckline of the linen shift shows at the neck of the gown which is finished with a pique edge embroidered in coloured silk. The undersleeves and forepart are of a figured woven silk but the turned-back sleeves and the edgings of the gown are decorated with applied thread

in a lattice pattern which creates the effect of a bold texture. It is a design which has been conceived in a quite different way to either the patterns created with applied jewels or the delicate patterns embroidered onto the cuffs of the shift sleeves.

Knot Patterns

During the mid-sixteenth century there was a great fashion for embroidering the basic linen undergarment — the man's shirt (4) and the woman's shift. The neckline was invariably either a high-standing collar or of a low square shape, and the cuffs were finished with a single ruffle. The garments were beautifully worked, and a few remain from the late sixteenth and early seventeenth centuries. One boy's shirt (5, 6), in the Victoria and Albert Museum, dates from about 1540 and is an excellent example of the garment depicted so clearly in many of Holbein's portraits. The body and the seams of the garment were embroidered, but this was never intended to show. The boy's shirt is worked in blue silk on white linen, but in other cases black or red silk were used, although occasionally other colours appear and gold was used for royalty. The knot pattern predominates and according to Holbein's pictures there were endless variations on this theme — no two are alike. They were intended to intrigue the mind and the lines twist in and out, sometimes incorporating flower heads or leaves, reminiscent of the complicated and delicate patterns of some Italian Renaissance artists. They are also similar to the patterns that are to be found in the

4. *(above left)* Drawing of Edward, 9th Baron Clinton, by Holbein; the shirt is embroidered in typical mid-sixteenth century style.

5. *(above right)* Boy's linen shirt embroidered with blue silk thread. English, 1540s.

6. *(right)* Detail of the collar.

decoration of the great Tudor houses. Plasterwork and woodwork was often decorated with cunning patterns, contained in a square or rectangle but made up of interlacing lines. Outside the house the knot garden followed the same form; the low hedges were planted around the herb beds so that they formed a similar overall geometric pattern. Although many of these patterns may have been derived originally from foreign sources, they have English characteristics in the choice of flowers and the lightness of design. Italian portraits depict embroidery of this type but it includes motifs inspired by the more florid decorations of Roman villas or by Arabic textile patterns. All these patterns had a great deal of movement in them, using stitches which were quick to work. The shirt in the Victoria and Albert Museum has the collar and cuffs worked in cross and double running stitches with overcast edges; the small knot patterns that cover the seams are worked in a knotted and buttonhole insertion stitch.

Blackwork

By the turn of the sixteenth and seventeenth centuries, any article of dress or furnishing might be decorated with embroidery. Blackwork, or black silk embroidered onto white linen, once known as Spanish work, became very popular and was used on bodices, doublets, detachable sleeves, coifs, night caps, handkerchiefs and

occasionally on collars (2). A few of the wide-falling collars depicted in portraits are of fine linen covered with blackwork patterns (7). Two rare examples of these are in the Middleton Collection in Nottingham; one is worked in herringbone stitch so that it is reversible.

All kinds of motifs were chosen for blackwork — a particularly suitable one was a spider's web. Seeding or speckling stitches were used to add shading to the motifs. Some of the best-known pieces, worked in this technique, were intended for furnishings. 'The Shepherd Buss' is a picture worked on a linen cover. The gentleman shepherd, who is a person of sensitivity and poetic feeling, has retired to a pastoral setting where he is surrounded not only by sheep and a vine but by books, musical instruments and other symbols of his intellectual pursuits. He represents the melancholy young man known from Elizabethan poetry. Flat vine leaves, held in the centre of spiralling stems, were a popular motif; these could be filled with tiny geometric patterns which added a patchwork of textures to an otherwise simple shape. These 'filling patterns' are based on simple stitches, particularly straight stitch, which is used in different directions. The viewer is drawn into a close examination of them, and once again the fascination is endless. Despite the miniature and shimmering qualities of much of this work, the overall effect of the designs can be bold. A long cushion cover, decorated with vine leaves and placed on a window seat or stool,

7. (left) Anonymous painting of two small boys with blackwork collars. English, late sixteenth century.

8. (opposite) Jane Seymour by Holbein: luxuriant English-style embroidery, especially on the edgings and sleeves of the gown. 1536.

9. Unfinished blackwork nightcap, showing drawing of original pattern. English, early seventeenth century.

would be noticeable. The boldness and intensity of the black and white patterns could add greatly to the decoration of dress.

There were two qualities of the black silk thread, used for this embroidery, as well as a third kind which consisted of a black and a white thread spun together. Many examples of black silk left to us today have deteriorated due to the quality of the dye. A lot of black dye was obtained from woad or was iron tannate black, two of the oldest dyes. Iron tannate is tannic acid extracted from alder or oak bark, then mixed with gall nut and used with an iron mordant base to give the black colour. Woad is used for blue, but if the dye bath is strong enough and vegetable matter is mixed with it, woad will also produce black. Logwood was beginning to be imported from the Americas but the dye obtained from it was not fast and it was not until later that it could be used successfully.

It is partly where the black silk has worn away and partly where the work is unfinished (9), that the drawing of the original pattern can sometimes be seen. The complicated pattern of spirals and flower heads had to be drawn out first, and the filling stitches might then be worked by counting the threads. A short straight stitch was generally worked over two threads. Normally the pattern was transferred to cloth by means of drawing the design onto parchment, and marking the pattern by pricking holes along the lines and using pouncing powder (10), often mixed with powdered charcoal. A fine, wet brush was then used to draw the line. A few pieces have the design printed onto the linen by the means of an engraved plate (11) but this method does not seem to have been very successful and such pieces

are rare. These designs tend to be heavy and lacking in freedom. They are the same motifs as those used for the pricking and pouncing method of transfer, but they have lost the naivety that is part of their charm. The same designs and themes were used for polychrome embroideries.

Arcadia

The melancholy young man may be more common in miniature painting and poetry than he is in embroidery, but flowers, insects and other motifs, inspired by pastoral themes, abound in all types of embroidery. The idea of a country retreat, where the gentle person could study and lead the supposedly simple life of a shepherd in the classical world, was partly inspired by Sir Philip Sidney's work *Arcadia*, started in 1580. This was also a period when there was a keen interest in horticulture and extensive plant experiments were taking place. Flowers and plant forms generally provided inspiration for both art and literature; in several of Shakespeare's plays groups of people retreat to the beauty and seclusion of islands or wooded dells. Scenes are also set in gardens or orchards and plants are used as symbols. In *Hamlet*, Ophelia, in her madness, explains what some common plants are thought to symbolize. Many of these are country superstitions which a gentle person such as herself would not normally have known.

Most large gardens were divided into kitchen gardens, herb gardens and orchards. Flower gardens were a

10. Panel traced for embroidery. English, early seventeenth century.

11. *(right)* Linen coif printed from engraved plate and embroidered. English, early seventeenth century.

luxury although one which was becoming ever more common.

The canvas work valances (12), which went around the top of the great beds, tell us something about the gardens of great houses. They usually illustrate a Bible story or one drawn from classical mythology. It may be the visit of the Queen of Sheba to Solomon or the story of Venus and Adonis, but the scene takes place in the garden of a sixteenth-century European house. At one end is the knot garden and trellised walk with climbing roses. Next, further away from the house, is a mound with a decorative fence or summer house and perhaps a fountain in the Italianate style. Behind is a wide vista of mountains in cool grey and blue colours. Finally, this cultivated garden opens into a wilderness or park; a cottage may be glimpsed in a clearing, and perhaps a shaded pond. The great table carpets, also worked on canvas in tent and cross stitch, often had borders which included pastoral scenes. Hunting or other country pursuits are carried out in a landscape of hills with small white clouds floating across a blue sky.

The embroiderer used every type of flower and plant with no regard for where they grew or at what season or for their scale. Flowers and insects were treated in the same way that they were in herbals. They were either repeated across the cloth as a spot pattern or joined by curling stems. A linear design of green fern leaves could be made to shimmer, as if they were wet, by applying spangles. This design would look well curling all over a lady's jacket bodice or on bed hangings. The prickly holly leaf was used as a spray, either worked in black silk and gold thread as a spot pattern, or in green and red wool as a bold trailing pattern on hangings. Among the other plants which embroiderers favoured especially were the pansy, sometimes known as 'three faces in a hood', cornflowers, honeysuckle, roses and the strawberry which was shown both in flower and in fruit, the latter adding a bright colour.

Although much embroidery was done in professional workshops or by the ladies of a great house, working together, the smaller pieces have an intimate quality and were sometimes worked as gifts and keepsakes. The small purses and sweet bags with their beautifully plaited handles, the coifs and nightcaps, the covers for miniature prayer books and gloves were among the small items which were so encrusted with embroidery that they became jewel-like. Richly coloured floss silk is mixed with purl (a tightly coiled wire) sequins, seed pearls which were being imported in quantities from the Americas, and silver gilt bobbin lace. Larger pieces were worked as gifts too. Mary Queen of Scots worked a crimson satin petticoat while she was Queen Elizabeth's

12. Detail from a canvas work valance, one of a set of three. French or Flemish, late sixteenth century.

prisoner, and made a gift of it to the Queen in the hope of softening her. She would have had her ladies-in-waiting to help her with large items of embroidery. While she was in prison in England, she also had a professional embroiderer working for her. In England these craftsmen were members of the Broderers' Livery Company, incorporated in 1561. A master craftsman would have his own workshop while others would travel from house to house, helping the ladies to start work on large pieces. While Mary Queen of Scots was at Hardwick, under the care of George Talbot, 6th Earl of Shewsbury, she and his wife, Elizabeth or Bess, worked the famous hangings now known as the Oxburgh Hangings. The designs for these are of a far more exotic nature than many of the floral and knot patterns mentioned so far. The drawing of the designs to a certain extent still re-

flects the style of the contemporary Natural History illustrations and wood engravings from which they were taken. They include such strange animals as 'a great monkey' and a 'bird of America' which is a toucan, as well as a cactus and other botanical specimens that by the standards of the time were comparatively rare.

The embroiderers' patterns were often obtained from herbals, illustrated Bibles and other books. Perhaps one of the best-known books is Jacques Le Moyne de Morgues, *La Clef des Champs*, published at Blackfriars in 1586. It contains woodcuts of animals, birds, flowers, plants and fruits with titles to the plates in English, French and Latin; there is little text apart from the titles. In the dedication there is an explanation of the book, which says that it was intended to be of use to noble patrons and craftsmen, especially goldsmiths, embroiderers and tapestry makers.

In the early seventeenth century more pattern books began to appear and the amateur embroiderer was better catered for. Thomas Trevelyon's folio of designs was completed in 1616; it contained designs for embroidery, carpentry, and one for gardens entitled 'The Green Dragon'. In this section some of the embroidery designs are repeated. He does not give directions for stitches but his 'drawn workes', as he called them, are in full repeat. Patterns for night-caps embroidered to shape, complete with alternate borders are included among the designs. During the seventeenth century other pattern books followed. Some of the best-known were *A Schole House for the Needle* by Richard Shorleyker published in 1624, and James Boler's *The Needle's Excellency* which had reached twelve editions by 1640.

Court Dress

At the beginning of the seventeenth century much informal dress was embroidered and portraits show us how these items of dress, were assembled. Although it was not 'full' dress, it was none the less very grand. Margaret Laton's jacket is preserved in the Victoria and Albert Museum, with a portrait of her wearing it. She has a cap embroidered to match it; it is edged with silver gilt lace as is the jacket. The silver gilt lace on the cuffs and the neck of the jacket is hidden by the white linen ruff and cuffs. The basques of the bodice are obscured by a whitework apron or kirtle, which is worn so that it gives the dress the high-waisted line of the 1620s. The jacket bodice is stretched smooth and made on a firm base of linen. Despite its smooth appearance, the exotic, brightly coloured birds are raised so that they stand away from the surface. Pieces of parchment or waxed threads were used to raise the motifs. The bodice has gussets in the basques but otherwise there is nothing to interfere with the embroidered pattern. The seams are covered with applied gold braid. This type of embroidery, executed in a great variety of colours and stitches, was generally intended to be seen flat and not draped.

Formal dress was often jewelled and embroidered with gold thread which was a fine wire. It was either couched on with Maltese, or some other matching silk thread, or it was drawn through to the back of the cloth and caught with a silk thread. Goldwork, for formal dress, was usually executed on a silk damask cloth. Italy, Spain and France were all producing figured silks by the late sixteenth century. The goldwork often echoed the design of the silk to which it was applied. The designs were generally of a heavier and more formal character than the flowers, spirals and geometric motifs used for informal dress. Heavy formal embroidery was not intended to be draped; it was usually applied as a border pattern or just to the parts of the garments which showed. The undersleeve might have ovals of embroidery which would show where the seam of the outer sleeve was left open.

Gloves were an indispensable part of court dress from the early sixteenth century onwards. The decoration was kept mainly to the gauntlet, and consisted of motifs worked on silk and then applied to the glove; the cuff was then lined with silk. Sometimes the motifs fit into the tabs of the gauntlet and usually there is a central motif in the main part of the gauntlet. Gloves were often perfumed and given as expensive gifts. The rates of the London Customs House list many ready-made and embroidered accessories which were imported from France and Spain. Although a great number were produced here too, the demand for accessories apparently could not be met.

The great court masques of this period brought employment to the embroiderers. Very few garments that were made for masques remain; they can be seen in portraits and in the designs which Inigo Jones made for the Jacobean masques. It is difficult to tell from these sources which of the textiles were embroidered and which were painted. However, it is known that large numbers of professional embroiderers were brought to court when a masque, or some other festivity, such as a tilt, was planned.

The portraits by William Larkin and the miniatures by Nicholas Hilliard and Isaac Oliver have left us an excellent opportunity to study the dress that was generally worn. All these artists were capable of minutely depicting an embroidered jacket or cap, and in the case of William Larkin, the full dress down to the embroidered handkerchief, shoes and hose.

The handkerchief (13) was a symbol of gentility and was not for actual use; the silk embroidery and lace edgings were usually very fine. An embroidered handkerchief might be presented as a gift and its value and significance is illustrated in Shakespeare's *Othello*, where part of the plot hinges on it.

The sixteenth-century linen hose, in the Victoria and Albert Museum, are embroidered with a thick green

thread in French knots and running stitches. The hose (15) worn by Richard Sackville, 3rd Earl of Dorset, when he was painted in 1613 by Larkin, are of a very different character. The elaborate clocks are of delicate curling patterns and flowers, while the motifs embroidered on his shoes match those on his doublet and the gauntlets of his gloves. Another motif is used for the decoration of his breeches; while his shoes are finished with great rosettes and his standing collar with a deep lace border. He was painted in miniature by Isaac Oliver in 1616; his clothes are just as decorative and this time the clocks on his hose are in gold.

Bold Designs and Sombre Shades

There was a tendency for the decoration of dress to be bolder in the early seventeenth century. Elizabeth Howard, Countess of Banbury, was painted by Daniel Mytens in a black and white dress. Her petticoat and bodice are white, embroidered with a pattern of black tendrils and leaves; her gown is embroidered with the same pattern in black on black and is trimmed with ribbon that matches the petticoat. Her ruff and cuffs are

embroidered with a black spot pattern and her cap, handkerchief and veil must necessarily be white to complete the ensemble. Although the embroidery is of the delicate and curling kind, the over-all look is one of comparative simplicity and boldness. If a lighter form of embroidery was being used, it might only consist of gold thread couched on in a vermicular pattern.

Diana Cecil, Countess of Oxford and Anne Cecil, Countess of Stamford, who were twin sisters, were painted wearing identical dresses, by William Larkin. They too have favoured a bold approach in the decoration of their dresses (16). Yellow gold-coloured silk has been embroidered in large chevrons, onto white satin. The satin has been slashed. A gentleman's cloak, in the Victoria and Albert Museum, is decorated in a similar manner, although the embroidery motif is different. The slashing (14) was evidently done by the tailor, after the embroidery had been completed, for it follows the direction of the motifs.

The black silk used for blackwork was gradually replaced by red silk and by the 1630s this had given place to red crewel wool which was worked on a heavier quality of linen. Larger patterns were required

13. (opposite) Linen handkerchief embroidered with silk: a decorative mark of gentle birth. English, early seventeenth century.

14. (right) Cloak, embroidered and then slashed. Italian, 1600–20.

15. Richard Sackville, 3rd Earl of Dorset, by William Larkin. Intricate embroidery adorns all his clothes. English, 1613.

16. Diana Cecil, Countess of Oxford, by Larkin. Her gold-coloured silk dress has very striking embroidered ornament. English, early seventeenth century.

17. Bed from the Great Chamber at Parham Park, Sussex. Coverlet and back canopy are late sixteenth century; curtains c. 1615.

for this type of work. Crewel wool was quick to work and great flower heads and spirals were worked in one colour so that they trailed and swirled across hangings. The speckling stitches were still used to add texture, enhanced by the twisting of the crewel yarns with a white linen thread (19). Now the emphasis of the design was on the weight of the motif and the massive quality of the over-all pattern. This type of embroidery not only filled the large areas of furnishing textiles, it also suited the bulky quality of the great swelling sleeves of the bodices and doublets. The waist was high and the basques of the bodice were long and full. Silk bodices and doublets of the same shape were also embroidered with sequins and couched thread, often in stripes.

By this time there was a reaction against the elaborate dress of the early years of the century. Some garments were embroidered but Charles I set a fashion for simple elegance. His courtiers were painted in plain sombre-coloured satins; decoration consisted mainly of ribbons, lace and pearls. Deep rich blue and crimson colours also remained fashionable. Although black was worn a lot, the fashion for small sharp black and white patterns or a riot of bright colour was not to return until later. Accessories were still embroidered – shoes, especially the informal mules, gloves and gentlemen's low-crowned nightcaps – might all be embroidered. Ladies would embroider work bags, which they would keep with them, thus adding further decoration to their dress and to the room. These, too, would often be embroidered in wool on linen but the design did not sprawl as it did on the hangings, as it was controlled by the rectangular shape of the bag, the flowing pattern being contained within it.

Embroidery of several kinds was still used to decorate the home and classic patterns, such as flame stitch were used for upholstery and hangings. The colours often followed those of the fashion and at this period they were sombre. The choice of colour was important as the optical effects in these patterns can be quite altered by the use of colour. The appearance of bed furnishings embroidered with subtle colours will be that of soft shadows, whereas upholstery fabrics, stretched flat and worked with chevrons of bright red and yellow, have a more vital appearance. The great bed at Parham Park has curtains worked in Hungarian point in a flame design, but the rest of the bed furnishings are of silk embroidery. Thus two contrasting types of embroidery (17) are used for the furnishings of one bed. This was not unusual, and an embroidered coverlet and valances might be used with curtains of damask.

Embroidery for upholstery was still executed in cross or tent stitch on canvas, but the design no longer had the naive quality of the earlier work. It was closer to the designs made for woven tapestry and owed something to the Baroque. A set of chairs with walnut frames might be upholstered with scenes illustrating classical myths (18). Groups of people, in a type of classical dress, feast in halls with black and white marble floors sur-

18. One of a set of four chairs upholstered in canvas work at Parham Park. English, *c.* 1635.

rounded by Baroque architectural motifs. Around the scene will be sprinkled the floral motifs, always loved by the embroiderer.

The political unrest in England in the middle of the seventeenth century led to even more embroidery being done by the skilled amateur. There was little money available for new clothes or grand schemes of redecoration. Time, skill and imagination were available and many of the most notable pieces of embroidery from this period are examples of stumpwork or other pieces which are on a small scale.

A Fine Art

It was at this time that embroidery first became a work of fine art and the finished picture was framed and hung upon the wall. Some pieces are exactly like miniature portraits (**20**); the floss silk is worked so that it looks like smooth flesh tones. Other pieces, particularly those in stumpwork, often have a charming naivety about them. Many small household objects were covered with tiny embroidered scenes. Among the most popular pieces were caskets, mirror frames and pictures. As ever, Bible stories were used as a source for inspiration. The figures in the scenes, however, are usually dressed in contemporary dress, and the central characters are sometimes portraits of Charles I and Henrietta Maria,

19. Woman's bodice of linen embroidered with crewel work twisted with linen. English, *c.* 1635.

appearing as Solomon and the Queen of Sheba, as well as other well-known characters. Stumpwork is usually done on a white or ivory-coloured satin ground, a variety of materials being applied to it. Often the choice of colour is again in a sombre key. Tawny oranges, deep yellows and greens are mixed with dusky pinks and blues and scattered over the white ground. The figures in stumpwork have clothes of figured or embroidered silk, their faces and hands may be of embroidered satin or of carved ivory or wood, tiny pieces which have been applied with the mass of other materials. Their clothes may be embellished with seed pearls or glass beads. Around them are fantastic castles and cottages, fountains and bowers, creatures and birds of both the real and fantastic kinds, fruit and flowers. They all have a sculptural quality – where a motif is raised it is stuffed with cotton or wool; where a piece of applied silk fabric is required to stand away from the ground a wire is stitched to the edge. Sometimes the petals of a flower are worked in detached button-hole stitch so that they too stand away, or a small artificial silk flower is applied. Naturally these fragile pieces, representing as many hours of work as the larger pieces, were not for use – simply to be looked at.

Once a little girl had completed her samplers to the required standard, her next task might well be to work a casket in which she could keep her toys or precious miniature pieces, including her needlework tools. She would already be well acquainted with the Bible stories which she worked on the outside of the box. Then the inside had to be worked too; each drawer might be covered with silk and embroidered with a floral motif, while the lid might contain a complete garden.

This type of work has a very English character to it. During the years of the Civil War and Commonwealth, England was fairly isolated, and the energy and novelty which were put into English design give it a freshness and individuality. Things that were familiar and much loved were included – the tulip which everyone was planting in their gardens, rainbows and fashionable fruits. It is also set apart from foreign embroidery by the love of fantasy which is characteristic of stumpwork.

Much of the work which was done on the continent was closer to the movements in architecture. Border patterns reflected those used in the carvings on Italian Baroque buildings and the floral motifs were more stylized. The pictorial designs tend to be heavier and bolder than the English ones, and although they too have a charming and naive quality, they often lack the elegance and romance of the English versions.

Later there were many influences on English design from abroad. The Royalists, returning from exile in the

20. Embroidered miniature portrait of a lady, with flesh tones rendered in floss silk. English, mid-seventeenth century.

1660s, brought ideas from the Netherlands and from France. French Protestants, who belonged to the Huguenot church, had been leaving France to settle in England, Holland and other parts of northern Europe since the sixteenth century. Many of these people were craftsmen, and among them were silk weavers and other textile artists who were to have great influence on English design. In 1685 the Edict of Nantes, which had to a certain extent protected the interests of Protestants in France, was revoked, and the number of refugees increased enormously.

Eastern Influences

The importation of goods from the East also steadily increased; the pieces were often made for the Western market and included things that Eastern artists thought Western people would like. In their turn, Western designers learned a great deal from the East and embroiderers increasingly selected quick stitches, such as chain stitch, which predominated in Indian work. Previously, quick stitches had been reserved for working the parts of the design which gave an over-all effect rather than requiring detailed examination.

From the seventeenth century onwards, Indian chintz was highly prized, and the East India Company's trade was brisk. Occasionally a design used for a painted Indian chintz will also appear as an embroidery. An Indian chintz of 1690–1700, in the Victoria and Albert Museum, has a design of hunters and shepherds among rocks. Some of the animals and plants are distinctly Western – they include a strawberry plant, recognizable

21. Man's doeskin coat embroidered with silver thread. English, early 1680s.

22. Man's coat of wool embroidered with silver thread. English, 1720.

from English sixteenth-century embroidery. In the Museum of Fine Arts in Boston, one can find the same design (but in reverse) on a piece of English crewelwork hanging. John Irwin has suggested that it is possible that a pattern book was the source of both designs. One was owned by the English embroiderers who thought that they were executing an 'Indian' design, and the other was owned by the Indian painters, who were working for the Western market. Another example of a haphazard mixture of Eastern and Western motifs is on a quilt in the Victoria and Albert Museum. It is Italian quilted linen, embroidered with floss silks, and among the exotic-looking flowers are four motifs based on Buddhist symbols.

The great traveller, Celia Fiennes, always described the beds which she saw in the state rooms of great houses. In about 1698 she visited Lowther Castle, near Penrith, and remarks that she saw three handsome chambers. One had its walls hung with scarlet striped cloth, and the hangings matched. In another room there were hangings of flowered damask which were lined with fine Indian embroidery, and in a third room

there was a blue satin bed embroidered with a great deal of silver and gold thread. She usually commented if the embroidery had been done by a member of the family; as she does not in this case, we may presume that it was the work of professional embroiderers. Some amateurs still worked yards of embroidery for hangings and Celia Fiennes greatly admired the embroidery done by Queen Mary II and her maids-of-honour, when she saw it at Hampton Court.

Metal Thread and Silk

By the 1670s men's dress had undergone a considerable but gradual change and the suit, made up of breeches, waistcoat and coat, was established. The coat and waistcoat were long and full-skirted, so that they incorporated large plain areas which warranted decorating, they were usually embroidered with metal thread in a stylized pattern. The leather buff coat, trimmed with gold or silver braid and often including silk sleeves, predominated in Civil War portraits (21). There are also surviving examples. The practice of embroidering straight onto leather was not unknown, and an example of this art is a doeskin coat embroidered with silver thread, in the Museum of London, which dates from the early 1680s. Silk was used for coats and waistcoats but the most usual textile was wool, which would take the weight of the metal thread embroidery (22). The embroidery outlined the front edges of the coat, the hem, the side vents, the pocket slits and covers the large, turned-back cuff, and the work on the waistcoat would follow the same pattern. The doeskin coat has quite dense bands of embroidery. However, in some examples the coat simply had a little decoration around the buttonholes.

Embroidery did not feature to such a great extent on ladies' formal dress. Figured silk, trimmed with lace or braid, was a more usual form of decoration. The woman's silhouette was much slimmer than it had been and the open gown was favoured again. The stomacher, which was pinned over the opening of the bodice of the gown, was sometimes embroidered. Its elongated triangular shape meant that the design could be one of flower heads which became smaller in scale towards the bottom, or one of tendrils and flowers which grew up from the bottom of the triangle. There are several examples of stomachers (23) and embroidery patterns preserved from the 1670s and 1680s. They show naturalism in the design and are once again worked in rich bright-coloured silk.

A Variety of Approaches

Despite the great fashion for figured silks and needlepoint lace at the turn of the seventeenth and eighteenth centuries, it is also a very interesting period in the history of embroidery. During this period many different techniques and designs were worked.

Layettes of linen were worked with quilting and couched threads, in patterns of a suitably small scale. The same techniques might be applied to the decoration of adult garments or household items. Embroidered accessories could be worked in almost any technique. There are examples of shoes and mules (26) worked in silk embroidery, flame stitch or metal thread on velvet. Hose often had small embroidered clocks on them. The hanging pocket, which was tied on around the waist under the ladies' petticoat, was beautifully worked even though it did not show. They were worked for gifts or just for pleasure and were of stout linen twill with either silk or wool embroidery in one or more colours. Despite the smallness of the area the design is quite free.

A number of larger garments for ladies' informal dress were also decorated with embroidery. The

23. Stomacher embroidered with brightly-coloured silk threads of flowers and leaves, c. 1675.

decorative apron was an important part of informal dress and examples vary from very fine whitework to coloured silks and metal thread worked on a plain silk. Some of them are in a very decided colour scheme such as autumnal browns or reds; others include many colours and tones, the grading of the colours adding to the realism of the flower heads. These colour schemes do not necessarily give any indication of the colours of the dress with which the apron was worn.

The jacket bodice was worn for informal dress throughout the eighteenth century. A panel from an unfinished bodice, in the Victoria and Albert Museum, has a small waist, narrow armholes, and the front edge is cut rounded. It is made from three layers of linen which were to be quilted. The embroidery, worked in silks, is of a floral pattern in a small scale, which is in keeping with the small quilted pattern and the slimmer line of the dress. The lines for the quilting are drawn in, likewise the seam lines so that the embroiderer knew where to stop work. The seam allowance was narrow; material was never wasted and fashionably dressed people were not expected to wear their clothes for very long. A deep seam allowance denoted a cheaper garment as the wearer might want to let it out later, regardless of whether it was still fashionable or not.

Decorative Household Textiles

Some of the finest English quilts were embroidered during the early eighteenth century. They were worked for the state beds, or the beds in the grandest rooms of the house kept for visitors. They were looked after with care and when these rooms were not in use the textiles would have been covered. The finest coverlets were worked on narrow pieces of sheer white satin which were joined together before work was started. The normal width of hand-woven cloth is 48 to 53 cm (19 to 21 in), although occasionally a quilt is made from a piece of cloth which is of a greater width. Many quilts were worked on thicker and harder-wearing linen. They were worked, very often by the gifted amateur and frequently included a signature and date or a monogram, perhaps in honour of a marriage.

Among this group of embroideries are the exquisite sets of bed furnishings, known as marriage sets, consisting of a coverlet and four cushions (**24**). The design would be a formal one, perhaps a gold shell pattern which forms a trellis for richly coloured flowers, gathered together in dense patterns in the centre and in the corners. The same design, in a slightly modified form, would be worked on the cushions. Although the frames of these grand beds were of a simple plain structure, they were hidden entirely by the elaborate hangings which surrounded the sets of embroidered coverlet and cushions. Silk damask or cut velvet was used as a base to cover the headboard, tester and for the hangings. These were tied and nailed into swags and trimmed with fringe and braid, as well as being embroidered.

Embroidered bed hangings of a very different type were beginning to appear at this time. At Levens Hall, south of the Lake District, there is a piece of patchwork made from Indian chintzes which date from the late seventeenth and early eighteenth century. The daughters of the house worked it in the early eighteenth century and it is the earliest piece of known patchwork in this country. Later, patchwork was associated with the servant's rooms or cottage furnishings.

One of the most popular motifs for embroidered hangings, workbags and parts of dresses was an island of earth with a tree growing from it. Sometimes it was treated as one motif and the tree would grow up the fabric or it could be used as a small motif repeated all over the cloth. The plant always sprouted leaves and

flowers of an exotic kind and the mounds of earth were striped tones of greens or browns. This motif was used in all forms of textile design; in embroidery it ranged from bold versions worked in crewel wools to silk embroidery of a more delicate sort. It would usually be worked in rich colours on a white ground. This motif probably originated in Chinese art but came to England through Indian art, in the same way that several motifs of Persian origin had done.

Floral Motifs

Ladies' skirts swelled again in the 1720s and were once more embroidered, although plain silks, damasks and brocades were very fashionable. Ladies adopted the fashion for wearing side hoops or panniers under their skirts in the 1730s, and they were most fashionable between 1740 and the mid-century. For formal full dress they wore a mantua (**25**) or robe with a matching petticoat. The back of the bodice of the robe was sewn down in pleats and the narrow train of the skirt was pinned up, so that an expanse of petticoat showed. It had to be embroidered all the way round and larger designs were adopted. They might include architectural motifs, rococo curves or shells, worked in metal thread with flowers embroidered in coloured silks around them. The motifs on the bodice had to be of a smaller scale so that they would fit in between the pleats, and they also appeared on the robings, the facings, down the front edges of the bodice, and around the neck. Embroidery was thus a convenient way of decorating the mantua because the motifs could be adapted to fit the construction of the garment.

Mrs Delany, embroiderer, artist and correspondent, designed and embroidered her own court dress with trails and bunches of coloured flowers on black silk. As well as being a gifted needlewoman, she had great powers of description and her letters contain some very interesting comments about dress and embroidery. In 1741 she attended a gathering held by the Prince and Princess of Wales at Norfolk House. Out of innumerable grand dresses, she described Lady Scarborough's dress as being very fine but she found the embroidery pattern, which included festoons and pillars, 'unmeaningful'. However, the Duchess of Queensberry's dress she wished she had thought of herself. It sounds, from her description, very like the type of motif which was worked on hangings. It consisted of brown mounds of earth covered with foliage, and a tree with twining flowers growing out of it, from the bottom to the top of the petticoat, which was repeated on each width of cloth. It took seven widths of cloth to make a robe and

24. Cushion from a 'marriage set' of bed furnishings. English, early eighteenth century.

petticoat if panniers were worn, and at this period and at such a function, it is fairly certain that the Duchess would have worn them. The Duchess's clothes were apparently of white satin embroidered with chenille and gold. The flowers included nasturtiums, ivy, honeysuckle, periwinkle and convolvulus. The sleeves and bodice were decorated with the same flowers in loose trails. The smaller motif on the robings and facings consisted of green banks covered with foliage.

Although it would seem that the Duchess of Queensberry's petticoat was embroidered in separate widths; often an elaborate border pattern was worked continuously across the seams, after the petticoat had been made up.

There are also examples of beautifully embroidered waistcoats from this period. The waistcoat was still long, full-skirted and often had sleeves. They were usually embroidered to shape before they were made up; the silk was stretched on the frame and the front of the waistcoat was drawn out so that the pattern for embroidery could be placed on it. The fronts were

embroidered with dense floral patterns, and the pocket flaps and the cuffs were also embroidered. The large coloured flower heads were worked in silk and were intended to look smooth and glossy; to achieve this, long and short and satin stitches were commonly used. A great variety of stitches was used for the metal thread which often acted as a ground for the flowers, whereas chenille thread would add texture and an extra intensity of colour.

Chair seats and backs were also embroidered to shape. A set of canvas-work chair seats might be worked with illustrations following a story so that each one had a different scene depicted on it.

Although the devoted amateur occasionally worked these large pieces, they were more often worked by professional embroiderers. The amateur usually worked smaller pieces such as pocket books or shoes which were then sent away to be made up.

During the first half of the eighteenth century there was a close relationship between design for embroidery, figured silks and lace. As the century progressed the motifs became lighter and were scattered across the cloth; ribbons, baskets and posies of flowers replaced the floral trails and architectural motifs.

25. Embroidered mantua, petticoat and court train, worn for a wedding. Dutch, 1759.

Additional Techniques

Whitework remained very fine and the pattern continued to be quite dense. It included a lot of cutwork and drawn-thread work, with buttonhole and darning stitches featuring among the very many other stitches. The emphasis, as in lace, was on fine textures. White cotton thread was often used on muslin or cambric (a fine linen) to create aprons, neckerchiefs and flounces for caps and sleeve ruffles.

Quilting was another popular form of embroidery used for both dress and furnishings during this period. A quilted jacket bodice or waistcoat might be worn for informal dress which was a fashion favoured by young girls in particular. The fronts of the jacket were caught together with ribbon ties and the neckerchief would be pulled through the front opening. The basques of the jacket were deep and full, and there were either vents or inverted pleats from the waist. The waistcoat or jacket was cut to the shape of camisole stays, which were less rigid and not as heavily boned as stays for formal dress. The quilted petticoat was an equally informal and comfortable garment; it was worn shorter than a petticoat for 'full' dress, and either with a small round hoop or no hoop at all. The hem had a deep and elaborately quilted border pattern which gave place to a simpler geometric pattern in the upper part. Thus informal dress often consisted of quilted garments worn with whitework accessories. Quilted garments might be worn in summer as well as winter; darker colours, tawny orange, yellow or dark green, were winter colours, while white or pale blue were for summer. Other clothes made from quilted satin included such garments as a gown of redingote type, a hood and cloak, a man's waistcoat and a nightgown which was like a twentieth-century dressing gown.

The gentleman's suit, heavily embroidered with gold thread, was retained particularly for court wear in France and Italy. Some of the motifs were raised which added to the texture and to the glitter of the work. As the line of the suit became narrower and the coat and waistcoat (27) sloped away from the waist line, the use of embroidery became rarer and the suit was trimmed with applied braid.

Ladies' gowns were still very decorative in the 1760s. Elaborate trimmings were applied to figured silks which were dyed to match the colours in the silk, and artificial

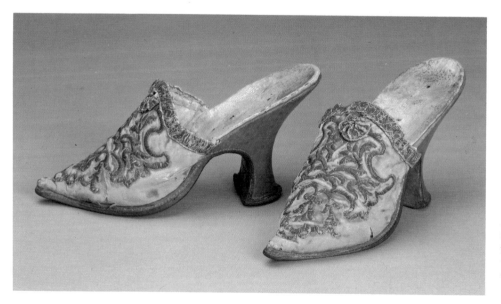

26. (left) Silk mules embroidered with silver thread. English, c. 1750.

27. (opposite) Man's velvet suit embroidered with silk thread, worn with a satin waistcoat also embroidered with silk thread. English, 1775–7.

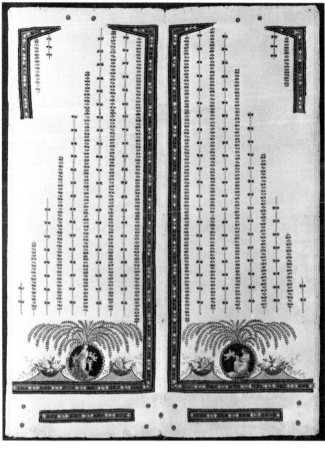

28. *(above left)* Double-fronted waistcoat with a neo-classical design. French, late eighteenth century.

29. *(above right)* Waistcoat fronts embroidered with silk thread in a neo-classical design, using applied spangles, ribbons and engraved medallions. The embroidery would be completed to shape, before cutting out and making up the waistcoat. English, 1790–1800.

30. *(left)* Details of the hangings on the neo-classical state bed at Osterley Park House, London. Late eighteenth century.

silk flowers, silver lace and sequins were lavishly applied onto the dress.

Cotton Embroideries

From the middle of the eighteenth century there was a decline in embroidery generally. The types of fabrics required for dress changed as lighter weights of cloth with more drape to them suited the new styles. In the last quarter of the century very little quilting or crewel work was done, and they were replaced by lighter cotton embroideries. Around 1760 tambouring was introduced into Europe, apparently from China. The fabric was stretched onto a round frame, hence the French name *tambour* (drum) was adopted for it. The thread was pulled through with a fine hook and formed into a chain of stitches.

Throughout the century there was great interest in introducing novel materials into embroidery which created quite a new effect. Straw, quills, hair and ribbon were among these materials, and later in the century, tiny pieces of metal foil were also incorporated into the design. Knotting was also worked; the thread was wound onto a shuttle and tied into knots, and it was then couched on to form a highly textured embroidery.

Patterns were on a smaller scale than before. A ladies' court dress of the 1770s would usually only have embroidery down the fronts and around the hem. Sprays of delicately drawn flowers were worked in chenille and silk on a white ground, and although the colours were still rich, a pastel-coloured ribbon might be included. The flowers themselves were cultivated or wild European ones, and an accessory would have one spray, placed centrally upon it, which would be very carefully drawn. Great attention was paid to the delicacy of the stems, leaves and tendrils and the realism of the flower heads (31). A detailed piece of work of this sort was not intended to create an overall look of grandeur: it was to add romance and sensitivity to a simpler style of dress.

The light cotton fabrics used for dress in the 1780s were sometimes embroidered by the yard. There was a short-lived fashion for ladies to embroider the muslin for their own gown. Coloured silk sprays were worked in quick stitches all over the gown 'piece', or the hem was worked in a border pattern. The muslin was light enough to be transparent and was often worn over a coloured silk base which matched one of the colours in the embroidery. Narrow lace or a matching silk ribbon trimming completed the effect. However, embroidery and figured weaving were both beginning to be replaced by printed cottons.

Waistcoats

The braid trimmings on men's suits became narrower and often the buttons were the only decoration left on the coat, but the waistcoat was still embroidered (28). It was short and had lost its skirts, the fronts sloped sharply away from the waist, and the embroidery tended to be concentrated on the front edges and the pocket flaps. Each button might be embroidered with one flower or bud which was repeated over the front of the waistcoat. The French favoured figurative scenes and tiny pictures of gardening or sailing boats spilled out over the floral border into the front corners. There are several examples of waistcoat fronts that have been embroidered but not made up. Possibly this is due to the change in mens' fashions which took place at the end of the eighteenth century. Fashions were beginning to change more quickly and men turned to a style of simple elegance which relied on cut and precision rather than decoration, but they continued to wear the embroidered three-piece suit for court dress. The court suit was heavily embroidered, often on a base of cut velvet or figured silk, in a spot pattern. Great delicacy was again applied to the drawing and the execution of the embroidered flowers, but the scale tended to be larger than that used for ladies' dresses. The slightly sombre colours and the slim line of the suit were in keeping with daily wear but the gorgeous decoration was not. The waistcoat worn for normal fashionable dress might be decorative but in an understated way; woven striped patterns were popular or embroidery of one colour in a simple pattern might be used.

Needle Painting

Embroidery of a smooth and regular type was used for pictures which have been described as examples of 'needle painting'. The picture was generally small and often worked in an oval; it was intended for an interior designed in the neo-classical style and the size and the shape would complement the general scheme. A silk ground and flat stitches were used, and often details would be painted in watercolour to add to the realism. There were also larger copies of paintings executed in worsteds in long and short stitches, which lent the work something of the qualities of a painting; a portrait could thus be copied very faithfully.

An example which brings together many of the best qualities of embroidery during the neo-classical period is the state bed at Osterley Park House (30). The bed was designed by Robert Adam in 1776 as a part of his scheme for the house. The hangings are of silk and

31. Tambour embroidered muff with delicate flower designs. Early nineteenth century.

velvet worked with silk, chenille and silver-gilt thread in stem, satin, long and short, and split stitches, with French knots, laid and couched work. The hangings are trimmed with thick silk fringes and tassels. The embroidery lends a lighter touch to the bulk of the bed. On the coverlet, narrow border patterns lie above small wreaths with medallions, and the velvet hangings have larger wreaths embroidered on them. The colour is a cool green with richer colours mixed in. The bed is surmounted by a large dome, which was originally hung with great wreaths of artificial flowers which must have made the embroidered wreaths appear even smaller and more delicate. Horace Walpole doubted the classical authenticity of this design and likened it to the work of a milliner.

The fashion for classicism affected dress, and instead of flowers, a muslin neckerchief would be decorated with a whitework pattern of curling stems and acanthus leaves or a Greek key pattern. The embroidery on a light muslin dress would be reminiscent of a Roman grotesque painting. Sometimes medallions, like cameos, were used as a central motif surrounded by swags and plants in the classical manner (29); the cameos might be painted or printed from engraved plates, while the rest of the design was embroidered. The high waistline of the dress invited a heavily embroidered border, and the low square neck line and the short sleeves were usually decorated with a narrow band of simple embroidery. A gown embroidered all over with a sprig or spot was known as 'sewed muslin', and tambouring was very popular for this.

Several different types of embroidery were used for the decoration of dress. A description of the fashions for

February 1815 in *La Belle Assemblée* makes it clear that embroidery played an important part in dress:

> The form of the pelisse we have already described; the trimming of one which we thought particularly elegant, was an embroidery of oak leaves in chenille: the dark-green of the trimming formed a happy contrast to the delicate mouse colour of the pelisse, which was buttoned down the front with dark green silk buttons; the embroidery went up the front on each side, round the sleeve, and round the bottom of the pelisse. The mantle was composed of cloth to correspond, lined with white sarsnet, and trimmed with a similar embroidery to the pelisse.

Acorns are used as an embroidery motif on a French cotton dress of 1806, now in the Victoria and Albert Museum. Acorns and oak leaves were used as motifs in classical art and in this case they are mixed with vine leaves and tendrils. Napoleon used oak leaves and acorns as devices and they became especially popular in France just after his coronation in 1804. Fashions spread very quickly from France to England, despite the English dislike of Napoleon.

The Early Nineteenth Century

John Heathcoat's invention in 1809 of a machine which produced net by twisting three threads together into a hexagonal shape preceded a number of inventions which were to revolutionize the manufacture of net and lace. The net could be produced in large pieces and then embroidered by hand (32), either to imitate

32. (*opposite*) Princess Charlotte's wedding dress. Silver tissue and net embroidered with silver thread. English, 1816.

33. (*opposite inset*) Wedding dress of silk embroidered with metal thread. French, 1828.

34. (*below*) Embroidery pattern for a border from Ackermann's Repository. English, 1810.

lace or in coloured silks or chenille; this was particularly fashionable for evening dresses between 1807 and 1810. The stitches used for either silk or cotton embroidery tended to be simple – French knots were popular for spot patterns, and satin and outline stitches for the figures.

The pocket book or magazine was well established by the early nineteenth century. As well as showing fashion plates and giving lengthy descriptions of the fashions, they also produced embroidery patterns. These usually consisted of border patterns (34) intended for flounces, handkerchiefs, collars and cuffs to be worked in white embroidery.

Other accessories were produced by amateur or professional embroiderers. The long, narrow shawl was sometimes worked to imitate those imported from India, but many shawls were woven with a pattern instead. Shoes, stockings and ribbons might be decorated with silk embroidery, and occasionally so were kid gloves. Beads could be added to the embroidery or threaded onto silk and knitted. The comparative lightness of dress materials meant that a hanging pocket, worn under the dress, made a bulge so ladies preferred a small purse or reticule, which was often bead-embroidered or knitted. There was a great variety of beads – the round glass beads came in three sizes and were known as pound beads because they were sold by the pound. The smallest size was used for dress accessories, and the larger ones for panels, screens or other pieces for the house. Among the other types of beads there were tube-shaped bugle beads which were cut from rods of glass, ceramic beads, jet, freshwater, seed and artificial pearls, and metals such as silver and cut steel.

During the 1820s the construction of garments became very important and contributed a great deal to the decorative qualities of dress. The line of the dress was still slim with a high waist, but the skirt had a wider hem as it was cut in gores. The attention was therefore focused on the border pattern which was given sculptural qualities. It consisted of leaves and other padded shapes made from the same material as the dress, or swags of net attached with artificial flowers might be added to an evening dress. Yards of satin ribbon were used for edgings and pipings on the bodice, and were formed into cunning shapes for the border of the skirt. As the waistline returned to the right place and became more pronounced, the sleeves became much larger. Embroidery was used mainly to decorate the front and hem of the skirt. The grandest dresses (33) were still embroidered around the skirt with metal thread in heavy patterns inspired by classical art.

Wide collars and pelerines were worn over the great puffed beret and gigot sleeves, and were worked with white embroidery, sometimes with deep cuffs worked to match. Although the finest of these were of Ayrshire work, cheaper versions became possible when Heilmann (whose father owned a factory, specializing in whitework, in Alsace-Lorraine) invented the first successful embroidery machine. The machine had 130 needles which embroidered simultaneously. It was awarded a medal by La Société Industrielle de Mulhouse in May 1829, a year after it had been invented. It later proved a great success when shown at the Paris exhibition in 1834, and was soon being made and used in other countries, Henry Houldsworth of Manchester introducing it into England. Other machines followed, and in 1841 Leavers produced a machine which could embroider almost any lace pattern onto net. Handwork had to be very fine to compete with these new machines. China was still famous for cheap fine hand embroidery and garments were sent out there to be embroidered, but the patterns were no longer inspired by Eastern art. The workers were provided with the patterns for romantic floral designs in keeping with the interest in picturesque dress of the 1830s and 1840s.

The amateur embroiderers now mainly confined themselves to Berlin woolwork pictures and small accessories. The pictures were worked to a coloured pattern and needed little skill except the ability to embroider evenly. The accessories and other small decorative pieces for the house gave more scope for imaginative and varied work. Card cases, chokers, wristbands and garters were among the pieces which were worked on fine canvas (37), while a young woman was expected to embroider a pair of slippers for the man she was engaged to.

There were a number of different materials used as base fabrics for the embroidering of such articles as pictures and blotters, among them flannel and other cloths with a smooth surface. The narrow silk ribbon which had been used earlier for embroidering dresses and waistcoats was still popular at this period. It was dyed deep, rich colours, sometimes shaded, was slightly less than a quarter of an inch wide, and was called china ribbon. It was sewn with a crewel needle and was often worked on a satin ground using satin stitch.

During the early years of the nineteenth century there were strong feelings of nationalism in many countries. In most European countries some kind of traditional folk dress had gradually become established as a national costume (38). Although based on very old forms of dress, some of the garments were influenced by fashionable styles. The textile patterns also originated

35. Embroidered wedding smock. English, nineteenth century.

36. *(below)* Child's coat and dress by Mrs Latter Axton. English, 1888.

years before and it can be that the design of the textile gives the costume its national character, rather than the cut of the garment.

In England the embroidered smock (**35**) was the only real form of national dress. The smock, worn by countrymen, was hand-sewn from rectangular pieces of cloth. It was mainly embroidered on the shoulders, sleeves and the smocking was used to gather the material on the yoke. Linen thread was used on natural-coloured linen so that the design had to rely on form and texture for effect and not on colour. The patterns, which included rope, basket, wave, chevrons, and box and curls, were bold and yet formed intricate designs. The stitches included running and stem stitches, chain and variations of feather stitches, with French knots on the panels.

Later in the nineteenth century these stitches were worked on children's clothes and often a small child was dressed in a simple and colourful version of a smock. The simplicity and fresh country approach was thought suitable for children's clothes (**36**) and some-times smocking would be combined with a design of wild flowers on a little girl's dress. Smocking has never since disappeared from children's clothes.

It was possibly the great interest in folk dress which led to the fashion for decorating women's dresses, boys' suits and men's smoking jackets with applied braid, of the type used in some northern European countries. The large area of the crinoline skirt provided a plain ground which could be filled with bold decoration. By the mid-1860s the fullness of the skirt had moved to the

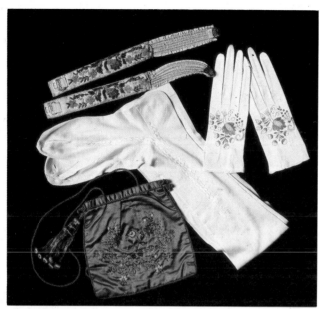

37. Embroidered accessories worked in the 1830s.
38. Traditional festival costume. Spanish, 1830s.

back, and was sometimes worn with a bolero jacket and Swiss belt which was in keeping with the applied braid. The princess-line dress was also fashionable; the dress had no waist seam so again the simplicity of the line provided an excellent base for braid decoration. For evening wear the crinoline might be decorated with artificial flowers or transparent materials, such as net, which were machine embroidered. These embroidered designs for evening wear tended to be backward-looking and usually consisted of floral motifs.

Both sewing machines and embroidery machines were being developed by the middle of the nineteenth century and most dress embroidery was handled by a professional embroiderer on a machine. As machines took over, the standards of hand embroidery deteriorated, with coarse workmanship and unimaginative design. As early as the 1840s some designers were advocating that embroiderers should look at historic needlework for inspiration, in order to learn a greater variety of stitches, and in 1840 Mrs Elizabeth Stone published her book, *The Art of Needlework*, which looked at the finer needlework of the past.

William Morris

One of the foremost figures in the renaissance of embroidery design and technique was William Morris. While he was studying at Oxford, he and a group of friends became aware of medieval art, and felt that it was superior to classical art because it was a representation of nature. They developed ideals concerned with life and art which Morris tried to achieve all his life. One of his chief aims was to make available to everyone, the love of art and the satisfaction of artistic fulfilment. Although he was a noted designer of all forms of textiles, he started to experiment with embroidery techniques early in his career, in the 1860s when he was living with his wife Jane, in the Red House at Bexleyheath, Kent. The house had been designed for them by their friend, Philip Webb, but when they came to furnish it they had great difficulty in finding suitable furnishings and so they decided to make things themselves.

Morris learned to embroider and then taught Jane and later their daughters. One of the first embroideries was a daisy pattern, worked in couched wool on dark blue serge which later inspired Morris's 'daisy' wallpaper. Another undertaking was a series of figures based on Chaucer's tale, *The Legend of Good Women*. These were

39. (opposite) William Morris's bed at Kelmscott Manor with hangings and coverlet embroidered by his wife Jane and his daughter May. Late nineteenth century.

designed by Morris and worked by Jane and her sister Elizabeth, the figures being finished and then applied to serge. Jane described how her husband taught her to lay darning stitches closely together so that they covered the ground smoothly and radiated outwards. Morris experimented with seventeenth-century crewel work techniques and vegetable dyes. Although knowledgeable about antique textiles, his design was very individual and is easily recognizable. The strength of his drawing, his love of graceful curves, and of birds and flowers inspired by Gothic art, are combined with muted colours in shaded tones.

He did not live for very long at the Red House but moved to Hammersmith and Kelmscott Manor, Oxfordshire, where a number of his embroideries were executed. Embroidery always played a very important part in the work of the firm, Morris, Marshall, Faulkner and Company which he founded in 1861. Morris's daughter May took over the embroidery section of the firm in 1885. She was a very individual designer and held strong views on technique and aesthetic qualities. The firm employed a team of embroiderers and to be economically viable they had to produce small pieces as well as large hangings. They therefore produced cushion covers with the designs drawn out and the silks or wools supplied. Thus Morris's designs were made available to those who could only consider working from a coloured pattern.

One of the greatest illustrations of Morris's approach to embroidery are the hangings on his bed at Kelmscott Manor (39). They were embroidered between 1891 and 1895 by his wife Jane with May and a group of friends, in wool on linen. The trellis pattern on the curtains was derived from an early wallpaper design by Morris, and the birds were drawn by Philip Webb. The valance has a poem worked on it which was composed especially for it by Morris. Jane worked the coverlet and signed it 'Si je puis Jane Morris Kelmscott'. It too has a quotation worked on it from Morris's poem, *A Garden by the Sea*. It seems quite possible that Morris's family tried to create a memorial to his work when they planned these embroideries.

One of the curtains was exhibited in the Arts and Crafts Society exhibition of 1893. Embroideries had been shown on equal terms with the other crafts since the first exhibition of the society in 1888. Several well-known designers and architects exhibited embroideries as they wanted to create interiors which were complete units and they were therefore prepared to design everything for them.

Among these designers was Ballie-Scott who included embroidered panels in his decorative schemes.

He felt that embroidery should not imitate other art forms. He selected natural materials, often of the cheap and hardwearing kind, which he laid next to one another. He believed that embroidery should be uncluttered and the materials allowed to stand on their own. Glass beads and metal cord might be applied to a stout cotton ground in large flat shapes. He was interested in the effects of different colours and textures working together and was against naturalism and shading.

During the last years of the nineteenth century several rural workshops were opened which produced all kinds of crafts supposedly based on peasant designs and techniques.

Few of the artists who exhibited in the Arts and Crafts exhibitions in the 1890s designed clothes but the house of Liberty produced dresses in the 'aesthetic' style. Ladies who worked crewel work or linen appliqué hangings wore equally artistic dress which was unlike fashionable dress. Tight corsets were not needed as the line of the dress was free and graceful, often ending in a short train. The dress might have a Renaissance or medieval appearance (40) and sometimes took the form

40. Detail of a Renaissance-style bridesmaid's dress by Liberty, tucked and embroidered with pearls. English, 1906.

41. Detail of a mantle by Jessie Newbery. Linen embroidered with crewel wools, and drawn thread work border. Scottish, late nineteenth century.

of a tunic or tabard. True to its aims of introducing new and artistic ideas, the house of Liberty was among the leaders in this fashion. In 1884 it opened the highly successful 'Artistic and Historic Costume Studio', which continued to produce 'artistic' dresses into the early years of the twentieth century. The embroidery on these dresses was usually confined to the neck and yoke, the belt (if there was one) and the hem. The motifs might be of flowers (lilies were popular) or of patterns inspired by Celtic or medieval decoration – spirals and linear knot patterns. Lightweight materials were often smocked. Liberty's was famous for its children's smocks.

The Glasgow School

The work of the group of designers, now known as the Glasgow School, developed a style which again was quite a new approach to art and design. It was functional and in keeping with many of the ideals of contemporary art. This group of artists collected around the Glasgow School of Art. The new building, designed by Charles Rennie Mackintosh in 1897, clings to the side of the hill in Glasgow like a Scottish castle. Despite the avant-garde qualities of the design, Mackintosh was also interested in the traditional Scottish ways of building. His work often involves soaring vertical lines which are reminiscent of the Scottish baronial style and of Scots pines. He had been a student at the school before he was commissioned to design the new building

by the director, Francis Newbery. Among his fellow students was Jessie Rowat who married Francis Newbery. As Jessie Newbery she became a very well-known designer of metalwork and embroidery, introducing embroidery classes at the school. Like William Morris, she too was very interested in old forms of embroidery and much of her early work was crewel work (**41**). She also used the techniques of needle-weaving and appliqué early in her career. All her life she continually searched for new stitches and studied folk embroideries for this purpose, and was especially inspired by Russian folk embroidery. Her designs were original and yet in keeping with the ideals of the Glasgow movement. Nothing was left to chance, each form was balanced against another, one line gently curved against a straight line and often a quite straight line ended in a circle. She never used figurative forms but did introduce some heavily stylized roses and often included lettering in her work. She was an excellent colourist and her soft pinks, mauves and sage greens applied to an off-white ground never become insipid; sometimes they are enlivened by touches of a glittering, peacock green. Many of her other colour schemes are deep and rich in tone. She made clothes for her children and friends as well as herself, and preferred them to be hand sewn. Many of them were small pieces such as belts and collars, and when she made a dress the embroidery was usually around the neck and belt. The materials might be expensive silks or simple, cheaper fabrics but they were always of good quality. Her feeling for materials was as individual as the rest of her design. She planned the whole garment so that the fastenings complemented the embroidery, introducing silk cords with glass beads and Russian clasps as well as a more basic fastening consisting of a silk loop and glass bead. Her students were greatly influenced by her teaching but she always encouraged them to take an individual approach to design. With Mrs Christie and a number of other embroiderers who were at work during the early twentieth century, she helped to bring about a quiet revolution in needlework education.

Embroidered decoration on fashionable dresses was of a coarse and limited kind during this period. Lingerie was often made from yards of machine-embroidered cotton or silk (**42**). The installation of bathrooms and the increased knowledge of hygiene meant that the white linen underwear, which could be boiled, was no longer essential and underwear could become a pleasure to wear.

42. Camiknickers. English, *c.* 1915.

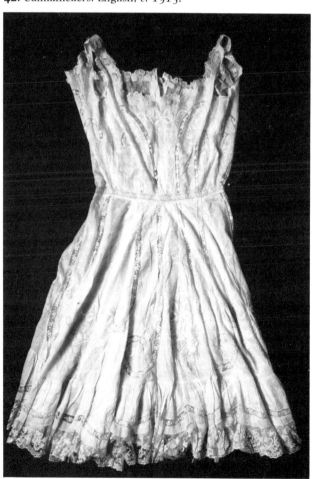

Haute Couture

The fashionably dressed lady sometimes selected an embroidery pattern based on an old design but it was consciously done to create a feeling of nostalgia. A dress of fashionable cut with slim skirt, small waist and high neck-line would have an Elizabethan style, standing collar, epaulettes and embroidery in the style of blackwork so that it had a truly romantic appearance.

Evening dresses were often covered with sheaths of net, heavily bead-embroidered. A method had been developed in Luxeuil, in France, which made it possible to embroider sequins by machine; however, beads still had to be tamboured, the work being done by hand under sweated conditions. During the early years of the century, attention was drawn to the plight of these workers and conditions were very gradually improved.

The house of Worth was known for very grand dresses of an ostentatious kind, but also made quieter dresses. Simpler dresses for day, in embroidered cottons (**43**), and evening dresses which relied for decoration on a few beads applied to the chiffon sleeves, were as much a feature of the house's work as the sumptuous bead-embroidered gowns and the tea gowns with floating panels of chiffon and embroidered net.

Very little embroidery had been used on men's clothes for a long time but occasionally an embroidered waistcoat might be worn by a gentleman who did not mind being thought flamboyant or eccentric. A French waistcoat (**44**), made by Creed & Co., now in the Victoria and Albert Museum, is embroidered on canvas. The shape of the garment is short and the fastenings are concealed so that nothing interferes with the design on the fronts. It is worked in cross and vertical tent stitches on canvas, and pieces of silk chenille are laid, edged and decorated with couched silk cord. The design is typical of the French Art Nouveau movement; linear slender shapes flow from the shoulder to the hem and curve around the armholes. Although textiles designed in the Art Nouveau style were often printed or stencilled there were also energetic and graceful embroideries.

In 1909 Diaghilev's *Ballet Russe* was first seen in Paris and Léon Bakst's exciting costumes, inspired by Oriental clothes, were the centre of attraction. Paul Poiret, already a recognized leader of fashion, also used bright colours and Oriental inspiration in his designs for chic and daring young women. His softly draped high-waisted bodices which did not need corsets under them, lampshade tunics with wired hems, hobbled skirts and harem trousers were considered outrageous. The embroidery motifs for these clothes were bold and

43. Embroidered cambray day dress by Worth. French, c. 1880.

exotic but they were used sparingly. A few large stylized floral motifs would be placed across the front of a tunic, while coloured bead embroideries would shimmer against black satin. Simplicity was his key note. The fashion for Russian dress continued and the Russian blouse, decorated with folk embroidery, was very popular even among the less wealthy. Indeed, there was great interest in all folk embroideries as well as embroidered cloths imported from India and the Far East.

There was also a revival of ribbon embroidery which was used especially for girls' party dresses. The narrow silk ribbon (45) was usually in shaded colours and formed into small rosettes, the ribbon being taken through to the back of the cloth in small stitches and held in place with running stitches.

The beaded evening dress continued to be worn, the short flat shape of the 1920s dress making an excellent base for elaborate bead embroidery. The beads were mainly of glass and the patterns made with them often reflected the functional geometric shapes associated with architecture of the period. Other designs reflected Egyptian art which was much used in all forms of textile design, after the opening of Tutankhamen's tomb in 1926. An evening gathering consisted of women dressed in a glittering mass of soft colours punctuated with gold, silver and black.

Possibly some of the most opulent and romantic bead-embroidered dresses were produced by the Parisian house of Callot Sœurs. The couturier dressmakers had always worked closely with the silk mills of Lyons and at this time luxury fabrics might be produced especially for a single fashion house. The three sisters, who directed the house of Callot Sœurs, were known for their controlled and confident use of these fabrics. Their father had dealt in antique fabrics and they always respected delicate materials. Their dresses (46) were covered with translucent beads which had been applied to a softly coloured ground so that they did not become harsh. A chiffon, printed in subtle yet rich colours, would have the printed motifs outlined with beads. These bead embroideries were mixed with trimmings and insets of silver and gold lace. After the First World War the house also introduced Chinese embroideries into their designs.

At this time a firm link was also being established between fine artists and the world of fashion. Well-known painters designed textiles and Schiaparelli used the work of artists including that of the Surrealist painter, Dali. Schiaparelli selected a different theme for her work each season; among her liveliest embroideries were those based on the circus. Appliquéd elephants with sequins and beads all added to the glitter of her 'circus' collection. She was also interested in new developments in textiles and included some of the new metalic threads in her embroideries.

Sparkling New Designs

In the early part of the century metal threads mainly consisted of finely drawn wire or thin ribbons of rolled metal sheet known as tinsel. Tinsel or wire was also

44. *(above left)* Waistcoat by Creed. Canvas embroidered with cotton and applied silk chenille and cord, edges bound with silk velvet. French, 1900–5.

45. *(above right)* Detail of a girl's dress of shot taffeta embroidered with ribbon. English, 1920s.

46. *(below left)* Bead-embroidered evening dresses by Worth (left) and Callot Sœurs (right). French, 1925–8.

47. *(below right)* Evening dress by Schiaperelli in embroidered silk organza with appliqué flowers. Italian, 1953.

48. *(right)* Wedding dress and jacket by Sue Rangley, quilted and bead embroidered. English, 1984.

used, wrapped around a textile core. During the 1930s further textile experiments were carried out in Germany; among the most successful was a regenerated cellulose obtained by the viscose or cuprammonium process and bonded to aluminium foil. At the same time cellophane was being developed in America and a little later acetate film. These threads were lightweight and pliable and the experiments led to lurex being developed after the Second World War. Lurex was stronger than any previous man-made thread because it was based on a polyester film; the centre layer, the supposedly metalic part, is clear polyester vaporized with aluminium in a high vacuum.

One of the notable features of women's evening fashions in the 1930s was the startling geometric pattern. Sequins were lavishly applied all over dresses, jackets and pyjama suits in fish-scale and radiating patterns, and formed into vertical or diagonal lines of strongly contrasting colours. Designers were using everything they could in new ways and in 1937 Charles James made his now legendary white satin quilted jacket filled with eiderdown. Quilting had not been a fashionable form of embroidery for many years; now it was used in such a way that it created a piece of abstract sculpture. The cut and the stitching of the jacket had to be planned together. The vast bulk of the garment and the great curves that it was quilted into, were a new concept in embroidery. However, it has a touch of romance, in the heart shape quilted on the back.

Embroidery of the mid-twentieth century could be very romantic. Motifs on lingerie varied from a simple monogram in a contemporary style of lettering to flowers or courting doves. Shadow embroidery was popular for lingerie; the motif was cut from coloured material and applied behind the translucent fabric of the garment. The motif was then outlined and embellished either by machine or by hand embroidery.

The Machine Age

Rebecca Crompton's highly experimental approach lent itself well to machine work. With help from Dorothy Benson, who was in the vanguard of teaching machine embroidery, she created embroideries, which despite the speed with which they were worked, were conceived like pieces of fine art. Her interest was chiefly in creating an immediate effect, and so she used the simplest materials and applied them with large stitches which would add to the final restless and yet magical quality. This type of embroidery had not yet been used in dress and although established in the 1930s it did not become well-known until after the Second World War.

During the long evenings of the 'blackout', those people who had materials saved from before the war worked at home crafts. Embroiderers appliquéd motifs onto childrens' clothes–ducks to brighten up dungarees, lambs onto nightdresses. Pre-war magazines could also be searched for transfer patterns and, with the limited materials available, tray cloths and chair backs were worked.

It was not until after the war that the embroiderer could really turn to experimental work again. Domestic embroidery machines were being developed and by the late 1950s they were marketed at prices which many people could afford. The freedom that had entered embroidery design before the war was in keeping with the so-called 'contemporary' interior design. The effect was one of spontaneity and excitement.

Romantic clothes soon returned after the war. In 1933 Norman Hartnell had designed a 'fairy-tale'

49. Dress by Courèges, machine embroidered with the fashionable daisy motif. French, 1967.

wedding dress for Miss Margaret Whigham, later the Duchess of Argyll. It was of white satin and silk tulle with cut-out and applied stars, each one edged with tamboured pearls and bugle beads. The stars were graded so that they became smaller towards the end of the train, the effect being one of stars floating on clouds of tulle. Hartnell's fame for bead embroidery and the most romantic wedding dresses was well-established when he designed H.R.H. Princess Elizabeth's wedding dress in 1947. Like Worth he used painting as an inspiration when he was designing, and some of his embroidery motifs are inspired by such artists as Botticelli.

The glamorous ball gown returned soon after the 'New Look' had changed fashion. A ball gown made by a couturier house would have up to three hundred hours of work in it. A crinoline skirt has always made a good base for applied decoration, and these dresses often had artificial flowers liberally scattered over the skirt. Some had silk organdie petals which stood away from the skirt (47); while their stems and leaves were machine embroidered, other floral motifs were worked in gilt or beads. These designs were imitated in man-made fibres for the mass market with plastic beads used as an alternative, as apart from their relative cheapness, their lightness and evenness made them easy to use.

During the war years some designers had been working in comparative isolation in America. While the 'New Look' and romantic evening dresses swept across Europe to America, some new ideas also travelled back across the Atlantic. Mainbocher had produced a typical wartime cardigan but had made it special by embroidering it with beads. The idea of a knitted casual garment embroidered with beads, silk or wool, became acceptable. Adrian, the designer of dresses for films, opened his own house and included an American gingham dress in each of his collections from the spring of 1942 onwards. The fashion for gingham reached a peak in the late 1950s when it was smocked or lavishly trimmed with broderie anglaise.

Although the 'mini', vinyl boots and jeans of the 1960s are associated with the Space Age, embroidery on dress did not disappear. Romantic evening dresses were still required and a slim long skirt was often teamed with a high-waisted bodice or jacket encrusted with beads. The fashionable daisy motif (49) and abstract forms were also applied to smart day wear. They might be in strident colours or have a black-and-white optical effect, but they were simple and bold, in keeping with the functional quality of the clothes. As the line of the dress softened again in the next decade, designers turned once more to India and the East for inspiration. There was also a fashion for the small-scale floral printed cotton, which was often quilted for winter wear and for furnishings.

During the second half of the twentieth century, embroiderers have continued to work pictures. Each of the movements which has taken place in fine art has been translated into embroidery. Sometimes the pictures have illustrated the mood of literature too, particularly that of the metaphysical literature popular in the 1970s.

Designers of embroidered dress have taken an entirely new approach by creating garments which are built up of embroidery rather than the embroidery being used as an adjunct to the garment (48).

Since the Second World War Britain has again become famous for embroidery of all kinds. This is due partly to the attention paid to needlework education in the early part of this century, and later on, to a flourishing craft movement. Once again a school of British embroidery has been formed and is recognized all over the world.

BIBLIOGRAPHY

Birmingham Museums and Art Gallery *Textiles by William Morris and Morris & Co., 1861–1940.* Exhibition catalogue 1981

Buck, A. 'The Countryman's Smock', *Folk Life* 1963

Edwards, J. *Bead Embroidery*, London 1966; New York 1974

—'The Beaded Dress: La Belle Epoque', The Costume Society, Proceedings 1967

—'Embroidering by Machine: Early Victorian Costume, 1830–1860', The Costume Society, Proceedings 1969

—*Crewel Embroidery in England*, London 1973

Hall, M. *Smocks*, Shire Album No. 46, Princes Risborough, Buckinghamshire, 1972; Cincinnati, Ohio, 1984

Marshall, B. *Smocks and Smocking*, Sherborne, Dorset, 1980

Nevinson, J. L., and S. Levey *Embroideries at Hardwick Hall, 1560–1650*, London 1987/8

Parry, L. (series ed.) *How to Make Historic Embroideries*, London 1986

Seligman, G., and T. Hughes *Domestic Needlework*, London 1926

Tarrant, N. *Smocks in the Buckinghamshire County Museum*, Aylesbury, Buckinghamshire, 1976

ABCDEFGHIKLMNOPRSTVVXY IANE ROSSICK

ALICE·LEE·WAS·BORNE·THE·23·OF·NOVE

NG·TVESDAY·IN·THE·AFTER·NOONE·1596

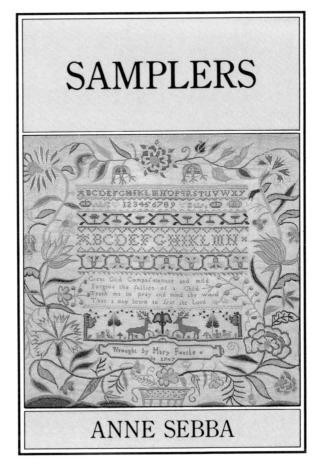

SAMPLERS

ANNE SEBBA

Samplers have a long history; almost since cloth has existed there has been an urge to embellish it. The sampler arose out of practical necessity; in the days before printed pattern books which could record and suggest designs and stitches, it was devised both as a reference sheet for patterns and as an experimental practice ground for new stitches. The word 'sampler' comes from the Latin *exemplum*, meaning: 'something chosen from a number of things, a sample . . . an example to be followed, a model.'

Historical Records

The earliest surviving example is thought to be an ancient Peruvian sampler of early Nazca culture, which has been dated approximately at between AD 200 and 500. This specimen is worked in cotton and wool on a cotton cloth and portrays some seventy-four figure motifs, all worked in running stitch. Some of the motifs overlap each other, perhaps because the need for the earlier ones had disappeared or perhaps because new motifs were added by later generations – it is impossible to know. Fragments of decorated material have also been found in the tombs of the ancient

Egyptians and these illustrate that samplers have roots in the Near East as well. These examples are believed to have been made around AD 400–500, clearly early pattern samplers. The remains of an Egyptian sampler kept in the Victoria and Albert Museum in London and probably worked in the fifteenth or sixteenth century has geometric patterns in double running and darning stitches in silk on linen and includes two motifs, the 'S' and the 'X', which were later commonly used both in continental and British samplers.

For centuries, needlework was an essential skill for women of the leisured upper classes, who looked on sewing as a prized accomplishment, and for the needy lower classes for whom it was often a means of survival in a harsh world. Thousands of women in countries quite remote from each other have made samplers. Although the printed pattern books were initially costly and rare, remarkable similarities can be traced in sampler motifs and border patterns once these books began to appear. But each country has its own peculiar traditions. Danish sampler makers specialized in exquisite drawn and pulled work and other varieties of whitework. Spanish embroideresses excelled at elaborate and densely worked blackwork. Highly religious motifs such as a crucifix and other symbols of The Passion are usually seen only in German and Spanish varieties. In America, the well-designed pictorial sampler flourished as nowhere else. Regional differences notwithstanding, the repertoire of stitches was largely the same throughout Europe.

1. *(opposite)* Detail from the earliest dated sampler known. Made by Jane Bostocke as a gift for two-year-old Alice Lee of metal thread, pearl beads and silk thread on linen. English, 1598.

2. *(above)* Mary Postle's sampler used coloured silks on a wool background. English, 1747.

Needlework in England before the sixteenth century was centred almost exclusively on the Church. However, encouraged by the geographical discoveries of the age, domestic embroidery suddenly assumed considerable importance and eclipsed the fine traditions of ecclesiastical embroidery, *opus anglicanum*, of previous centuries. As Renaissance explorers returned with hitherto unimaginable stuffs, dyes, spices, jewels and furs, a new and wealthy merchant middle class was growing up, aspiring to join the ranks of the aristocracy. Needlework, almost exclusively the concern of the noblest ladies in the land, was of prime importance in giving otherwise bare Tudor households a feeling of opulence and warmth; the amount of decorated upholstery and curtains in a house was the surest indication of a family's level of affluence.

Coinciding with the expansion of trade was the development of printing methods, which was to have a crucial effect on needlework. The most popular of all the sixteenth-century pattern books was, for English workers, Johann Sibmacher's *Schoen Neues Modelbuch*, first published in 1597 in Nuremberg. Books on natural history, especially botany, were also very useful for embroiderers as were woodcuts, herbals and illuminated manuscripts. The needleworker would sometimes copy patterns for herself or, if she were rich enough, employ a professional to do this for her. But, in spite of the tentative availability of pattern books, the best way to ensure that an attractive new embroidery pattern was not forgotten was to take a piece of cloth and reproduce it there. The cloth would be rolled up and put away in a needlework box when not in use.

Valuable Pieces

The very high cost of textiles, silk and metallic thread in sixteenth-century England explains why samplers and other embroideries were accorded such a high place in inventories and wills. There are several sixteenth-century literary references to samplers. Shakespeare evidently noticed women at work on samplers as he referred to the fashionable practice in *Titus Andronicus* and *A Midsummer Night's Dream*. This reference interestingly suggests the likely practice of working a sampler from both ends. Another contemporary account, *Of Phylotus and Emilia* by Barnabe Riche (1581), reveals how a wealthy lady would turn to her sampler after dinner and study it before deciding:

> Whiche worke would doe beste in a ruffe, whiche in a gorget, whiche in a sleeve, which in a quaife, which in a caule, which in a handcarcheef; what lace would doe beste to edge it, what seame, what stitch, what cutte, what garde.

3. Susan Nebabri's delicate band sampler has cut and drawn threadwork with needlework fillings. English, *c.* 1580–1600.

But in spite of the documentary evidence for early samplers hardly any have survived from this period. A band sampler of cut-and-drawn threadwork with needlepoint fillings, believed to have been made in England in the last quarter of the sixteenth century, is now housed in the Museum of London (3). It comprises fifteen rows of different designs worked in silk, linen and metal threads on a linen background. The top row of this exquisite piece has two large 'S' motifs either side of a rose and is in red silk and gold thread. The name of the worker, Susan Nebabri – which might suggest Spanish or Italian ancestry – is in the fourth panel below the royal arms of Queen Elizabeth I and the initials E.R.

The earliest surviving dated sampler (1), which was discovered only in 1960, was signed Jane Bostocke and evidently made as a gift for Alice Lee. It is a square sampler with motifs of a bear, a deer, a dog and a leopard worked in the top section. A castle has been traced from remaining stitch holes, where the silk has rotted, and this is believed to have been taken from an unknown printed pattern book; it was subsequently reproduced in a nineteenth-century continental sampler. There is an alphabet, lacking a J, U and Z as was common for the time, and an inscription in the middle of the sampler. Below this is the largest section containing more than twenty blocks of geometric and stylized fruit patterns.

The Golden Age of Sampler Making

Many fine samplers have survived from the seventeenth century. By mid-century at least they were often made by children, with the addition of names (or perhaps initials) and dates, indicating the beginning of the sampler's transition from reference sheet to display piece. Several needlework pattern books were by now available. One of the most popular was *The Needle's Excellency*, first printed in 1631, and by 1636 already in its tenth edition. All these works tried to satisfy the appetites of Stuart embroideresses for small creatures such as birds, caterpillars, frogs, butterflies, snails, beetles, as well as larger species such as peacocks, lions, rabbits, snakes, deer, swans and fish. Soon samplers were being made by children as young as eight. Clearly, if eight-year-olds could produce such well-executed pieces, these were not merely trial grounds but probably represented an end product; dexterity with a needle was evidently learned at a very tender age.

In general, seventeenth-century samplers can be divided into two types – band samplers and random or spot motif samplers. Human or semi-human figures

4. The earliest dated random sampler to contain human figures. English, seventeenth century.

5. A spot sampler of coloured silks, silver and silver-gilt thread on linen. First half of the seventeenth century.

such as mermaids began to make their appearance at this time. The earliest dated sampler containing people (**4**) shows a man and a woman, perhaps the parents of the worker, holding hands. The initials C.R. for the reigning monarch Charles I are embroidered above them. An undated spot sampler (**5**) with many geometric and figurative patterns also includes a porcupine, a reclining stag, a mermaid with looking glass and a rare falconer. The initials M.R. are worked in the centre of the piece. Several random samplers have designs drawn but not worked. One undated example has geometric designs at either end and a section of floral and insect motifs in the centre worked sideways to the length. Two pieces of linen have been joined together for this with selvedges at opposite ends.

The undated and unnamed random sampler (**6**) is an excellent example of a rich, densely worked piece. The embroideress has used coloured silks and silver and silver-gilt threads for a variety of motifs such as a unicorn, mermaid, rabbit, peacock and several flowers. Among the geometric, repeating patterns can be found fleur-de-lys, swastika, diamond and 'S' patterns. The repertoire of stitches used is no less impressive and includes cross, tent, Florentine, double running, rococo, Cretan, eyelet, Hungarian, chain and raised plaited braid. (The last stitch is one of the most complicated, involving some five successive stages.) There is also some pulled work and various interlaced and interwoven techniques in metal threads add to the complexity of the piece.

6. A random sampler of coloured silks, silver and silver-gilt thread on linen. The embroidered creatures include a rabbit, a unicorn, a mermaid and an insect. Mid- to late seventeenth century.

Mixed Samplers

It is not uncommon to find samplers combining a section of spot motifs and bands of patterns for use as borders both on costumes and domestic linens. The length of these samplers varied little, being decided by the maximum loom width of the day; 50 cm (20 in) is average but a sampler as long as 105 cm (42 in) is known. The width varied from 15 to 30 cm (6 to 12 in) and was usually just wide enough for one large pattern or two-and-a-half repeats of a smaller one.

There were geometric and formal floral designs and some of the carnations, roses, strawberries, and pansies seen on the spot motif varieties were now worked into border patterns. Sometimes pairs of birds made an attractive arrangement and the acorn, an important symbol in British folklore, is one of the most popular motifs. The pea flower, with open pods, was often turned into a stylized sampler border pattern, perhaps because the relatively new garden pea had now become a common vegetable. Detached buttonhole stitch was much in vogue on these samplers, used chiefly for rose petals on band samplers to give the bloom a realistic effect of a double flower.

Many band samplers had a line reserved for small men walking sideways carrying a flower-like object. Because of their usual attire – shorts and a vest – and their pose with one arm raised, they have been nicknamed 'boxers'. The unknown maker of the band sampler (8) made her boxers into highly fashionable creatures. She worked two rows of these little men with padded and painted satin faces and bodies of detached stitches worked over padding. Their knee breeches were edged with looped fringes, made by detached buttonhole loops, a fashion detail which has led experts to read the confusing date of this piece as 1663 rather than 1683.

The lavishness of court costume during the reign of James I meant that the demand for lace was still extremely high. The designs for lace edging can often be matched with those on contemporary openwork samplers. Several mid-century samplers of linen thread on linen might include bands of geometric whitework using counted satin stitches, as well as cut-and-drawn work with darned and detached needle-made fillings. Vellum was often tacked to the back of such samplers to support the band to be worked and, on one or two surviving examples, is there still.

Towards the end of the century, rows of alphabets and numerals became more common, suggesting that the piece might have been made in the schoolroom. In addition, from about 1650 onwards, the introduction of religious and moral inscriptions tells us that the use of a sampler as a pattern record was becoming secondary. Dates, signatures and sometimes the ages of the worker appeared. By the late seventeenth century some children began to acknowledge a debt of gratitude to their parents. Two surviving seventeenth-century samplers commemorate historical events, doubtless also inspired by teachers. In 1694, Mary Minshull embroidered the following inscription:

> THERE WAS AN EARTHQUAKE
> ON THE 8 OF SEPTEMBER 1692
> IN THE CITY OF LONDON
> BUT NO HURT THO IT
> CAUSED MOST PART
> OF ENGLAND TO
> TREMBLE

Many samplers from this century have remained in exceptionally good condition (9), the colours still vibrant, partly because they were rolled up and put away. But sometimes the remarkable neatness of the work made the reverse as fine as the front, and a later generation, framing the piece, might sometimes display what was in fact the wrong side, thus preserving the front.

Samplers as Statements of Achievement

Eighteenth-century samplers are today often considered schoolroom products with a pervading air of drudgery; they had come to represent neither records of fine stitchery and elaborate designs nor trial grounds for difficult techniques. According to the eighteenth-century dictionary definition by Samuel Johnson, a sampler was '. . . . a piece worked by young girls for improvement'. The most notable change was its shape, which, in order to look suitable in a frame, now became squarer, and, at the same time, a border was usually added to set off the piece. The middle of the piece could be filled with a verse and a few symetrically arranged motifs of birds, flowers and trees. These were often in pairs and rather sparsely scattered. The need for economy had apparently vanished. The vast majority were made in schools and so alphabets and numerals were learned through needlework. As the sampler workers became younger, the pieces, were, not surprisingly, no longer such a formidable technical exercise. Even six-year-olds were often expected to have one sampler to their name.

Although linen was still the main background material used for samplers, by mid-century, most were worked on a fine woollen cloth called 'tammy'. However, this fabric was susceptible to moth damage and its popularity was shortlived. Cotton too, was occasionally used at the end of the century. Mary Postle's sampler of 1747 well illustrates the influence of the printed oriental designs and their imitation in crewel work (2). Her naturalistic flower border, rising from a basket at the bottom, is the focal point of the piece, but she also includes alphabets, numerals and some border patterns in the centre, and a verse:

> Great God compassionate and mild,
> Forgive the follies of a child.
> Teach me to pray and mind thy word,
> That I may learn to fear the Lord.

In some early eighteenth-century samplers, just a fraction of a border was sometimes included to fill in space on either side of a panel and, as such, it was a logical development of a band sampler. But gradually, from 1720, as the decorative potential of the border was grasped, three and then four sides of the sampler were surrounded. One of the earliest border designs used was an arrangement of trefoils, but stylized flowers and geometric patterns, often rather thin and boring, quickly became the almost universally accepted surround. Anne Haskins set off the beautiful design of her sampler with an unusual border. She worked panels of stylized flowers, a row of fleur-de-lys and an alphabet followed by the Creed; below this she embroidered a country house, set in a park with animals, trees and flowers. Two thick, vertical bands of finely worked Florentine stitch edged the whole scene. This sampler is dated 9 October 1732.

Popular Themes

Although the choice of border was probably decided by the schoolmistress, many of the most popular styles were those with age-old symbolic meanings. It is doubtful if the countless thousands of children sewing these motifs and patterns were aware of their deeper significance. One of the easiest to recognize is the trefoil, often transformed into trilobe-shaped flowers symbolizing the Holy Trinity, which is sometimes also represented by three flowers on one stem or three sprays in a vase. A flower which lent itself particularly well to this idea is the tri-coloured pansy, rivalled only by the strawberry for its popularity in sampler border patterns.

The crown motif too now began to appear regularly in samplers. Sometimes a variety of coronets took up a whole row, but a single crown was extremely useful in filling up a small space. Doubtless, the frequency of this motif owed something to the necessity of marking linen belonging to the nobility, with the type of coronet accorded to the family's rank. But many a sampler contains a row of different crown patterns with the following initials either above or below: L D Q GR P E B standing for Lord, Duke, Queen, George Rex, Prince, Earl and Baron. Generally, coronets are no more than a decorative pattern in eighteenth-century samplers, although it is possible that a sampler containing just one type of crown indicates that the maker came from noble stock. Occasionally, crowns were turned into a border pattern with alternate ones worked upside down. An unusual unsigned early eighteenth-century sampler (7) features a richly-dressed lady surrounded by hills and trees, but with the familiar bands of pattern above including a row of coronets.

If the flowers, birds and crowns had an air of uniformity to them, the increasingly popular vogue for representations of the embroideress's home or even her parents, enabled the child to display some originality. Jean Murray worked a sampler, dated 1740, of her house with a weathervane on the roof, a servant on the steps as well as numerous dogs, trees, peacocks and flowers, a thistle, roses, coronets and verses (10).

7. This sampler picture makes a strong visual impact, but its educational purpose still remains clear. English, early eighteenth century.

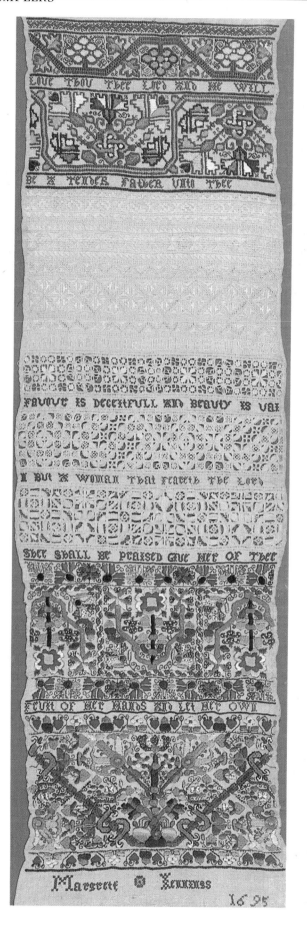

8. *(opposite left)* A band sampler of linen embroidered with coloured silks. The two most striking bands of this sampler contain small figures known as 'boxers' with padded and painted satin faces and bodies of detached stitches worked over padding.

9. *(opposite right)* A fine example of a coloured and whitework band samplers by Margaret Jennings. English, 1695.

10. This transition sampler includes a thin, conventional floral border and is made of silk on wool. Scottish, 1740.

MR and MS above the initials probably stand for Mister and Mistress.

Instructions for Upright Living

The character of eighteenth-century samplers derived chiefly from their sentimental and moralizing verses. Needlework was clearly of secondary importance to the instructions for upright living. Some samplers at this time offer advice on the correct form of behaviour towards the opposite sex. Sarah Grimes counselled in 1730:

> Keep a strict guard over thy tongue, thine ear and thine eye, lest they betray thee to talk things vain and unlawful. Be sparing of thy words, and talk not impertinently or in passion. Keep the parts of thy body in a just decorum, and avoid immoderate laughter and levity of behaviour.

By mid-century, most inscriptions were in verse form, largely taken from the writings of Dr Isaac Watts,

11. Eleanor Speed's sampler, with later alterations to the Christian name and dates, which should be 1733–4. English.

Philip Doddridge and John Wesley. Watts' *Divine and Moral Songs for Children*, published in 1720, set the tone for the majority of samplers in this century. Believing that what was learned by heart remained longer in the head, Watts hoped his verses would prevent the young from seeking 'relief for an emptiness of mind out of the loose and dangerous sonnets of the age.' The samplers of two eight-year-olds show that, in spite of their extreme youth, they had been taught to focus already

on the next life. This is hardly surprising, bearing in mind the high mortality rate for eighteenth-century children. A popular verse, embroidered by Elizabeth Raymond in 1789, helped many children come to terms with the loss of a sibling or close friend.

> Lord give me wisdom and direct my ways
> I beg not riches nor yet length of days,
> My life is a flower, the time it hath to last
> Is mixed with frost and shook with every blast.

The most popular eighteenth-century religious passages were the Ten Commandments, the Lord's Prayer and the Creed but many other lengthy extracts from the Bible were often embroidered on samplers. These would usually be set within tablets similar to those painted and hung in contemporary churches; they were often flanked by biblical figures such as Moses or Jesus. A sampler with the name Eleanor Speed (11) includes a number of moral precepts as well as extracts from Exodus. But both the Christian name and the dates on this piece have been subsequently altered, indicating that this sampler may in fact have been the work of a relative which Eleanor wished to pass off as her own.

From about 1770 onwards, map samplers were often made in schools (12). Sometimes just a small district or county was featured; others shared two hemispheres, one marked The Old World, the other, The New World. Most of these maps were oval and many were in some way or other inaccurate, partly because the outlines were often drawn freehand by the children. Eleven-year-old Anne Brown cannot have been taught by a geography teacher as she thought the coasts of England and France were joined. It was possible to buy commercially printed map outlines which were usually on satin, but these have often perished with age. Those made on linen or gauze have fared better. A map of Africa, made in 1784 at Mrs Arnold's Fetherston Buildings, is surrounded with a border of embroidered flowers and bows embellished with 'spangles', the eighteenth-century term for sequins. The map is full of evocative if obsolete place names such as Grain Coast, Tooth Coast and Slave Coast. Other novelty samplers dreamed up by imaginative needlework teachers were acrostic, rebus and almanac samplers. These kinds may have demanded little in originality but called for considerable technical competence.

Work of High Quality

Of all eighteenth-century samplers, darning and hollie point samplers stand out above the rest. Not only do they contain some fine and elaborate examples of

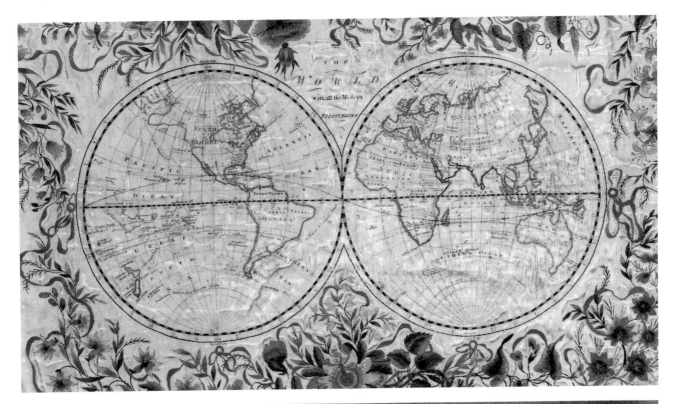

12. *(above)* A map sampler, printed on a satin background in black and embroidered with coloured silk. *c.* 1800.

13. Sarah Gerney's square sampler contains cut circles and square filled with hollie point and detached buttonhole fillings. 1727.

14. These eight darns provided useful practice for household repairs. The date 1798 is also darned in.

needlework but they are also closer approximations of the original pattern record sampler. Some darning samplers were quite simple and obviously a response to the need for making fine darns in damask table linens. But many darning pieces contained elaborate floral arrangements worked in pattern darning with stem and chain stitches used to outline the leaves and flowers. The bouquets would be placed in the centre of the darns, which were themselves worked in contrasting colours to give a most attractive effect. Adult needlewomen are generally thought to be responsible for these fine pieces.

The darning sampler illustrated (**14**) has eight darned crosses with three sets of initials: EL, TB and EB, and the date, 1798, worked into the top right-hand darn. The flower sprays around the edge and the bouquet in the middle enabled the worker (or were there three?) to display proficiency with a variety of other stitches, mostly chain, feather, pattern darning and couching. Samplers of hollie (or holy) point are equally delicate (**13**). To make these patterns, circles or

squares would first be cut from the background fabric and edged with buttonholing, then rows of buttonholing would be built up one into another. The pattern was made by missing stitches, which appear as pin-pricks on an even white ground.

However, the tone of Mary Cole's verse in 1759 reflected contemporary values most accurately:

> Better by far for me
> than all the Simpster's Art
> That God's commandments be
> Embroidered on my Heart.

In Service

The importance of needlework for girls growing up in the nineteenth century can hardly be underestimated. For a poor girl, who dreaded the thought of spending her days in a grimy factory, entering service with a family where plain sewing would be a vital part of her duties could perhaps be the only alternative. Simultaneously, the woman who employed her was expected to concern herself only with child-bearing, handwork and management of maids.

Most maids had at some time to mend and mark household linens. This explains why so many of the new schools for poor children, far from dispensing with the sampler as a piece of elaborate sewing from a bygone age, developed it for the new needs of their charges. A group of samplers made at orphanages well illustrates this. They are densely worked pieces on linen, all in either black or red thread, containing several rows of aphabets and numerals and perhaps as many as eighty rows of simple border patterns worked in cross stitch. A moralistic verse would usually be added as well. Extreme neatness was demanded of the girls who made these pieces, well equipping them for marking household linens of all kinds.

Sarah Catherine Drew may have been preparing for a lifetime in service when she made her thirty-row sampler in 1816. She was allowed only one colour – red – but her competence with a needle is apparent from the neatness and delicacy of the embroidery. She used running, cross and back stitch as well as Algerian eye stitch. Her verse was not unusually gloomy:

> Fragrant the Rose is but it fades in time
> The violet sweet but quickly past the Prime
> White Lillies hang their Heads and soon decay
> And whiter Snow in Minutes melt away
> Such and so withring are our earthly Joys
> Which Time or Sickness speedily destroys.

Nineteenth-century Samplers

English samplers in the nineteenth century had become so much a standard form of school exercise lacking in originality, that dictionaries could define precisely what should appear in a sampler. There were also some pattern books which teachers could use for the purpose, or a pupil teacher might be set the task of making a master pattern for all the girls to copy in their own work. Samplers signed by pupil teachers are rare but Eliza Sophia Newton made one in 1808 comprising a map of Norfolk with the county divided into hundreds. After her name she embroidered 'pupil teacher, 1st year'. The map is thought to have been made for the children to copy.

In general, school samplers did not differ dramatically from those of the late eighteenth century. Some motifs such as twin birds, stags, a parrot on a spray and fruit trees, and border patterns of strawberries and honeysuckle, were little changed even from the sixteenth and seventeenth centuries. More buildings made an appearance in the nineteenth century; sometimes these were representations of the worker's home or school but more often they were copied from an embroidery picture book (16). Several of these were called Solomon's Temple. The name of the school was mentioned more frequently (15) and domestic animals such as dogs, cats and horses often featured in later pieces. They were made almost exclusively in cross stitch, frequently in wool instead of silk, on a coarse mesh canvas. Some schoolgirls made samplers in the form of multiplication tables, or pounds, shillings and pence charts – these types were invariably executed in only one stitch. Cross stitch is often termed sampler stitch because of its usefulness for large amounts of lettering.

One school, a Quaker (Friends) school at Ackworth in Yorkshire, produced an original type of sampler, worked entirely in cross stitch and usually in monochrome silks on a woollen background (17). These contained a series of medallions, garlands and motifs with a border of half medallions or half motifs. Some of the garlands contained initials, a date or a motto. It is interesting to note that the only other schools where

15. A rare piece of contemporary information on a sampler: Elizabeth Rooke was a pupil of Market Bosworth Boarding School, Leicestershire, in 1814.

16. Sophia Stephens' square sampler of silk on a wool background, crowded with different motifs inside a double border of stylized fruits and flowers.

samplers with similar designs are known to have been made were the Quaker schools in America – Westtown in Pennsylvania and its sister school in New York, the Nine Partners Boarding School.

The pervading sense of gloom and doom in samplers persisted (20) although a small group of samplers was concerned with death in a rather specific way. These were made by people who believed in the Second Coming of Christ and who were predicting an imminent end to the world. There were a large number of millenarian movements in England from the 1790s onwards and a favourite slogan of followers of the American Adventist William Miller was: 'Prepare to Meet Thy God' (a verse from Amos). The Millerites believed that this meant they were to be ready for the Second Coming of Jesus in 1844. A sampler made in Cotgrave, Nottingham, by Louisa Ann Morris in May 1843, is inscribed:

> Prepare to meet your God
> That Heaven may be your home.

Others have survived from this date with similar messages. Evidently, British morals and educational standards were exported to the colonies (18). Lucy Grant, living in Regent Town, Sierra Leone, in 1840, chose a typical verse:

> Father what e'er of earthly bliss
> Thy sovreign will denies
> Accepted at thy throne of grace
> Let this petition rise.
>
> Give me a calm a thankful heart
> From every murmur free
> The blessings of thy grace impart
> And make me live to thee.

As a rule tantalizingly little is known about the origins of a sampler maker. However, a group of samplers made by the Brontë sisters, featuring lengthy Bible extracts, is now owned by the Brontë Parsonage Museum in Yorkshire. Worked in greenish-black silk on rough canvases, the pieces are totally without ornament apart from a Greek key border. Although plain and undecorative, these samplers are fascinating when seen in the context of the bleakness of the land around the parsonage in Yorkshire where they lived, and the tragedies that had three times struck their family. A similarly plain sampler of letters and numbers might

17. *(above)* An example of a sampler from the Quaker school at Ackworth, Yorkshire. Usually these were in monochrome colours, but Frances Rae worked hers in silks of different colours. Nineteenth century.

18. Sampler made by eleven-year-old Helen Price. Kirkee (Poona), East Indies, first half of nineteenth century.

have little interest were it not known that the maker, Frances Maria Grevis James, of Ightham Court in Kent, later fell in love with a handsome tenant farmer from her father's estate. The marriage caused a furore in her family and her father moved away from the neighbourhood.

The Berlin Craze

From the 1830s onwards, a rage for Berlin woolwork originating in the German city of that name, captivated almost all needleworkers. Its popularity derived partly from the squared paper patterns, sold with the wool, which were easy to follow simply by counting, and enabled the worker to achieve a high degree of realism

19. *(below)* A good example of Berlin work, with a variety of stitches and patterns. English, mid-nineteenth century.

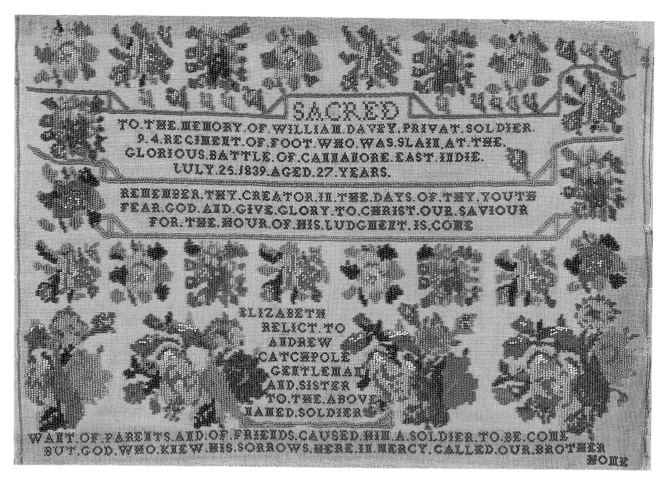

SACRED
TO.THE.MEMORY.OF.WILLIAM.DAVEY.PRIVAT.SOLDIER.
9.4.REGIMENT.OF.FOOT.WHO.WAS.SLAIN.AT.THE.
GLORIOUS.BATTLE.OF.CAMIAORE.EAST.INDIE.
LULY.25.1839.AGED.27.YEARS.

REMEMBER.THY.CREATOR.IN.THE.DAYS.OF.THY.YOUTH
FEAR.GOD.AND.GIVE.GLORY.TO.CHRIST.OUR.SAVIOUR
FOR.THE.HOUR.OF.HIS.LUDGMENT.IS.COME

ELIZABETH
RELICT.TO
ANDREW
CATCHPOLE
GENTLEMAN
AND.SISTER
TO.THE.ABOVE
NAMED.SOLDIER

WANT.OF.PARENTS.AND.OF.FRIENDS.CAUSED.HIM.A.SOLDIER.TO.BE.COME
BUT.GOD.WHO.KNEW.HIS.SORROWS.HERE.IN.MERCY.CALLED.OUR.BROTHER
HOME

20. Elizabeth Catchpole's beadwork sampler – a tribute to William Davey, slain in battle. English, 1839.

through shading. But the wools, too, found favour with Victorian needlewomen as they were much softer and took a more brilliant, faster dye than the hard-twisted worsteds previously available. The influence of Berlin work is easily noted on children's samplers which, by the end of the century, often contained floral bouquets of large blooms, buildings, or the domestic pets which were extremely popular for working on cushions and firescreens. There also exists a group of long, woolwork samplers (**19**) containing many different floral and geometric patterns worked on double canvas by adult needlewomen, and perhaps sold in the fancy needlecraft shops for amateurs to copy. These pieces contained a wide variety of stitches, chiefly cross, tent, satin, Hungarian, Florentine and brick with some couching, laid and plushwork. They were made on long, narrow strips usually bound at the edges with silk ribbons, and sometimes with a piece of silk attached to the top to cover the sampler when rolled up.

North American Samplers

Seventeenth-century American samplers are almost indistinguishable from their English counterparts in terms of style, technique and design. The early colonists still looked very much to the mother country to set the fashion and provide the supplies. The settlers took few possessions with them, but a sampler, being both sentimental and practical and taking up little space, was often included.

However, by the eighteenth century, although the moralizing inscriptions and verses continued, a sense of design and colour turned American samplers into much more original and decorative pieces than their English equivalents. Their makers were less concerned with formality, discipline and symmetry, more with local and family history, artistic form and unrestrained liveliness. Also, after about 1800, samplers were imbued with the spirit of republicanism and featured symbols of liberty, the American eagle and other patriotic themes.

Elizabeth Rush, believed to be the great-aunt of Dr Benjamin Rush, one of the signatories of the Declaration of Independence, made her sampler in 1734 (the '3' is

21. Sally Bott was eleven when she worked this pictorial sampler. It typifies Stivour School work. American, 1784.

22. *(below)* Detail from Elizabeth Rush's English-style band sampler. The needlework is of a high standard although the 3 in the date is reversed. American, 1734.

reversed). It clearly illustrates the sampler in transition as the older formal stylized bands are well executed but she also included verses and a vine border (**22**).

American samplers depended considerably for their originality on the talents of the particular school-mistresses, several of whom were newly arrived from England. The best of the pictorial sampler work was done by girls aged twelve to sixteen at the female academies, the select schools which took in both boarding and day girls. The earliest and finest of these were along the eastern seaboard, especially in the Boston area. Silk was the most popular embroidery thread for American samplers, and some of the silk had an unusual, crinkly appearance which gave the work a shimmering effect. Those pieces worked at Miss Sarah Stivour's school in Salem, Massachusetts, are all notable for a very long stitch, particularly in the background areas, in crinkled, or ravelled silk. It is no coincidence that samplers using this thread were made in Salem, a port of some significance at the time for its trade with China and Japan from where the yarn undoubtedly came.

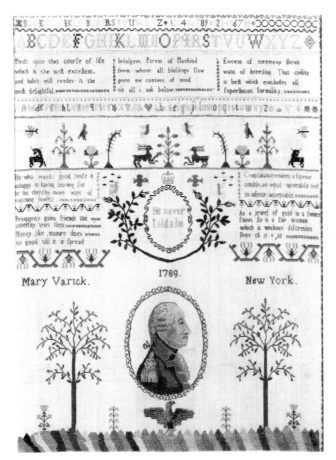

23. Mary Varick's patriotic sampler shows a profile of George Washington dated 1789, the year he assumed the presidency. New York.

group of American samplers. Balch School samplers (**25**) combined detailed architectural motifs with landscape, figures and occasionally a maritime scene, thus achieving some of the most elaborate effects ever seen on samplers. Although many have 'Providence' embroidered on, none specifically names Miss Balch. The background of these samplers is usually worked in diagonal pattern darning, a demanding stitch over large areas for young girls. The focal point of the pieces is, however, a public building in the area usually flanked by elegant pillars or arches. The building is often worked in simple stitches but has the appearance of being three dimensional through clever use of colour and perspective. Beyond the pillars was a graceful, floral border, often growing out of pots or urns.

Susan Smith, who was born on 28 May 1783, made her large, ambitious sampler apparently in just six months when aged eleven (**28**). The background is entirely filled in with satin stitch and the central building portrayed the First Baptist Meeting House of Providence, worked in tent stitch. The arch is in cross stitch and the sky in rice stitch.

But Balch School samplers were not restricted to buildings. Occasionally a copious basket of fruit was the main subject flanked by the familiar columns as well as a floral border and verse. Most had just one or two aphorisms such as:

> Honour and Renown
> will the ingenious crown.

> or

> May spotless innocence and truth
> my every action guide
> and guard my inexperienced youth
> from arrogance and pride.

The favourite Balch Academy maxim was 'Let virtue be a guide to thee'.

Regional Differences

A third distinctive group of samplers comprised those made at schools in Pennsylvania. These often named the teacher concerned, the most famous being Mrs Leah Meguier who taught at Harrisburg. The borders of these samplers were divided into about twenty 2·5 cm (1 in) squares, each containing motifs such as the traditional hearts, flowers, birds, a basket of eggs, geometric shapes or butterflies. An inscription would usually take up the bottom two or three squares. For example, Barbara A. Baner worked the following text below a panel containing her name, her parents' names,

Samplers with this 'Stivour stitch' were mostly arranged in a similar fashion. There might be a landscape at the bottom with, perhaps, a man and a woman, some sheep, and a floral border with large blooms emanating from trees on either side of the central square. Long blue and white stitches overhead indicated the sky. The central section, all that remained of the English type, contained alphabets, a short verse and the maker's name and date, but was far from being the focal point of the piece. Two of the earliest examples worked by Stivour pupils, Nabby Mason Peele and Ruthey Putnam, were both dated 1778 and named the school. Sally Bott, who made her sampler in 1784, did not name the school. She filled in the whole border areas with the diagonal ravelled silk threads behind people, flowers, birds and trees, giving the piece considerable depth (**21**).

Samplers made at the school run by Miss Mary (Polly) Balch in Providence, Rhode Island, are perhaps the best known and most sophisticated of any single

her birthplace and date, the name of the school and the date she made the sampler (26):

> And must this body die this mortal frame
> Decay and must those active limbs of
> Mine lie mouldring in the clay. And there
> for to remain until Christ doth please to come.

Meguire samplers also featured a central pictorial section usually of a woman, perhaps garlanded with roses. Sometimes the picture was of a couple sheltered by a weeping willow, a tree common in the area.

There are many regional characteristics which make it possible to group some American samplers even if the name of the teacher or school concerned is not known. For example, Pennsylvania girls often specified that their work was a present for their parents, such as Elizabeth Miskey who embroidered: 'Respectfully presented to Anthony and Elizabeth Miskey by their affectionate daughter Elizabeth Miskey done in her twelfth year, Philadelphia, 26 April 1822.' Bow knots

24. This Dresden (or drawn work) sampler (undated) by Frances Pashal combines drawn work and cutwork, with chain stitch. American, late eighteenth century.

holding up swags of roses were a typical Connecticut hallmark. The quintessential American symbol of patriotism from the revolutionary war onwards was the eagle with outstretched wings. Surprisingly, not many of these found their way on to samplers and most that have survived were not worked until the nineteenth century. Mary Varick of New York managed to combine several different motifs (23). She featured two medallions, one with a bust of George Washington and another, above this, containing the words, 'He never told a lie'. She embroidered an eagle below, and also, strangely, a royal crown. She dated the piece 1789, the year Washington assumed the presidency. One of the most amusing American samplers was stitched in 1800. 'Patty Polk did this and she hated every stitch she did in it. She loves to read much more.'

25. A fine example of silk on linen needlework from Polly
Balch's School, Providence, Rhode Island, depicting, in silk
on linen, the first Congregational Church there.

26. A beautiful squared-border sampler — a typical example from the Leah Meguier school in Pennsylvania, 1812.

27. *(below left)* Genealogical tree sampler by Lorenza Fisk, with family names and dates stitched on the yellow fruit. American, early nineteenth century.

28. One of the most ambitious of the Balch samplers portrayed the First Baptist Meeting House. Made by Susan Smith in only six months between 1793 and 1794.

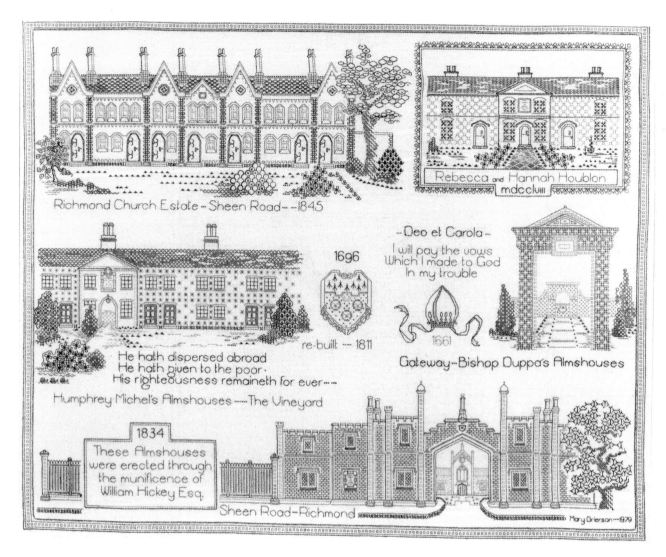

Richmond Church Estate – Sheen Road – 1845

Rebecca and Hannah Houblon
mdccluiii

1696

re-built – 1811

...Deo et Carola...
I will pay the vows
Which I made to God
In my trouble

1661

Gateway – Bishop Duppa's Almshouses

He hath dispersed abroad
He hath given to the poor ·
His righteousness remaineth for ever ——

Humphrey Michel's Almshouses ——The Vineyard

1834
These Almshouses
were erected through
the munificence of
William Hickey Esq.

Sheen Road – Richmond

Mary Grierson – 1979

After about 1800, the family record or register became a very popular, if less decorative type of American sampler. The names of the dead relatives were usually embroidered in black silk and spaces were often left for deaths to be recorded at a later date. The genealogical sampler (27) was sometimes made in the style of an actual tree with each name taking up a separate fruit. Another design featured pillars at the side and possibly an arch over the top. These supply interesting sociological information such as that second and third marriages appear to have been quite common.

There were a few lacework samplers made in America (24), mostly in the Philadelphia region in the late eighteenth century. They are reminiscent of the exquisite cut-and-drawn-work samplers of seventeenth-century England but display a peculiarly American flavour. This is chiefly because they were made in the form of well-designed pictures instead of featuring

29. Mary Grierson's sampler of almshouses, uses different techniques of blackwork to convey accurately and imaginatively various architectural details.

several rows or bands of techniques. Again, the most popular design was a basket of flowers – a favourite American motif in several crafts – with the stems outlined usually in chain stitch and the blooms filled in with drawn- or Dresden work. Executed in white silk or linen thread on a fine linen or cotton fabric, the technique of Dresden work required that several warp and weft threads be cut away; the remaining threads were embroidered together into lacy stitches.

Chronicles of the Times

Come the twentieth century and women found themselves freed from the drudgery of plain sewing by the increasingly widespread application of sewing machines. Those who wished could concentrate entirely on needlework as an art form. The early part of the century saw a revival of practical samplers used by those involved in church decoration or in preparations for special royal occasions. As in Elizabethan days when gold and silver were so popular, metallic thread is still costly and difficult to use and requires experience. A sampler with silk, gold thread and spangles on purple velvet was made in 1952 to illustrate the designs and methods for the embroidery on the coronation robe of Queen Elizabeth II.

Adult amateur needlewomen making samplers to-day are often spurred to creativity by some particular event to be commemorated, be it royal or personal. Mrs Louisa Robins of Cardiff composed her own verses and designs for her sampler (31) commemorating the coronation in 1937 of King George VI. Although full of period charm the age-old acorn is used for a border pattern. For American needleworkers, one of the most stirring events of the early part of the century was the first nonstop solo flight from New York to Paris made by Charles A. Lindbergh in May 1927. Several sampler maps were made at this time, tracing the route taken by Lindbergh's aircraft, *The Spirit of St Louis*.

Original Designs

Mary Grierson's training as a botanical artist gave her a keen eye for detail in her needlework projects, many of which are drawn to scale and executed in blackwork. In making a sampler picture of the seventeenth-century church of St Mary at Lambeth, she returned several times to the building to ensure that she had accurately portrayed the beautiful stained-glass windows in stitchery. Her sampler of 'Tudor Chimneys' at Hampton Court Palace also relies on blackwork to convey the intricate patterns of the stone and brickwork with imagination and yet great precision too. In the sampler illustrated (29) a piece full of interesting social and historical detail, Miss Grierson has translated another architectural theme. Each of the five almshouses in this embroidery was worked out first on graph paper with a grid to match approximately the threads of the evenweave fabric on which it was worked. Most of the embroidery was done using a single thread of stranded cotton across two threads of the material, although in some cases, where greater detail was required as in the coat-of-arms, it was worked over a single thread. Great care has to be taken in the choice of stitch to create variety and interest with blackwork. Texture and pattern were achieved in the 'Almshouses' sampler by using the three base colours of black, blue and stone, and interposing them with different shades. Tonal values in black were achieved by different qualities of thread and one or two important features were picked out in silver. Silver thread, couched down, was also used to good effect for the border of this picture. The stitches used are almost all traditional – varieties of backstitch with some cross stitch – but the weave of the back-ground can be used to create different effects by counting, spacing and the quality of thread. Upset at the slow pace at which this complicated project was being completed, Miss Grierson embroidered three snails into the shrubbery.

Joan Syrett, another modern needlewoman fasci-nated by the sampler form, has created some highly original interpretations. An Egyptian astronomical papyrus in the British Museum inspired her first sampler (30). Taking a length of Dupion furnishing fabric as her background, she machine-stitched it at

30. A modern sampler by Joan Syrett based on an Egyptian astronomical papyrus.

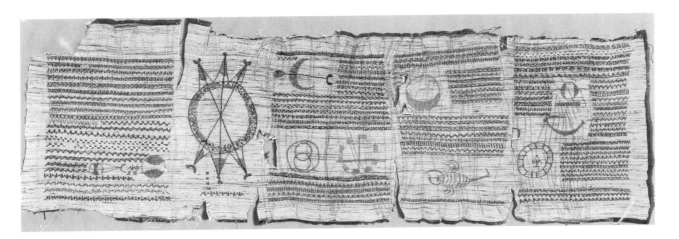

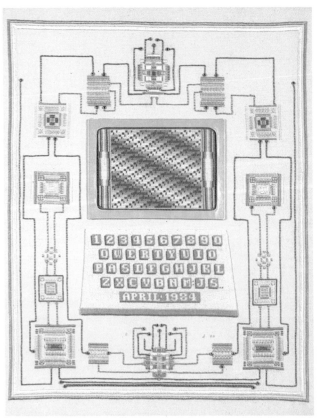

31. *(above left)* Sampler by Louisa Robins of Cardiff celebrating George VI's coronation, 1937.

32. *(above right)* A computer sampler by Joan Syrett worked in cotton on linen.

33. A modern commemorative sampler designed and made by Rosalie Sebba as a gift for her granddaughter. The background stitch is taken from a fifteenth-century German embroidery.

random to give it texture; she then worked the script in black, red and green sewing cotton, using eighty-five variations of herringbone, most of them invented. When finished, she backed it with black chiffon to suggest wear and shadow and applied the whole to red taffeta, finally making several cuts and tears as in the original. The effect is remarkably realistic.

Taking a more modern idiom, Mrs Syrett has also designed and made a computer sampler (32). She began by collecting and studying the various spare parts that make up a computer system and then transposed her idea on to graph paper. The centrepiece of this sampler is a screen with raised satin-covered frame, displaying vivid computer graphics. Below this is the keyboard, a piece of canvas worked in tent stitch later applied to the background. Mrs Syrett kept the traditional aspects of a sampler very much in mind in designing this picture. The keyboard enabled her to include a date and an alphabet (albeit not in alphabetical order) and the border, an electrical circuit with bronze coloured beads to convey connecting points, is, after all, a variation on a highly stylized floral border. Green, being the colour of flower stems, was used for the wires.

Commemorative birth samplers are popular today and offer the needlewoman wide scope for symbols to be included. Rosalie Sebba has made a series of five highly

individual examples, one for each of her grandchildren. Some of these feature their houses and smaller motifs such as clocks showing the times when they were born, particular trees in their garden, favourite pets, or, in one case, a map of Australia as the child moved there within months of his birth. A draughtsboard, using a different stitch for each of the sixty-four squares, was another of Mrs Sebba's ideas. In the sampler (33) made for Henrietta Amy's birth, the two houses are exact replicas of where she was born and where she now lives. The traditional American eagle is included as the child is an American citizen, the violets are her birth flower and the deer, one of the oldest of sampler motifs, is a reminder of the many that roam in Richmond Park, near to where Amy now lives. At least twenty different stitches have been used in this piece.

All the modern samplers rely in some way on traditional techniques or designs. Samplers are unlikely ever again to be used as an essential part of a young child's school curriculum. Today's sampler makers are adult needlewomen who turn to embroidery through choice rather than compulsion. Although the purpose of samplers has radically changed in five centuries, the high standard set by modern embroideresses, in both originality of design and in technical mastery of complicated stitches, makes them worthy heirs of a great but gentle tradition.

BIBLIOGRAPHY

Ashton, Sir A. Samplers, London and Boston, Mass., 1926
Bolton, E. S., and E. J. Coe American Samplers, National Society of the Colonial Dames of America, Massachusetts Branch, 1921
Christie, A. G. I. Samplers and Stitches, 3rd edn, London 1934
Clabburn, P. Samplers, Princes Risborough, Buckinghamshire, 1977
Colby, A. Samplers, London 1964
Dreesman, C. Samplers for Today, New York 1964
Horner, M. M. The Story of Samplers, Philadelphia, Pa., 1963
Huish, M. B. Samplers and Tapestry Embroideries, London 1900

King, D. Samplers, London 1960
Krueger, G. A Gallery of American Samplers, New York 1978
—New England Samplers to 1940, Sturbridge, Mass., 1978
Oddy, R. Samplers in the Guildford Museum, Guildford, Surrey, 1951
Payne, F. G. Samplers and Embroideries in the National Museum of Wales, Cardiff 1939
Sebba, A. Samplers: Five Centuries of a Gentle Craft, London, New York 1979
Tarrant, N. The Royal Scottish Museum Samplers, Edinburgh 1978

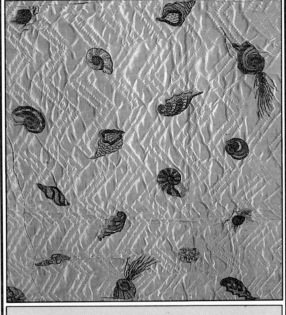

PATCHWORK
AND
APPLIQUE

SHIELA BETTERTON

Appliqué, patchwork and quilting in some form are to be found in almost every country in the world, and although quilting is usually associated with bedcovers, this form of needlework can be employed for many other purposes. A quilt, or a piece of quilting, is usually defined as a textile sandwich. The three layers consist of a top and a backing with a filling between. The top may be of whole cloth, appliqué, patchwork, or a combination of these, and the quilting is the pattern worked in running stitch which holds the three layers together. Quilting is the last process in the making of a quilt.

Patchwork and quilting are often mentioned in literature. In Shakespeare's *Henry IV* the Prince asks Falstaff, 'How now blown Jack, how now quilt?' — no doubt a reference to his size. Jane Austen wrote to her sister Cassandra about pieces for the patchwork bed-cover they were making, and it is still to be seen in Jane's old home at Chawton in Hampshire. In 1836 Robert Southey's daughters covered books with cotton cloth. He called it a 'cottonian library' and remarked that 'no patchwork quilt was ever more diversified'. In 1882, when Oscar Wilde was lecturing in the United States to 'select groups of women' they were reported as making 'Oscar Crazy quilts' where at the centre was a lily, daisy or a pansy, flowers that symbolized the Aesthetic Movement. Of poems and songs which have been written with quilts as the theme, perhaps the most famous is the song written by Stephen Foster:

In the sky the bright stars
  gathered,
On the banks the pale moon
  shone,
And 'twas from Aunt Dinah's
  quilting party,
I was seeing Nellie home.

Both British and North American painters have incorporated patchwork and quilting into their pictures. During the eighteenth century many well-to-do families commissioned family portraits which later became known as 'conversation pieces'. The grouping was fairly standardized, with the lady of the house seated, her husband standing beside her and usually a child or two and a little dog. The lady's dress was arranged to show her beautifully quilted underskirt. The great American painter, Winslow Homer, spent two years from 1881 living at Tynemouth on the Northumberland coast and painted a number of pictures of the fisherwomen wearing their quilted skirts.

QUILTING

Like so many other forms of textile art, quilting comes from the East and the Middle East. In *A Voyage to East India*, written in the mid-seventeenth century, Edward Terry makes the observation that 'the natives show very much ingenuity in their manufactures, also in the

1. *(opposite)* Detail from the top of an uncompleted multi-coloured quilt with chintzes inlaid in cream calico. Eire, *c.* 1860.

2. *(above)* Detail of a white satin quilt embroidered in silk with shells. English, eighteenth century.

excellent quilts of their stained cloth, or of fresh coloured taffeta lined with their prints, or of their satin with taffeta, betwixt which they put cotton wool and work them together with silk.'

During the Crusades, quilted jackets were worn under metal armour for comfort and light troops often had no protection but a quilted jacket. One of the earliest pieces of quilting in existence in England is the jupon belonging to the Black Prince, who lived during the fourteenth century. It is made of red and blue velvet, heavily embroidered with gold, and quilted lengthwise. Unfortunately it is too fragile for public display, but a replica can be seen in Canterbury cathedral.

In 1540 Katherine Howard was given by Henry VIII twenty-three silken quilts as a token of royal favour. Quilts for persons lower down the social scale would at that time have been made of linen or wool, or a combination of both known as linsey-woolsey. Throughout succeeding reigns quilting for both dress and furnishings was fashionable. Towards the end of the seventeenth century it became the custom to quilt the ground fabric of a bedcover in small patterns, often using yellow silk, and over this were embroidered sprays of flowers in brightly coloured silks. A seventeenth-century quilt at Blickling Hall, Norfolk, a National Trust property, is made of white satin, but instead of flowers, has embroidered on it many shells, each one different (2).

During the eighteenth century quilted clothing was high fashion; women wore quilted petticoats or under-skirts, usually of silk with a homespun linen backing and sheep's wool for filling. The skirt of the fashionable dress fell from the bodice and curved open over the hips, to show the underskirt. Quilted bodices and pockets for women as well as quilted waistcoats (vests) and breeches for men were worn, but as fashions changed quilted clothing faded away except in some of the more remote country districts. Women in the Welsh valleys, in the Isle of Man, fisherwomen on the north-east coast and bondagers who worked in the fields in north Northumberland, all continued to wear their quilted underskirts and bonnets well into this century.

British Quilting Traditions

Although there was a quilting tradition in most parts of the British Isles at one time, it is only in the valleys of South Wales and the north-east of England that it has survived without interruption, albeit very nearly dying out early in the twentieth century. The traditional quilt was of whole cloth, of a solid colour, the quilting pattern being distinctive of the area in which the quilt was made, for example, quilts from the north of England used

lovely feather circles and feather borders usually closely quilted with a background of diamonds; while quilts in Wales were stitched with running spirals in Carmarthen and curved leaves in Glamorgan. Quilting patterns in the West of England were usually taken from nature—flowers and leaves. In Ireland and the Isle of Man quilting was very simple; coverlets invariably were of two layers quilted in 'waves' — just chevrons or zig-zags sewn over the whole coverlet, irrespective of the pattern on the top. The edges of most British quilts were finished by turning in the top and the backing and sewing them together with two rows of running stitch.

In the north of England, quilting was considered the finer art and a true quilter would seldom make patchwork. The making of a plain colour coverlet, where the attractiveness depended solely on the design and stitchery, presented a far greater challenge to the needlewoman than the making of a patchwork one.

Towards the end of the nineteenth century quilt 'stampers' or markers plied their trade in the north-east. These were both men and women, who would mark out the quilting pattern on the top of the coverlet leaving the actual sewing to the customer. As well as quilts being made at home, there were professional quilters, often the village dressmaker. There were also quilt clubs, often connected with a church or chapel, where funds were raised by members making and selling quilts and 'hooky mats', and in some areas these gatherings took the place of whist drives as a social occasion. Quilts were sometimes made and presented to a member of the club on the occasion of her marriage. In Wales, there were in addition itinerant quilters who went round from farm to farm and to the great houses, making new quilts and mending old ones. Quilting 'bees' of the American type were unknown except in Ulster but in the north of England one quilt was made at home for a marriage, and in Wales, six quilts and one 'carthen' (woven coverlet) were made for the bride's hope chest, the local quilting experts often being brought in to help the family.

American Quilts

The Puritans looked upon needlework as a virtuous talent and women emigrating to America took their textile skills, including a knowledge of quilting, with them, but there is no mention in contemporary literature of patchwork. Before the American War of Independence, American quilts were similar to English ones, of whole cloth and solid colour, the only pattern being formed by running stitches which held the three layers in place.

Calamanco, a fine worsted fabric made mainly in East Anglia, was exported to the American colonies,

3. Detail of the wide border of a whole-cloth quilt of indigo-dyed glazed calamanco. American, c. 1770.

together with the sheep's wool for the padding. One must remember that there were no sheep in America before it was colonized and even well into the eighteenth century, so great was the demand for wool, that it was forbidden to kill a sheep before it was four years old. Calamanco was also one of the fabrics used for the tops of quilted petticoats and underskirts and the patterns on both articles were similar. Colours were simple: blues from indigo, reds from madder and browns from butternut. The quilt in the collection of the American Museum in Britain (3) is of indigo-dyed calamanco, numerous pieces having been joined together to make the top. The backing is of homespun linen and the filling carded sheep's wool. The centre portion of the quilt is beautifully sewn in a simple diamond pattern, but the wide border is quilted in a flowing pattern of leaves on a curving stem.

Additional Quilting Techniques

Homely, everyday bedcovers are often 'tied' or 'knotted' instead of being quilted. Two back stitches, taken one on top of the other, with the ends securely tied off, made at intervals over the quilt, serve to hold the three layers together. Such a coverlet is usually known as a comforter.

In addition to the wadded quilting previously discussed, several other forms of quilting can be employed in conjunction with, or instead of it. Italian quilting uses two layers of fabric: a top and an underlayer of fine loosely woven material such as butter muslin. The design always consists of two lines of parallel stitching, either running or back stitch, taken through both layers. From the back, soft cord is then run through the channel so made, to raise the pattern.

Cord quilting needs only one layer of fabric, under which a cord is held in one hand while the other works two parallel rows of back stitch, each one made alternately on either side of the cord, so that on the underside it is enclosed in a herringbone stitch.

Trapunto, or stuffed quilting, can be used to enhance an appliqué or pieced design and is often worked in conjunction with Italian quilting. When worked in white, on white, the effect can be most attractive. The pattern is outlined in running stitch and padding inserted from the back, through a tiny hole made by parting the fibres, or by snipping threads which are afterwards sewn together again.

APPLIQUÉ

Applied work was originally used to strengthen woven cloth, and rich fabrics were applied to one another with the details often worked in silk embroidery and metal thread. Applying fabric in this way for decoration was far less time-consuming than working embroidery and made an economical use of fine fabrics. During the sixteenth and seventeenth centuries design motifs were worked in wool on canvas and then applied to the woven ground. Applied work at this time was mainly ecclesiastical but was also employed on the bed furnishings and valances in the great houses of the day. The use of applied motifs on flags and banners continued from the Middle Ages.

From the seventeenth century onwards Indian palampores (cotton bedcovers) were imported into Britain through the East India Company, and were being advertised for sale in Boston as early as 1715. These fabrics were highly prized and when the bedcovers and furnishings were coming towards the end of their useful life, the best pieces were cut away and kept to be applied to a new background, thus making up another length of cloth. Many of the designs show Byzantine influence and one of the most popular was the motif known as the 'Tree of Life' or 'Tree of India'.

Sometimes each motif would be surrounded with a band of chintz simulating the sashing on a pieced

4. Chintz appliqué bedcover with a central motif of a bird, made from multicoloured chintzes and cottons. Eire, early nineteenth century.

coverlet, and sometimes a central motif would be framed with successive applied and pieced borders, as in the sophisticated bedcover made in County Dublin early in the nineteenth century (4). The central appliqué motif is surrounded by a garland of hexagons, the whole 'framed' in a sawtooth border. Obviously a bedcover such as this would have been made by a lady of taste with time to spare for elaborate needlework.

At the beginning of the nineteenth century cheap cotton became available for the making of appliqué motifs on quilt tops. It has often been said that appliqué quilts were for best, and pieced for everyday, but there is little evidence to support this view. It would seem that the quiltmaker herself designed her quilt in whichever technique she favoured and with whatever materials she had to hand. Side by side with traditional patterns and techniques for the making of appliqué and patchwork quilt tops are those which are derived from contact with North America. Returning emigrants brought back patterns with them and settlers sent back patterns to relatives at home.

Before 1830 few coverlets were made entirely of patchwork, being mostly of applied work or with applied work patterns included as highlights. The patchwork

5. 'The Sunday School Picnic'. Cotton appliqué, by Mrs Jennie Trien. American, 1932.

on many quilt tops is enhanced by an appliqué border, and the fashion for bows and ribbons on printed textiles was carried over into many of these appliqué borders. Generally they were made from odd scraps of plain or patterned fabrics which were folded into a strip from which the pattern was cut, thus ensuring that the sides of the shape were symmetrical.

Bold Patterns

The appliqué on a quilt top could make up one large design as in a painting, or smaller designs could be executed on 'blocks'; squares of fabric, which were then joined together in the same way as in pieced work. The patterns were often drawn freehand, as in the many floral and leaf patterns. In addition, abstract patterns could be made by the folded paper 'cut out' process which was used to great effect in some Hawaiian designs.

Pineapples were popular subjects, worked both in appliqué and quilting on many of the quilts made by the Pennsylvania German women in America. They were the descendants of the settlers from Switzerland and the Rhineland who brought with them to America a love of strong colour and design. The new colourfast dyes

6. Cotton appliqué quilt with pineapples – a typical Pennsylvanian German motif. A deliberate mistake has been made in this work: the third square from the left in the second row from the top has pineapples of a different colour. American, nineteenth century.

7. *(below)* Cotton appliqué of tulips with mauve and yellow petals. Northern Ireland, *c.* 1890.

of the latter part of the nineteenth century – strong reds, oranges and yellows – were here employed to great effect. The Germans in Pennsylvania and the Dutch in the Hudson Valley were among the few minority groups who preserved their own decorative motifs from being submerged into conventional colonial design. The motifs on the quilt (6) are typical of many worked on Pennsylvania German quilts. Pineapples were the symbol of hospitality and in Pennsylvania folklore the tulip represents the lily, a symbol of man's search for God and a promise of bliss in paradise.

The orange pineapples in this quilt have been meticulously cut out and applied and they are offset by green sashing stripes and meandering border. The quilting is simple, but neat, so as not to detract from the appliqué. Many women made a deliberate mistake in their work, noticeable in one block of pineapple shapes which is a different colour from the others. The quilt was part of the trousseau of Amelia Mellick of Light Street, near Bloomsburg, Pennsylvania, and in indelible ink in the bottom left-hand block is the message 'Remember Me, Harriet C. Wade.'

The simple outline tulip pattern was attractive and presented no difficulties even for an inexperienced needlewoman. It also forms the basic pattern on a quilt made in County Antrim in 1890 (7), the pattern for which was sent home by an aunt who had emigrated to Philadelphia. The petals of the appliqué tulips are of yellow and mauve print and the foliage turkey red cotton. The backing is white and although there is no padding, the two layers have been quilted in the usual 'waves' pattern.

Needlework as Documentation

Throughout the years topical events have been portrayed in needlework and embroidery, from the medieval Bayeux Tapestry to the modern 'Overlord Embroidery'. These needlework histories just as often portray everyday life, and as appliqué has more flexibility than geometric patchwork it can be used to great effect to tell a story, as shown in the quilt (5) aptly named 'The Sunday School Picnic'. Made in Nazareth, Pennsylvania in 1932 by Mrs Jennie Trien it shows the Sunday School picnic being held on the church lawn. The maker first laid down a foundation of blue for the sky and green for the grass, with birds and trees button-hole stitched on. Then she began to make her picture. Over the whole piece are delightful little vignettes: the maker's mother bringing to the picnic her speciality – a loaf of home-made bread; the maker's mother-in-law bringing her speciality – coffee in a coffee-pot; little boys playing ball; a young boy bringing home the cows; a little girl watering plants; and surrounding the whole all the people who are going to the picnic. They are dressed in the fashions of the day and no two are alike. The quilting is simple, just diagonal lines in the centre so as not to detract from the picture, but the blue border is intricately quilted with a chain pattern.

Of recent years the best-known example of appliqué and fabric collage has been the 'Overlord Embroidery'. This magnificent piece of work commemorates 'Operation Overlord' the name given to the organization which culminated in the invasion of Normandy on 6 June 1944. Consisting of a series of thirty-four panels, each of them 2·4 m long by nearly 1 m high (8 ft by 3 ft). The story starts from the aftermath of the Battle of Britain in 1940; eleven panels tell the story of Britain's struggle to avert the threat of invasion; a further thirteen panels illustrate the Channel crossings and D-Day landings by international forces from Britain, the U.S.A., Canada and Free Forces of many European countries. The remaining panels show how the German armies were defeated in France. The work was commissioned by Lord Dulverton and designed by Miss Sandra Lawrence, and the embroidery took twenty ladies of The Royal School of Needlework five years to complete.

The panels have a linen base and pieces of material were cut to shape and sewn down in the appropriate place, then edged with cord and embroidery thread, echoing the techniques of the medieval embroideries. Many diverse materials were employed including khaki battledress fabric and gold braid; authentically embroidered cap badges distinguish the various forces.

The panel illustrated (8) shows an easily recognizable General Eisenhower talking to men of the U.S. Airborne Division while paratroops of a British Airborne Division synchronize their watches prior to attack. Gliders can be seen in the background. The clever placement of the fabric gives a three-dimensional effect to the figures, shadows on faces and clothing being effected by a build up of different fabrics and nets. Couched cord simulates the camouflage netting over the men's tin hats.

Another exquisite modern appliqué and embroidered hanging is the 'Longleat Tree'. Designed by a young Wiltshire woman and worked by the Royal School of Needlework for the 6th Marquess of Bath, it shows in the

8. 'Overlord Embroidery'. Panel 15, showing preparations for the airborne attack. English, 1968.

central panel a beech tree with lacy branches and leaves of a delicate green, and within the roots a cartouche giving the date of the completion of Longleat House – 1580. The house is pictured at the top of the panel and the border consists of a series of leaves, each representing an occasion in the history of the house. Vines and leaves intertwine and at the foot of the panel are embroidered wild flowers which grow in the vicinity. The background is black and the fresh greens of the leaves and the brightly coloured embroidered flowers make a charming picture.

An outstanding modern appliqué hanging was made in 1973 by Miss Audrey Walker, commissioned by the City of Bath. It commemorates one thousand years of monarchy in England from AD 973 when Edgar, first King of all England, was crowned in Bath Abbey. The panel (9), which is hand worked, is divided into nine sections, each representing a reigning house from Saxon to Windsor, and the royal figure at the head is applied in padded gold kid with lettering in gold and silver kid, all sewn down with a variety of gold threads. At the foot, appliquéd in gold and silver kid, are the names of all the monarchs from Edgar to the present Queen. The centre consists of scenes from the nation's history. Stitched on a background of unbleached cotton canvas, the applied fabrics range from flimsy chiffons to stouter furnishing fabrics, and embroidery stitches such as herringbone, Cretan, seed stitches and French knots are used as highlights and to help the design to flow from one scene to the next. The colours are delicate – shades of turquoise, blue, green, white, cream and gold. The panel can be seen in the Pump Room in Bath.

PATCHWORK

The earliest British patchwork was literally patched work, where one piece of fabric was utilized to repair a threadbare spot in a woven material. The mosaic type of patchwork with which we are so familiar today is not a great deal more than two hundred years old, dating from the time when fabrics, particularly cotton, became so much more easily available. The scarcity and cost of materials in the past had made the piecing of quilt tops, and sometimes the backing also, a necessity. On many traditional quilts the top was of solid colour fabric to show off the fine quilting, but patchwork made an economical backing.

The choice of fabric, its colour, design and texture, plays an important part in the success of any pattern.

9. 'Monarchy 1000' marking one thousand years of monarchy in England. Made for the City of Bath. English, 1973.

10. A pattern pieced from turkey red and white cotton. English, c. 1890.

In the past women made use of pieces of fabric from their scrap bags, but often in such a way that patterns and colours were co-ordinated. The introduction of the 'turkey red' dye late in the eighteenth century heralded the making of many startling red and white quilt tops. Long known in the East, the brilliant red colour, which was the first fast red dye, was first produced in Glasgow by a Frenchman named Papillion, and in 1829 the dye was introduced into America.

A quilt made in Yorkshire about 1890 is a master-piece of construction (Bowes Museum). White diamonds make a six-point star and the addition of red squares and white elongated diamonds create circles which interlock. The pattern repeats over the whole of the top which is surrounded by a wide red border of solid colour. This pattern is not an easy one and the careful piecing has been achieved by using a paper template for each patch. The quilting pattern of Mother of Thousands, as it is known in the north of England, or Clam Shell has been worked over the whole quilt top with complete disregard for the piecing (10).

Throughout the nineteenth century great advances were made in perfecting a huge range of dyes, and with the development of roller printing on cotton a whole new spectrum of colours and fabrics was made available.

However, the modern quilt 'A Walk Around the Garden' made by Pat Novy (11) demonstrates clearly that it is not always necessary to employ multicoloured and patterned fabrics. Made by an Englishwoman, of traditional American block patterns set in asymmetrical fashion, this quilt is a variation of a sampler quilt (a quilt wherein each block is of a different pattern). The title, which was given after the quilt had been finished, explains the many arrows which represent movement

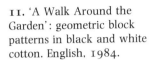

11. 'A Walk Around the Garden': geometric block patterns in black and white cotton. English, 1984.

round the garden. The fabrics used in the construction were black and white cottons, the patterning of stripes, spots and other designs giving the impression of shades of grey. The backing is cotton which has a small black and white print. The maker found working in just the two colours very restful.

Patchwork tends to be nearly always geometric, straight lines being easy to sew and geometric shapes are economical of cloth; squares, triangles, diamonds and hexagons can be used on their own or interlocking in countless combinations.

Framed Patchwork

Patchwork tops made by the American method of joining pieced squares or 'blocks' together were not unknown in Great Britain, but the typical patchwork of England and Wales was of the 'medallion' or 'framed' type, where a central motif was framed in a succession of borders, often a combination of pieced work and whole cloth. Although a certain number of British quilts were made with hexagonal shapes, far more were made as framed or medallion quilts, a type which was not peculiar to any one area and was popular with rich and poor alike. Often the central motif was a star, or a block pieced from geometric shapes, or perhaps a panel which had been specially printed for the purpose.

A typical example of this type of quilt comes from County Durham (12). Made about 1870, entirely of cotton, it has a central pieced block, set diagonally, of red and white squares, surrounded by successive pieced and solid colour borders, each with contrasting squares in the corners. It is interesting to compare the placement of the squares with those of the Amish quilt (18). The

quilting of the County Durham quilt is beautiful, with different patterns in each border.

In north-east England 'strippy' quilts were common from the end of the nineteenth century and into the present one. These were patchwork in its simplest form, the top consisting of an uneven number of lengthwise strips, 15–20 cm (6–8 in) wide, in two alternating plain or patterned fabrics, joined lengthwise. The resultant top was then attached to filling and backing by quilting patterns which usually changed with the changes of the strips.

Another type of framed quilt made in the north of England had a centre of whole cloth, solid colour, beautifully quilted, with a wide border of patterned

fabric such as chintz. Sometimes a diamond, created from a narrow border fabric, was inserted in the centre of the quilted panel to create a diamond within the square, again showing a marked similarity to some early Amish quilts.

Several types of quilts are common to all areas of the British Isles, including those quilts made of chintzes, either appliqué or pieced. That made by Jane Pizar in 1850–60 (1) is a truly astonishing piece of work which was never completed, as it lacks backing and padding. It is therefore possible to see, from the underside, that the blocks are all pieced, and all the shapes have been oversewn (whipped) together. All curves have been neatly clipped so that the surface lies flat.

12. *(opposite)* Beautiful framed (or medallion) cotton quilt. English, *c.* 1870.

13. *(right)* Detail of a nine-patch chain with a border made from an English copper-plate chintz. 1832.

The central medallion, which is 66 cm (26 in) in diameter, consists of a compass pattern surrounded by a border containing hearts and doves, which signifies that this was probably meant to be a marriage quilt.

Varied Patterns and Designs

One of the first patterns a young American girl was taught was the four-patch — just four squares sewn together to make a larger square. She would then graduate to making a nine-patch — nine squares, five of one colour and four of another, set alternately, to make a larger square. Once a number of these squares, or blocks as they were known, had been assembled they were joined together in whatever pattern the maker wished. The nine-patch chain (**13**) contains over three thousand pieces of over one hundred different early printed calicoes. In this instance, triangles have been joined to the nine-patch blocks to form long patterned bands which move diagonally across the quilt. The border is an English copperplate chintz. The quilt was made in 1832 for a bride of English descent who was living in Chester County, Pennsylvania.

Triangles and diamonds were often placed together to make the popular 'lily' patterns. These usually occur in sprays of three and are considered by some to represent the holy lily — the Trinity. To make the poinsettia flower (**14**) six red diamonds and two green

14. Poinsettia flowers in red and green on white. American, nineteenth century.

15. *(below)* Pinwheels of blue, yellow and red cottons with white. American, 1840.

16. *(opposite)* Cotton quilt with appliquéd doves, hearts and four-leafed clovers – typical motifs of a marriage quilt. English, 1860.

have been pieced to make the flower, and white geometric shapes added to make the block, which has been set as a diamond. The leaves and stems have been applied. The alternate blocks are exquisitely quilted with pineapples. The quilt, which was made about 1840, has obviously been treasured as the red fabric of the flowers has been darned neatly wherever it has worn away. This quilt shows a good example of an attractive border – an inner scallop of red and an outer one of green. The two colours with white present an attractive and clear-cut design.

One of the most popular and widely used patterns is the star – sometimes one large star which covers the whole top of the quilt; sometimes made in blocks with a small star in the centre of each block. A large star covering the whole top of the quilt is known in America as the Lone Star, but when there is, in addition, a small star in each of the four corners of the top, the pattern is known as the Star of Bethlehem. Other stars are variously known as the Le Moyne Star, Texas Star, Variable Star and so on and these names have now been accepted worldwide.

Symbolism of patterns was an important factor in a quilt's design. For instance, it was considered unlucky to work hearts on anything but a bride's quilt; pine-

apples symbolized hospitality; clematis and grapes —
prosperity and plenty; pomegranates — fruitfulness. The
rose of Sharon (from the Song of Solomon) was a
popular pattern from brides' quilts.

Cumulative Skills

When a girl had mastered the simple geometric shapes
she was ready to learn appliqué and the piecing of
curved patches, a much more exacting technique. One
elaborate pattern made *c.* 1840 by an experienced
needlewoman is the Pinwheel quilt from Branford,
Connecticut (**15**). Curved patches of blue and yellow

calico make up the twenty pinwheels which decorate
the top of the quilt. These are bordered with a circle of
red and white triangles. The alternate white blocks are
quilted with leaf forms and occasional stars and
triangles. The whole quilt is bound in red.

In the United States of America it was the custom for
a young woman to try to have at least twelve quilts in
her hope chest, possibly even thirteen, the thirteenth
being the grandest one of all — her bride's quilt. In the
north of England it was usual for there to be one special
quilt made for a marriage, either by the mother or the
bride herself. Such a quilt is one made in 1860 by
Rebecca Temperley of Allendale, in Northumberland

(16). Here one can see how the simple piecing of a variety of cotton prints, the appliqué and quilting have been skilfully integrated. In the centre block the little birds perched on leafy sprays possibly represent doves, often used on marriage quilts. The four single heart motifs in the centre and those in the four corner blocks are supposed to represent the lucky four-leaved clover. The quilting is finely worked with several of the patterns echoing the applied design. The wide border has a lined twist quilting pattern within a border of diamond-set squares enclosing hearts and leaf patterns. The overall design is unusual, but could have been planned so that the piecing and appliqué lie on top of the bed while the quilted borders hung round the four sides.

Collective Efforts

During the nineteenth century Album quilts were common in North America. These quilts were autograph albums in textile form, where each square or block was made by a different person, who usually signed and dated the contribution. An Album quilt was a co-operative piece, and in many instances both men and women were signatories. Presentation quilts, as the name suggests, were made to honour someone of note, or to be presented to a minister, perhaps on his leaving the parish, or for a bride, in which case hearts would be incorporated into the piecing or the quilting. Freedom quilts were made for young men on reaching the age of twenty-one. Sisters and girl friends would join together to make the quilt top which he would keep until he became engaged, when he would give it to his bride to be included with those in her hope chest. In the United States a number of Legacy quilts were made. An outstanding quiltmaker in the community, as she got older, would make what could well be her last quilt, featuring patterns which she considered worthy of being passed on to others. This was her legacy to posterity, hence the name Legacy quilts.

In Britain Album quilts were made for hospital use. *Weldon's Practical Patchwork* published about 1900 comments:

> Hospital quilts are made of good sized squares of red twill and white calico placed alternately like squares on a chess board, the white pieces having texts written on them or scripture pictures outlined in marking ink; they are much appreciated, and prove a great source of interest to the poor invalids.

Sometimes this type of coverlet was known as a Bible or Scripture coverlet and several interesting examples are still in existence.

Victorian Fashion

During the second half of the nineteenth century, 'crazy' patchwork became the rage, 'crazy' meaning crazed or cracked as in crazy paving. Usually made with rich fabrics, silks, velvets, brocades and ribbons, the scraps were pieced together random fashion with colourful embroidery covering the seams. Women vied with each other to see just how much rich embroidery they could put onto one piece of work. Sometimes floral and bird motifs were painted on to the silk, and narrow ribbons took the place of embroidery floss. These pieces, sometimes called Japanese work or Kaleidoscope, were seldom used as bedcovers, but graced the Victorian drawing room. So highly were these pieces regarded that there was little time for cotton patchwork and a Mrs Pullman, of New York, writing in the 1859 *Lady's Manual of Fancy Work* comments:

> Patchwork is a favourite amusement with many ladies, as by it they convert useless bits of silk, velvet or satin into really handsome articles of decoration. Of the patchwork with calico I have nothing to say. Valueless indeed must be the time of that person who can find no better use for it than to make ugly counterpanes and quilts of cotton.

In England much the same sentiments prevailed as Caulfield and Seward in their *Dictionary of Needlework* state that 'satin, silk and velvet patchwork is used for cushions, handscreens, firescreens, glove and hankie cases. Cloth patchwork is for carriage rugs, couvrepieds and poor people's quilts.'

Crazy patchwork in its Victorian form does not appeal greatly to modern taste, but Helen Kelley, a quiltmaker from Minneapolis, has created her modern version of a Victorian crazy quilt by making a lifelike picture of Queen Victoria herself, using crazy patchwork techniques, with brocades, velvets, taffeta, lace, beads, chenille and yarn (17). This wall hanging is beautifully quilted, but the Victoria crazy patchwork was usually knotted or tied unobtrusively through to the back.

The Art of the Amish

A great deal of interest is being taken by quiltmakers, artists, antique dealers and collectors among others, in the quilts made by the Amish or Plain People living in Pennsylvania and parts of the Midwest.

Present-day Amish quilts are almost indistinguishable from those made by other quiltmakers, and many Amish women now buy fabrics instead of relying on their scrap bags. But, during the nineteenth century and up to 1940, Amish quilts had a strong identity of

17. Appliqué hanging of
Queen Victoria. American,
1983.

their own, using only solid colours, in unusual and exciting combinations; no patterns were allowed. All forms of decoration were frowned upon and clothing was simple and dark-coloured, but quilts were regarded as utilitarian objects and more latitude was allowed in their making. All Amish designs are non-representational and borders were wide with a great deal of exquisite quilting often sewn in black thread.

Patterns used for historic Amish quilts can be divided into three main groups. The Sunshine and Shadow pattern consists of hundreds of little squares of fabric sewn together to form a series of brightly coloured larger squares, arranged to give an alternate light and dark effect. Although this pattern is similar to one called A Trip Around the World, the Amish quilt always has a wide border.

For the Amish 'Bars pattern' wide lengths of fabric were arranged to form vertical bars, very similar to the north of England strippy quilts, in two different and contrasting solid colours. These were surrounded by an elaborately quilted border, but the actual quilting on the bars tended to remain very simple.

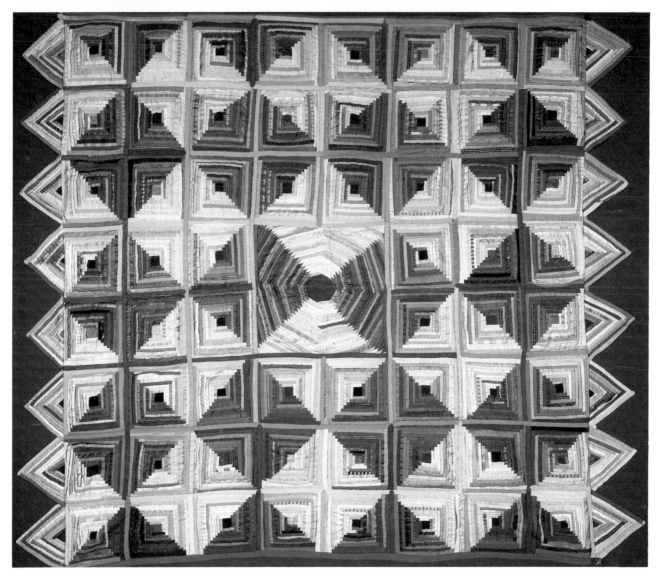

Opposite page:

18. *(above left)* Amish quilt 'Diamond within a Square', made of batiste and wool. American, Lancaster County, Pa., *c.* 1915.

19. *(above right)* Silk Lone Star quilt with Wild Goose Chase border. Canadian, 1865.

20. *(below)* Log Cabin quilt. Scottish, *c.* 1851.

21. *(above)* Patchwork coverlet, made of Welsh flannels, by Edward Tunnah. Welsh, *c.* 1820.

The third category was based upon a square, and 'the Diamond within a Square' (**18**) is typical of many Amish quilts. As a general rule only three colours were used. Here, the red diamond surrounded with green triangles has been framed with red rectangles enclosing green corner squares. This, in turn, is framed by a similar outer border, which keeps the continuity of the colour green out to the corners. Quilting has been worked in black thread and the borders presented a considerable challenge to the quilter who filled them with feathers, diamonds, cables stars and the ever-popular tulips among other patterns.

The quilts from the Lancaster, Pennsylvania, area were mainly of woollen fabrics, but many of the quilts made by the Amish communities of the Midwest use a polished cotton. Here the approach is more relaxed and patterned fabrics occasionally are used. Typical Amish colours were blues, maroons, pinks, deep greens, purple, mauves, red and black, but never white.

Variations on a Theme

Patchwork patterns in the British Isles have very few traditional names, in contrast to the many hundreds which are to be found in North America. As a consequence, the American names have been adopted in most countries of the world. American quilts produce more variations of basic patterns but many of them seem to have developed from traditional British patterns. The American named Log Cabin became especially popular in the middle of the nineteenth century after the American Civil War. It is sometimes known as ribbon patchwork because fine ribbons were used instead of strips of fabric, it was called Log Wood in the north of England, Log Pattern in the west of England, Folded

Patchwork in Ireland and Roof Pattern in the Isle of Man, where it is considered to be the true Manx pattern.

The block, which is supposed to represent the roof of a log cabin, is made by sewing strips of fabric, dark on two sides and light on the other two, round a central square, which traditionally was red to denote the fire. The light part of the block symbolized the firelight and the dark half the shadow. The size of the block could be changed by varying the width of the strips and also the size of the central square. As with most forms of pieced work, once the basic blocks have been made, they can be arranged to form a number of interesting patterns with names such as Barn Raising, Sunshine and Shadow, Straight Furrow, Courthouse Steps and many more.

An excellent illustration of this pattern (20) was made in 1851 of rich fabrics, silks, brocades, velvets, lace trims and ribbons by the girls who worked for Miss Jane Yeaman, a milliner of Forfar, Scotland. When business was slack the girls occupied their time by making patchwork, using up the scraps of fabric left over from their hatmaking. The centre of the bedcover is an elaboration of the basic Log Cabin block and is known as Pineapple Log Cabin. In addition to the strips on all four sides of the central square, there are subsidiary strips diagonally across the four corners, but there is no quilting.

Canadian Quiltmaking

There is a long quilting tradition in Canada, particularly in Ontario and the Maritime Provinces. At the time of the American War of Independence, those people wishing to remain loyal to the British Crown fled to Canada, taking with them their needlework skills and techniques, as did the Dutch moving north from New York. Subsequent waves of immigrants from Europe brought influences which helped forge a rich tradition of textiles of all kinds. By the time of the settlement of the western provinces store-bought goods were fairly easily obtainable so that not quite so much handwork took place. Today, however, quilting and patchwork are thriving hobbies and cottage industries.

In eastern Canada early quilts were made with homespun woollen materials. The people were poor and thrifty, so clothes were turned, cut down for children and finally cut into patches for quilts, which were heavily padded for warmth.

Thrift allied with rich fabrics and excellent taste go together to make the Lone Star quilt (19) made from taffeta dress silks, fashionable for the wide crinoline dresses of the mid-nineteenth century. The border

is made up of a pattern known as Wild Goose Chase. The quilt (which is backed with a fine dark printed cotton) has a light padding of soft wool, and the exquisite quilting is worked in silk in rosettes on a lattice ground with outline quilting on the star. The quilt was made by Janet Murray (Mrs Hugh Martin) in Clanbrasil, Haldeman County, Ontario about 1865.

Women in Canada made many quilts in blocks with similar patterns to those used in the United States, and during the nineteenth century it was the custom to make Friendship quilts, where each piece of fabric used in the making was donated by a friend.

Patchwork and Quilting by Men

A number of British patchwork and appliqué coverlets and hangings were made in the nineteenth century by men, but there are not many documented in the United States of America, although in recent years a number of men have come to the forefront, particularly in the design field. In Wales, tailors such as John Williams and Edward Tunnah made hangings from pieces of Welsh flannel and suitings, surplus to their tailoring requirements. John Williams used approximately 4,500 pieces of fabric in his coverlet, which was made between 1842 and 1852. It shows a number of biblical scenes and two of the great engineering features of Wales, the Menai Suspension Bridge and the Ruabon Viaduct. The coverlet is very colourful with an eyecatching chevron pattern at the sides.

Edward Tunnah, from Wrexham, North Wales, worked as a cutter at the Royal Shop in London during the reign of George III and made his coverlet with a compass star as the central motif, surrounded by a series of borders. Each patch has been outlined in red or black by inserting a very narrow strip of fabric between each of the shapes – a very intricate process as the whole work has been pieced in the traditional way by sewing on the wrong side (21).

In Scotland, too, soldiers and sailors made patchwork, and as during the nineteenth-century manufacturers advertised for sale bundles of heavy cloth from which uniforms were made, several bedcovers were made in hospital as occupational therapy. Sergeant Cumming made a patchwork cover out of squares cut from uniforms of the Highland Light Infantry while serving at Maryhill Barracks, in Glasgow, and other hangings of this type are known to have been made by soldiers in India when convalescing, and are often decorated with beadwork. A Scottish sailor, Nicholas White of Dundee, made a cotton quilt from what must have been cotton pattern books while serving on the whaling ship *Balena*. He used over one hundred different prints. John Monro, a tailor of Paisley, made a 'clothograph' which took eighteen years to complete. It consists of seven pieced and embroidered felt pictures each with separate mosaic patchwork borders, and the main border surrounding the whole is embroidered with the names of hundreds of famous men.

A Continuing Craft

Many factors contributed to the demise of fashionable patchwork and quilting in the British Isles, although these crafts continued to be practised in country and mining areas. The Industrial Revolution caused factory-made goods to be more easily available and home-made bedcovers were looked down upon. Many people would never admit to owning a patchwork bedcover – it was considered a sign of poverty. During the 1920s and 1930s efforts were made to revive quilting skills to give women a chance to earn some money by their needle during the depression. The second World War brought rationing of all clothing and textiles and apart from some very utilitarian work, embroidery and Needlecrafts came almost to a standstill. However, during the last ten years there has been a great renewal of interest in all forms of patchwork, and as women become more skilled at piecing, more and more are taking up the further challenge of quilting their work. In contrast, patchwork in the United States of America continued in popularity and the depression years produced very many quilts, often simple scrap bedcovers made from whatever was available, but carrying on all the traditions and patterns.

Much experimentation has taken place in all three techniques. Modern quiltmakers dye their own fabrics to achieve unusual colour combinations. Some quilting, where extra padding has been added to parts of the design to bring it into high relief, resembles sculpture. Clothing is made by one or more techniques and needlewomen are continually looking for unusual ways of assembling patterns and colours. They are combining modern fabrics, designs and colours into exciting bedcovers, wall hangings and clothing in ways which never could have been envisaged by their ancestors.

BIBLIOGRAPHY

Betterton, S. *Quilts and Coverlets from the American Museum in Britain*, Bath, Avon, 1978 and 1982

Bishop, R., and E. Safanda *A Gallery of Amish Quilts*, New York 1976

Burnham, D. *Pieced Quilts of Ontario*, Toronto, Ont., 1975

Clabburn, P. *Patchwork*, Shire Album No. 101, Princes Risborough, Buckinghamshire, 1984

Colby, A. *Patchwork*, London 1958

—*Quilting*, London 1972

Conroy, M. *Canada's Quilts*, Toronto, Ont., 1976

Cooper, P., and N. Buferd *The Quilters: Women and Domestic Art*, New York 1978

Finley, R. *Old Patchwork Quilts and the Women Who Made Them*, Philadelphia, Pa., 1929

Fitz-Randolph, M. *Traditional Quilting*, London 1954

Gutcheon, B. *The Perfect Patchwork Primer*, New York 1973; London 1974

Haders, P. *Sunshine and Shadow (Amish Quilts)*, New York 1985

Hake, E. *English Quilting Old and New*, London 1937

Hall, C., and R. Kretsinger *The Romance of the Patchwork Quilt*, New York 1935

Holstein, J. *The Pieced Quilt: An American Design Tradition*, New York 1973

Ickis, M. *The Standard Book of Quilt Making*, New York 1949

Irwin, J. *A People and Their Quilts*, Exton, Pa., 1984

Jackson, V. (ed.) *The Complete Book of Patchwork and Quilting*, London 1985

Katzenberg, D. *Baltimore Album Quilts*, Baltimore, Md, 1980

McKim, R. *101 Patchwork Patterns*, New York 1962

Montgomery, F. *Printed Textiles: English and American Cottons, 1700–1850*, New York 1970; London 1971

Orlofsky, M. and P. *Quilts in America*, New York 1974

Percival, M. *The Chintz Book*, London 1923

Safford, Carleton L., and R. Bishop *America's Quilts and Coverlets*, New York, 1972

Shipley Art Gallery *Patchwork in the North East*, Gateshead, Tyne and Wear

—*Quilting in the North East*, Gateshead, Tyne and Wear

Walker, M. *Quiltmaking in Patchwork and Appliqué*, London 1985

Woodard, T., and B. Greenstein *Crib Quilts and Other Small Wonders*, New York 1981

NEEDLELACE
AND
WHITEWORK

AUDREY FIELD

The earliest examples of needlelace, as we know it today, evolved from the needlework done in Italy in the mid-sixteenth century. Imagine, if you will, a plain handspun and woven linen altar cloth or bed hanging. It can only have been a divine spark that inspired the first person to draw some threads together and cut away some cloth, leaving geometric spaces to be decorated with needle and thread. Thus began an art which soon spread over Europe and has developed over the centuries, all the time changing with the nationality and skill of the maker and creating a challenge for each new generation of fashion.

First we must consider drawn work, which involved two different methods of working on a plain-woven linen ground. In one the design was left in the original cloth and the background was formed into a square network. This was done by drawing out some vertical and horizontal threads, usually in groups of three, and overcasting them with a separate linen thread sometimes of a different colour (3). By the other method, the threads of an entire panel were similarly drawn into

a mesh and the design was darned back into it, using a drawn-out thread (4). In each case the design was usually stylized figures, animals or birds. Buratto work was produced by darning similar designs into a specially woven cloth, one vertical thread interwoven with two horizontal ones.

Filet, or lacis work, had darned designs on a finely knotted cloth, like a traditional fish net. Earlier examples of this can be traced back to the darned netting altar cloths and burial sheets of the twelfth century. Most of the sixteenth-century pieces were for furnishing, but some very fine filet was used for fashion accessories, such as partlets (coverage for the exposed part of shoulders and neck) and hairnets. Queen Elizabeth I's wardrobe records show that she wore it in the form of 'white networke' and 'black networke'.

The table cover (5) is an exceptional example of early seventeenth-century French filet combined with whitework. It can be seen that great versatility was possible even within the geometric limits – note the bird in the oak tree, the mermaid's comb, the skull and crossbone, and the poacher's game, among other delights in the filet squares.

For generations lace historians have differed in their opinions of where embroidery ended and lace began. We must accept the fact that the dividing lines were blurred at this stage, until needlelace and whitework emerged in their different ways.

1. *(opposite)* Portrait of Queen Elizabeth I wearing a ruff of reticella and *punto in aria* starched so that it forms a frame to the face. By or after G. Gower, *c.* 1588.

2. *(above)* Miniature of Sir Walter Raleigh wearing a starched linen ruff edged with reticella and *punto in aria*. Nicholas Hilliard, *c.* 1585.

3. Detail from a linen panel with drawn background to the design. Italian, late sixteenth century.

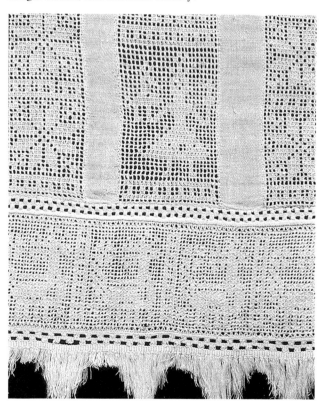

4. Detail from a linen panel with original fringe, showing figures and animals darned into the drawn-work background. Italian, late sixteenth century.

NEEDLELACE

Sixteenth to Eighteenth Centuries

If we return to the linen altar cloth the next stage of the development of needlelace involved more threads being cut away from the basic cloth, leaving a wider mesh to be decorated. The remaining threads were left in larger squares and others laid diagonally across them, to make a firm basis for rows of buttonhole stitches in endless variations of geometric design. This was the beginning of the North Italian reticella lace which has continued in varying forms until the present day (6). To recognize the earliest pieces, one must ascertain that the basic framework of the design is formed by the original threads of the woven material. Nearly all of it was linen but some silk lace was also made in various colours. It was used mainly to decorate the borders of church and household linens with the design confined to the straight edge of the cloth, but sometimes whole cloths were worked in squares, alternating with filet and cutwork in a chequerboard effect.

By the third quarter of the sixteenth century, lacemakers were working in other parts of Europe. The first pattern book was published by Frederico Vinciolo in Paris in 1587. The patterns were pinned to a hard pillow, and held on the lap or a table. Individual variations on these initial designs soon developed. Simple buttonholing was varied with Genoa stitch, a figure-of-eight twist on two or three threads, which gave a firmer foundation. By the first quarter of the seventeenth century, reticella was made throughout Europe, notably in England, with a plaited grid in place of the original woven ground. In 1591, Cesare Vecellio published a pattern book in Venice and four more before 1625; Isabetta Parasole and Bartolomeo Daniel followed, and, by the turn of the century the whole art of lacemaking had developed to its next stage.

Punto in Aria

Hitherto all the needle decoration on shirts and caps was narrow and straight, following the original cloth edge, as we can see from early portraits. However, with the invention of parchment patterns, the designs were released from the rigid geometric grid and the first pointed edgings appeared. Threads were laid along the lines of the design, drawn on the parchment, and tacked into position to make a framework for rows of buttonhole stitches, allowing freer, more elaborate designs. The outlining threads were overcast to make a raised rim to the design known as the cordonnet. The space

5. *(above)* Fine quality filet and whitework cover with bobbin lace border. French, first quarter seventeenth century.

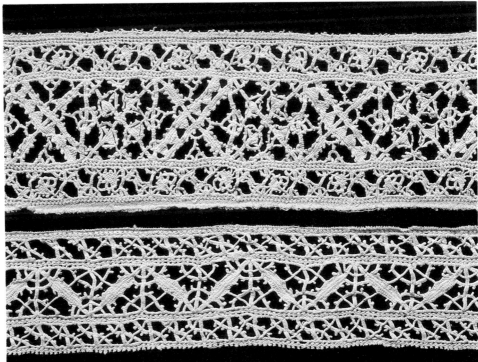

6. Two reticella insertions showing typical geometric design buttonhole stitched. Italian, late sixteenth century.

between was filled with row upon row of buttonhole stitches and the design was linked together with similarly worked bars or brides. The finished work was then removed from the hard pillow and, for the first time, the tacking threads were cut away from the pattern. The resulting lace was literally 'stitches in the air', which provided the name *punto in aria*.

This new development provided enormous scope for the leaders of fashion and it was not long before narrow pointed edgings, generally known as *passementerie*, appeared on costume all over Europe. By the latter part of the sixteenth century, they were most famous for the extremely fine, stiffened ruffs beloved of the Elizabethans in England (1, 2, 7, 8) and also worn in France and, most uncomfortably of all, in Spain. Towards the end of the century these were modified into more comfortable turned-down collars; some were wired to stand up behind the head into a more flattering frame. *Punto in aria* also appeared on the edges of tablecloths and other household linens.

Fine Flax

By now the published pattern books had made lace available to a greater number of people all over Europe and it soon became apparent that the Northern countries were generally making finer textured lace than the Italians, because an exceptionally fine flax was being produced. Indeed, the cultivation and refinement of

7. (*above*) An Elizabethan lady, Elizabeth Drury, aged seventeen years, in a fine embroidered dress with whitework, reclining on a blackwork pillow. Paul van Somer, *c.* 1516.

8. (*opposite*) Lady Scudamore wearing a cap and cuffs of reticella and *punto in aria*. M. Gheeraerts the Younger, *c.* 1614.

flax was a key factor in the development of the Flemish lace industry, and its success was both due to the ideal terrain and climate of the Netherlands, and also to the ingenuity of the local people. Santina Levey in her *Lace: A History* gives a graphic summary of the complicated procedure involved in its production:

Flax grown for seed was grown on different soil and was managed in a different way to flax grown for thread. The latter required a firm sandy loam or light soil, the careful control of the water supply and constant tending. In the Netherlands, the standing flax was sold to the flax dresser who weeded it, tended it and supervised its harvesting and subsequent treatment. At every stage, judgement and expertise were required: if the flax was pulled too soon, the fibre was soft and weak; if too late, it was harsh and coarse and difficult to spin. If dew-retted, the fibre was brownish or greenish-grey; if water-retted the fibre was a yellowish-white. Running water was needed for the best water retted flax and a more lustrous, stronger and whiter fibre was produced if a double-retting process was used. The fibre of the flax plant runs the length of the stem in a thin layer between the epidermis or outer bark and the coarse, woody fibres which adheres to the inner pith. Extracting it, even

Martij 12 mo
Anno Domini
1614

No Spring Till now

after retting, was difficult and it was easily damaged by poor husbandry and clumsy handling. Once extracted, the fibre was either wet or dry spun; stronger firmer thread was produced by dry-spinning but really fine thread had to be wet spun and then the thread had to be bleached . . . the best bleach in Holland . . . the process was a complex one and it could take as long as six to eight months to complete.

Venetian Needlelace

However, as far as design was concerned, Venice and the north of Italy continued to lead the field and, at the beginning of the seventeenth century, the wonderful flowing Venetian lace began to appear.

Venetian needlelace used the same techniques as *punto in aria*, but on a bolder scale. Needle-made tapes were laid upon the parchment patterns to form the foundation for a grander free-flowing design, built up with rows of buttonhole stitches and layers of threads then buttonholed over to create the famous padded ivory effect. Enormous stylized flower-heads were linked with buttonholed brides, sometimes with tiny picots in even more elaborate designs (**9** *top*).

Venetian *gros point* laces (not to be confused with the *gros point*, or cross stitch of embroidery!) were bold designs used in churches on altars and alb flounces where the grand scale of design was in keeping with the grandeur of the surroundings. They reached the peak of their fame in the third quarter of the seventeenth century when they were also used for household linens and for men's and women's fashions. The bold designs were well suited to the gentleman's flat square collar known as *col rabat*, resplendent in front and with a narrow strip of lace at the back of the neck, hidden behind the full wigs of the period. Again we must look to portraits to find that, as the fashion changed towards the end of the seventeenth century, so the laces became smaller in design, enabling them to be frilled and gathered more easily. Sleeve ruffles were now worn and linen cravats with lace ends replaced the collars.

Venetian *point plat*, or flat point as its name suggests, was similar in design to *gros point* but had no raised work, which gave it a better draping quality. This lace also changed from a large flowing design to a smaller and more delicate one. At the end of the century, a less attractive flat point with indeterminate trailing design was produced (**9** *centre*). It is said that a seaman's sweetheart first created the lace and named it 'coralline'.

The most elaborate and exquisite needlelace produced at the end of the seventeenth century was Venetian *point de neige*, based on the old *gros point* but on an incredibly small scale, with layers of tiny picots to resemble snowflakes and the most minutely decorated brides (**10**). *Point de neige* was a fashion lace, sometimes made in flounces but mainly made for the unbelievably high head-dresses known as *fontanges* which suddenly became fashionable. They were usually stiffened, pleated, and vertical fan shapes worn with trailing bonnet strings or lappets. These were to become an important item in eighteenth-century fashion.

Spanish Needlelace

At the beginning of the seventeenth century Spanish needlelace was strongly influenced by Venetian *punto in aria*. Early geometric designs soon incorporated Moorish characteristics from earlier textiles that were imported, with sun and wheel designs filling the framework of squares. These were usually made from gold or silver threads, which were wonderful against the silk and velvet of court livery and banners with heavier quality for horse trappings.

Spanish and Portuguese traders carried these laces to their colonies all over the world, and the typical sun laces are still made traditionally in many parts of South and Central America, the Philippines and the Canary Islands.

The Italian influence was still felt at the end of the seventeenth century, persisting in the Spanish *gros point*

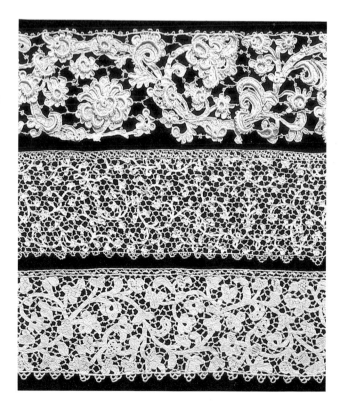

laces which were generally less padded than their Venetian originators. Narrow needlemade *passementerie* and insertions between loom widths of linen, for example on bed sheets, were known in Spain as *randas* and have remained traditional.

Although we are not concerned particularly with laces made on a pillow with bobbins, which by now were also being made all over Europe, we cannot pass the 1690s without noticing that at this time the two techniques were combined in a lace which was easier and cheaper to produce, namely *mezzo punto*. In this lace the outlines of the design were made with bobbin-produced tapes, and the fillings needle-made in great variety. The lace was usually extremely attractive and sometimes quite fine. It was produced mainly in Italy and England for domestic use (**9** *bottom*).

English Needlelace

Meanwhile lacemakers in England were also following the Venetian lead. The early reticella often had the plaited groundwork, and portraits show fine pointed edgings of cutwork and needlelace on ruffs and cuffs, sometimes in black. In 1624 Richard Shorlayker produced *A Schole House for the Needle* which showed rounded scalloped edges for the now fashionable soft falling collars. A flat needlelace with finely knotted buttonholing in tight rows (leaving small holes to form the design) was made in flounces for domestic use and as covers for boxes and prayer books. The designs often incorporated a profusion of fruit, flowers and acorns.

Hollie point was a very fine version of this lace used in the eighteenth century to decorate christening caps and vests. Little holes were left in the tightly knotted rows to form a design of tiny flowers or perhaps the name and date of birth of the baby. It is thought that the name of this lace is derived from the word holy.

French Needlelace

From the 1660s more and more Italian lace was exported to France, to such an extent that the government became increasingly alarmed by the amount of money being spent abroad by the French court. King Louis XIV appointed his minister Colbert to establish a lace industry. A number of Italian lacemakers were persuaded to settle in the Alençon area, where the first French lace was made.

As would be expected, for some time the patterns were based on established flowing Italian designs and some of the *point de neige* was probably made in France (**11** *top*). Gradually the French lace became lighter and more frivolous in keeping with the fashion of the court.

9. *Opposite page:*
(Top) Venetian *gros point* lace showing padded raised detail to the stylized flowerheads. Italian, mid-seventeenth century.
(Centre) Venetian *point plat* with smaller design and no raised work. Italian, last quarter of seventeenth century.
(Bottom) *Mezzo punto* showing bobbin-made tapes with needle-made fillings. English, *c.* 1690.

10. *(right)* Enlarged detail of a Venetian *point de neige* flounce: the fine buttonholed picots give a snowflake effect. Italian, last quarter of seventeenth century.

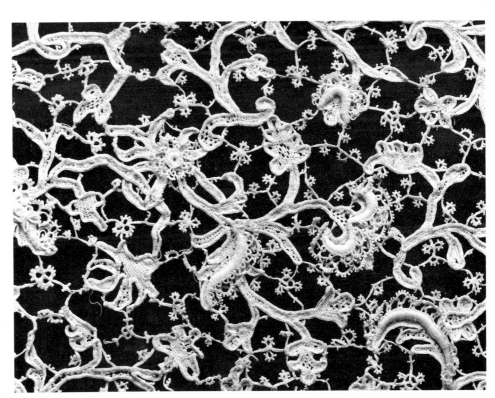

King Louis was evidently delighted and decided that only this French lace, to be named *point de France*, should be worn.

Point de France

Important and impressive flounces of *point de France* were made, with figures of the king under canopies, surrounded by angels or elaborate hunting scenes. The main difference between these and the Italian laces was the background to the design, made up of a hexagonal formation of picot brides, not merely connecting bars between the motifs as before, but an integral part of the design. This lace (11 *bottom*) was made until the first decade of the eighteenth century.

Other needlelace centres were started at Sedan and Argentan, and all the laces had this distinctive background reseau. However, the two main types of French needlelace, which were made throughout the eighteenth century, came to be known as *point d'Argentan* and *point d'Alençon*. Both of them had a finely buttonholed cordonnet surrounding flower sprays and pretty fillings in the design, and are easily identified by the difference in the reseau.

Point d'Argentan had a small hexagonal mesh reminiscent of the *point de France* but with no picots. There were normally five to ten buttonhole stitches on each side of the hexagon, which made a firm basis for the delicate flowers which were applied later (12 *top*). Towards the end of the eighteenth century, the reseau was more loosely worked and very often the buttonholing was sparse or replaced by a simple overstitch,

resulting in a deterioration of quality (12 *centre*). A variation of this was argentella, which had a larger, needle-filled honeycomb mesh, but comparitively little of this lace has survived. *Point d'Alençon* was much lighter and the reseau had a simpler single twisted buttonhole stitch worked in vertical rows (12 *bottom*).

Although *point d'Argentan* and *point d'Alençon* were finer than any needlelaces made before, Margaret Simeon reminds us in *The History of Lace*:

> They were considered to be winter laces by fashionable society in the eighteenth century. Although they were light in weight and delicate in design they still had the firm crisp texture of needlepoint lace which was thought to be more suitable for use with rich colours and heavier materials. The extremely fine and soft bobbin laces of Flanders and France were chosen for the lighter silks of summer . . .

As the eighteenth century progressed the decoration on the mesh became sparser. The fashion required more frivolous sleeve ruffles, or *engageantes*, caps, lappets and frills, so that the laces became more suitable for gatherings. Sometimes only the edge of the reseau was decorated prettily and a few dots were sprinkled over the fine mesh. Gone was the need for bold designs that needed to be laid flat for maximum effect, with the result that the Venetian lace industry was seriously threatened by the success of these lighter fashionable French laces. However, the Italians did produce one new lace in the early eighteenth century which was the only Italian needlelace with a reseau. *Point de Venise à reseau* was very much lighter than their earlier laces with dainty patterns and elaborate fillings on a fine

11. (Top) French needlelace at the transition stage from Italian design, with raised work and hexagonal mesh ground. French, *c.* 1700.
(Bottom) *Point de France* with exquisite buttonholed design and a variety of fillings. Made in Sedan. French, first quarter of eighteenth century.

12. (Top) Detail from *Point d'Argentan* lappet showing firm hexagonal reseau. French, *c.* 1725–50.
(Centre) Point d'Argentan border with loosely overstitched reseau. French, last quarter of eighteenth century.
(Bottom) Point d'Alençon border showing needle-made single twisted reseau. French, *c.* 1750–75.

13. (Top) Brussels *point de gaze:* part of a flounce with finely drawn and shaded flowers, leaves and ferns. Brussels, third quarter of nineteenth century. (Bottom) Brussels mixed lace, showing main outlines worked with bobbin-made tape, surrounded by vertical rows of twisted needle-made ground and an exceptional variety of buttonholed fillings and raised work. Brussels, third quarter of nineteenth century.

reseau made in horizontal rows. It was this lace that was later copied by the Burano Lace School.

Flemish Needlelace

Brussels was mainly famous for its bobbin laces but some needle point was made from about 1720. It was similar to French needlelace but the overwhelming difference was in the quality of the very fine thread, which resulted in a lighter lace. Its designs were mainly floral and exceptionally pretty and, until the middle of the eighteenth century, it had a simple twisted ground similar to *point d'Alençon*, with less raised work and only a loosely buttonholed cordonnet. From the 1760s the flower motifs were surrounded by a bobbin-made reseau, with four plaits to two sides of a very tiny hexagon, known as *vrai droschel* ground.

Nineteenth-century Needlelace

At the close of the eighteenth century, machines had been invented in England to produce fine netting, which suddenly made it possible to speed up the manufacture of net-based laces so rapidly that serious hand-made lace was no longer fashionable, except for the very wealthy. Laces were decorated with separate bobbin or needle-made flower motifs, which were stitched or stuck onto the net, and some extremely pretty effects were achieved (**19** *top*). Vast quantities of flounces, veils, stoles etc. were made and continued to be fashionable for most of the nineteenth century. As they were so much cheaper to produce, more people were able to afford them. However, there was a gap of two generations when muslin was more fashionable than lace, although attempts were made to revive hand-made lace.

Sadly, the real French lace industry had ended with the Revolution at the end of the eighteenth century. However, some *point d'Alençon* was made after the muslin fashion of the Empire period, and it was the Empress Eugénie who led the fashion for lace in the French court. The new *point d'Alençon* had quite a new character with flamboyant and romantic flower sprays, in keeping with the mood of the mid-nineteenth century and was mostly beautifully made.

At the 1851 Crystal Palace Exhibition, a new Brussels needlelace was launched in order to prevent the Flemish hand-made tradition from being totally submerged by the cheaper appliqué work, and as a rival to the exquisite Alençon lace. It was frivolous and pretty, with romantic floral designs which were skilfully drawn. Each spray was finely stitched and made separately with realistic shading to the flowers which were then surrounded by a very fine gauze, providing the name *point de gaze* (**13** *top*). Its popularity was outstanding and production soon overtook the French lace in quantity. Towards the end of the century, raised rose petals became a distinctive characteristic of this lace, giving it its other name of rose point.

At the same time, a mixed Brussels lace was developed, being a bobbin lace with needle-made fillings and often exquisite details (**13** *bottom*). Later in the century this was more cheaply produced by inserting medallions of *point de gaze*, perhaps with a rose spray, at strategic intervals in a Brussels duchesse bobbin lace for flounces, collars, parasols and fans etc.

The Venetian needlelace industry was given new life in the third quarter of the nineteenth century when a fashion was started for a revival of the old laces. A group of lacemakers on the island of Burano near Venice were encouraged to start making needlelace in order to earn a living during a time of miserable unemployment. A lace school was soon flourishing there, and an abundance of very fine copies of the seventeenth-century needlepoint lace was made. Sometimes it is difficult to distinguish the copy from the original, but as with all really old things, it is usually possible to feel the difference. Other needlelaces were also copied, for instance *point d'Alençon*, but the reseau usually had a distinctive, slightly cloudy appearance, due to the quality of the flax thread. Always, the genuine old laces retained their superiority.

More recently, at the turn of this century, a group of artists and craftsmen in Bologna formed *Aemilia Ars*, an organization to revise old crafts which continued operation into the 1920s. Reticella and *punto in aria* were their bestknown pieces. They also produced some filet.

A number of lace centres were formed in Vienna in the third quarter of the nineteenth century and some very fine laces were made, based on the old Venetian and French. Some were shown in the Paris International Exhibition in 1878, and the Vienna Lace School was then opened. This inspired lacemakers in other countries. The Art Nouveau movement had started in Switzerland and this very attractive style, with its emphasis on stylized flower motifs, lent itself very well to lace.

Little lace was made in Ireland in the eighteenth century and then it was mainly by a few keen amateurs who competed for coveted prizes awarded by the Dublin Society and charitable organizations. However, by the second quarter of the nineteenth century the Dublin Normal Lace School was founded and a lace industry developed which brought a great deal of relief to workers at the time of the potato famine. A rector's wife in Tynan, County Armagh, was inspired by a piece of old Venetian lace and opened a centre where needlelace

was made to such a high standard that it was shown at the 1851 Great Exhibition. The first convent lace school, in Youghal, County Cork, was opened in 1852 by nuns inspired by old lace. The lace, produced by talented children, usually had flat stylized flowers with intricate, interesting fillings, and was of an exceptionally high quality. New Ross in County Wexford, the other convent school, copied early Italian cutwork, *gros point* and flat point and later made fine copies of the smaller Venetian needlelace. In 1865 lace was made from locally grown flax thread at Innishmacsaint, County Fermanagh; it became a thriving industry for a number of years (**14**).

John Ruskin and a group of artist friends formed a craft centre in the Lake District in the 1890s. It is mainly famous for the needlelace copied from the sixteenth-century reticella, now known as Ruskin lace.

There was also an important revival in the popularity of filet, which had not been made in any serious quantity since the seventeenth century except as an amateur pastime. Nearly all was copied from the earlier designs, the majority with religious or mythological figures, stylized animals and flowers. It was mainly for domestic use as bedspreads and tablecloths, usually made in squares alternating with squares of white embroidered muslin, reminiscent of the seventeenth century. Dentate filet edgings were made for trimming underclothes and household linens well into the twentieth century.

Needlemaking

The exceptionally fine needlework and exquisite laces that have survived from so long ago should prompt us to wonder about the needles that made them possible.

In the Middle Ages, needles were made from iron, and needlemakers in England settled in areas where iron ore was readily available. From about AD 1200 a needle-making centre was established at Redditch in the Midlands. Usually the needles were made in the craftsmen's cottages and each laborious stage of the production was carried out by one man and his family. The process began with flat sheets of iron which were then cut into thin strips. They were then rounded with a hammer and rubbed down with sand and water into a thin wire, then cut into the required needle lengths. These were then pointed at one end and 'eyed' at the other, a lengthy process. After this tight bundles of needles were wrapped in a bag with pebbles, placed under a board, and rolled underfoot for polishing.

Needles were also brought into London from abroad, mainly from Germany, until the mid-sixteenth century

14. Detail from a needlelace collar showing Venetian inspiration with separately worked stylized flower heads linked with picoted brides, probably made at Innishmacsaint. Irish, third quarter of nineteenth century.

15. *(above)* Detail from a household linen border: a profusion of stylized flowers and foliage in a variety of built-up knots and stitches give a new texture. German, early eighteenth century.

16. *(left)* Linen sampler with 33 variations of pulled and drawn work, cutwork and reticella, buttonhole and flat embroidery, all on a single panel. English, early seventeenth century.

when an Act of Parliament prevented their importation. John G. Rollins, in his booklet *Needlemaking* tells us:

> Queen Elizabeth I, realizing that her realm was techno-logically backward, covertly encouraged her nobles to install foreign craftsmen on their estates. She did not want these foreign artisans set up in London where their activities could be monitored by their own ambassadors, but pre-ferred that they should work quietly in the provinces alongside native craftsmen who could learn from them.

Spanish craftsmen brought Arab techniques with them for producing steel needles which were highly prized. They were harder than the iron ones, as a result of a firing process which also made them more resilient.

Norman needlemaking families settled in the Mid-lands and introduced a new idea to needle production. Whereas up until then each craftsman had completed the entire process himself, these Frenchmen lived in rows of cottages and each family was responsible for one stage of development. Bundles of needles passed

from one cottage to the next, through a small hatch by the fireplace – the finished article emerging at the end of the row. The whole process constituted an early production line.

By the seventeenth century, water-driven machines were invented for pointing and polishing which speeded up the manufacture process considerably, making Redditch needles recognized as the best in the world. A century later a dry-grinding machine became the ancestor of the more mechanized industry of the nine-teenth century. We should be grateful to those crafts-men who created the forerunners of the needles we take for granted today.

WHITEWORK

Sixteenth to Eighteenth Centuries

We must now return our thoughts to the sixteenth cen-tury and follow the development of whitework em-broidery. White linen-on-linen embroidery was used ex-tensively throughout Europe to decorate church and household linens, shirts and underclothes.

Before the pattern books appeared the newest designs were recorded on examplers, or samplers, many of which have survived to give us a rich source of historical evidence of the very high standards achieved. The workers themselves divided long, narrow, vertical panels of linen into neat horizontal rows showing various de-signs for decorative borders, beautifully worked. Some early sixteenth century samplers were in silk on linen, but the majority from the seventeenth century were plain white linen on linen and were used to advertise and exchange patterns of cutwork, drawn-and-pulled work, needlepoint and other embroidery stitches (**16**). As we have seen from the evolution of needlelace, these designs were all constricted to geometric form as they followed the woven threads of the linen ground. All over Europe, mainly narrow borders were used to decorate caps, kerchiefs, collars and wristbands, and narrow decorative insertions were made at the seams of garments and bed linen. Some designs overlap with lace and some were used in conjunction with lace.

As soon as the first printed pattern books were published in Germany in the second quarter of the sixteenth century, followed by the Italian, French and later by the English, the samplers were no longer essential to the embroiderers and became a suitable pastime for ladies, and also were made by children. These were lovingly preserved by their families and indeed, a large amount of the English whitework from the period survives in this form.

By the end of the sixteenth and early seventeenth century, the linen was cut in bolder, less rigid designs and the spaces filled with a variety of simple buttonholing and more elaborate *punto in aria*; this was mainly for altar cloths and household linen cloths usually with *punto in aria* or bobbin lace borders. Whitework was made from patterns in the same way as needlelace. Fine linen was tacked to the parchment backing, which had the design drawn on to show through; the outline was then worked, followed by the fillings. As we have already seen from the needlelace beginnings, the designs were thus released from the geometric, providing enormous scope for the embroiderer's imagination. If we look again at the fine cover (5), this time with particular interest in the whitework squares, we can see that by the beginning of the seventeenth century very imaginative embroidery was worked on finer and more delicate linen fabric, often incorporating needlelace fillings to cut-outs in the design. Note the tiny beady-eyed birds, the caterpillar and the minutely detailed bee.

By now it was no longer necessary to cut the cloth or draw the threads together to provide interest; bold designs could be filled with a variety of built-up stitches to create a pleasing texture (15). This was used in the decoration of bed linen, but gentlemen's white linen or twill waistcoats had begun to be superbly decorated in this way, especially in Germany, Holland and England.

Hitherto, only the borders of garments and the parts that were to be seen had been decorated, but the new fashion for muslin aprons and kerchiefs provided a new challenge. Very delicate floral decoration on fine fabric led to a new look in whitework. Profusely patterned items were made to rival the exceptionally fine bobbin laces made in France and Brussels in the 1720s and 1730s. The first of these were very flat and densely worked and produced in Saxony. This extraordinarily imaginative drawn-and-pulled work came to be known as Dresden work, as this city was the main despatch point to other parts of Europe. Wonderful lappets, double sleeve ruffles or *engageantes*, and fichu borders (17) were made from fine linen, drawn, pulled and stitched in dense patterns with a profusion of different fillings in an all-over design, alike on both sides. The design was traced onto the material which was placed in a frame and the needle was passed from side to side, a technique similar to that of the early sixteenth century but on an incredibly fine scale. Its great distinction was the extraordinary versatility of the fillings. Dresden work dominated the whitework of the mid-eighteenth century and was copied in other parts of Europe, notably Scandinavia and England, but never seriously challenged.

Tambour Work and Traditional Embroidery

In the third quarter of the eighteenth century, muslin began to be imported into Europe from India, together with an embroidery technique which was to become

17. Detail from Dresden work fichu border. This embroidery is almost completely flat and relies solely on the versatility of the fillings for its immense charm. German, mid-eighteenth century.

18. Portrait of George Campton Courthope with his sister Emily Courthope seated, wearing a plain white muslin dress. English school, c. 1825.

most popular throughout the next century. A fine chain stitch produced with the use of a very small hook on muslin stretched over a tambour or frame became known as tambour work. The hook was held beneath the frame and the loops of thread were pulled through to the top of the fabric, so the work was far more easily and quickly produced than embroidery with a needle.

However, some countries continued to use the original geometric designs, which have remained their traditional embroidery for costume and household linens. In Denmark, the peasant Hedebo work has been used for linen shirt collars, fronts and wristbands, and for wall hangings and friezes from the sixteenth century. Similarly, Norwegian Hardanger embroidery was also used widely for decorating items, such as the neck and wristbands of traditional wedding shirts.

Nineteenth-century Whitework

The beginning of the nineteenth century saw another lull in the fashion for lace, and the high-waisted muslin dresses (18) of the Regency period provided ample scope

for delicate all-over embroidery of scattered flower sprays and leaves. A great amount of this whitework, known as sewed muslin, was produced by amateur ladies with the needle and tambour hook but it was also made professionally.

A flax-growing and linen-weaving industry had been started in Scotland c. 1800 and during the first quarter of the century, workers from the continent settled first in Glasgow and Paisley, then in Ayrshire and later spread to Ireland. They produced an exceptionally fine whitework, embroidered on a very fine but firmer muslin, which became known as Ayrshire work and was the most highly skilled white embroidery done in the nineteenth century.

The 1830s saw a fashion for double pelerine capes and collars which were perfect for showing off the embroiderer's art. By now the patterns were traced on thin cartridge paper, pricked round with a number of

pin pricks and laid firmly on the muslin for blue powder
to be rubbed through the holes. Separate pieces were
very often embroidered by the workers in their cottages
and later assembled. The main characteristics of Ayrshire embroidery were the very finely detailed flowers,
ferns, scrolls etc, and minutely buttonholed dentate
edges. The centres of the flowers in the design were
usually cut away and filled with needlepoint lace in
great variety. When the pelerine collars became unfashionable, the work was almost solely used for
superb babies' gowns and bonnets, many of which have
survived. The V-shaped bodice fronts and tiny frilled
sleeves were perfect for this small-scale embroidery. The
long skirts had triangular front panels of Ayrshire work
bordered with tiny dentate frills. The small caps usually
had elaborate crowns of Ayrshire work with beautiful
needle fillings.

Decorated Net

Machine-made nets that had been invented in England
and used in fashion since the turn of the century also
made a useful ground for both tambour work and
needle-run embroidery. Two new centres, at Carrickmacross and Limerick, were established in Ireland
where decorated net was produced in large quantities.

19. *(above)* (Top) Detail
from a bonnet veil with
needlelace flower spray
appliqué. Brussels, third
quarter of nineteenth
century.
(Bottom) Detail from a fine
net pelerine collar with
Limerick needle-run
embroidery showing typical
fillings, with bobbin-lace
border. Irish, second quarter
of nineteenth century.

20. (Top) Detail from a
small table mat with raised
satin stitch embroidery and
closely knotted fillings to the
flowers. France, or
Switzerland, last quarter of
nineteenth century.
(Bottom) *Broderie anglaise*
cuff showing bold cut-out
holes, some with Ayrshire
needlepoint fillings. Probably
Irish, last quarter of
nineteenth century.

From 1820 a special muslin appliqué lace, Carrick macross quipure, was made by tacking fine muslin onto a paper pattern. The design was first outlined with a thick thread as in early needle laces then over-stitched and joined together with buttonholed bars, before cutting away the unwanted muslin. The design was usually floral, and very delicate, most suitable for bridal wear. An alternative known as Carrickmacross appliqué had the flowers applied to a machine-made net, and the design varied with needlework fillings. Later in the decade, because labour was extremely cheap in Ireland at this time of great poverty, another centre was opened by an Englishman in Limerick, where they specialized in tamboured net and also produced their own needle-embroidered net with extremely pretty fillings (19 *bottom*). These muslin, appliqué, tamboured and embroidered nets provided an even cheaper alternative to lace appliqué nets. They were produced in varying forms in other parts of Europe and thus made available an undreamed-of variety of flouncing, fichus, bonnet veils, stoles and bridal wear, to women who had never before been able to afford frivolous clothes.

Popular Techniques

The bold new fashions of the second half of the century provided scope for three less-skilled techniques which were to remain popular for several generations. *Broderie anglaise* was a coarse hand-embroidered cotton largely used to trim the hems of full-skirted dresses and petticoats. The bold patterns were printed in rows on loom widths of fabric; usually huge daisy flowers with punched-out petals and leaves, which were buttonholed around. Strips were carefully cut away, as required, along buttonholed scalloped edges. This work was also used for children's dresses, collars and cuffs. The small cuff (20 *bottom*) also shows *broderie anglaise* combined with Ayrshire fillings, which is bold and effective.

Richelieu work also relied on cut-out design for its texture, but unlike *broderie anglaise* the design was buttonholed around the printed pattern first and then the background was cut away. Sometimes buttonholed bars held the design together; this was generally used to decorate household linens.

Unlike the previous techniques, Mountmellick work had no cut-outs but relied entirely on the exceptional knobbly texture of very thick, coarse cotton on a heavy cotton ground. Delightful rustic brambles and other fruit motifs were used on bedspreads, pillow-shams, sachets, runners and other domestic items, usually with added fringeing.

From the middle of the century, machines making whitework embroidery in France and Switzerland were also producing large quantities of pretty borders for underclothes, children's clothes and household linens. There remained a very few highly skilled workers, in those countries, who carried on the tradition of exquisitely embroidered muslin. The dainty little mat (20 *top*) has a beautifully worked flower design with raised knots. This, and very fine handkerchiefs with exceptionally close embroidery, were typical of the items produced for the very wealthy. However, as we have already seen from the story of lace through the nineteenth century, the advent of the machine also resulted in the sad decline of whitework. It was no longer possible to produce hand-made items in sufficient quantity to satisfy the clearly increased demand and so the old skills gradually died. The last word should perhaps, lie with John Ruskin:

The whole value of lace as a possession depends on the fact of its having a beauty which has been the reward of industry and attention. That the thing is itself a price—a thing everybody cannot have. That it proves, by the look of it, the ability of the maker; that it proves, by the rarity of it, the dignity of the wearer . . . If they all chose to have lace, too, if it ceases to be a price, it becomes, does it not, only a cobweb?

——————— BIBLIOGRAPHY ———————

Brooke, M. L. *Lace in the Making*, London 1923
Caulfield, S. F. A., B. C. Saward and A. W. Cowen *The Dictionary of Needlework*, 2nd edn, London 1972
King, D. *Samplers*, London 1960
Klickman, F. (ed.) *The Cult of the Needle*, London 1914
Levey, S. *Discovering Embroidery of the Nineteenth Century*, Princes Risborough, Buckinghamshire, 1979
——*Lace: A History*, Leeds, W. Yorkshire, 1983
Lewis, F. *Lace*, Florence 1980
Longfield, A. K. *Guide to the Collection of Lace: National Museum of Ireland*, Dublin 1970
May, F. L. *Hispanic Lace and Lace Making*, Hispanic Society of America, New York 1939
Rollins, J. G. *Needlemaking*, Princes Risborough, Buckinghamshire, 1981
Simeon, M. *The History of Lace*, London 1979; Totowa, NJ., 1979
Swain, M. *Ayrshire and Other Whitework*, Princes Risborough, Buckinghamshire, 1982
Symonds, M., and L. Preece *Needlework Through the Ages*, London 1928
Synge, L. *Antique Needlework*, Poole, Dorset, 1982
Walk, E. *Drawn Fabric Embroidery*, London 1979

ECCLESIASTICAL NEEDLEWORK

LANTO SYNGE

Religious devotion and conviction has been the inspiration for many of the greatest works of art, in the East, the West, the New World and developing countries where missionary zeal has revived artistic fervour of a spiritual kind. Indeed man has devoted his most serious efforts to expressing and creating wonders in art as a measure of his relationship with God and his piety.

The origins of fine textiles lie in the East and it is not surprising that the Bible contains a number of references to fine fabrics, dyes and costume. There are accounts of temple hangings, some of them no doubt of rich embroidery, and particularly well known is the account of Moses' veil in front of the tabernacle: 'blue and purple and crimson and wrought with cherubims thereon'.

From early in the Christian era weaving and embroidery were significant for enriching holy places and were especially valuable for their pictorial didactic qualities, being richly illustrative of narrative events, as were stained glass, murals and sculpture. Every church inevitably possessed decorations of these educative forms and the greater ones were very rich in them.

The earliest Christian remains include some remarkable Coptic embroideries of the seventh to tenth centuries, found in burial grounds in Egypt (2). The example illustrated shows in a roundel the Annunciation by the angel Gabriel and also the Visitation to the Virgin Mary, within a border of flowers of timeless design. The needlework, in satin stitch, covers the linen ground densely and the vitality of the drawing is enhanced by the changing directions of the stitching. Four small panels in the Cleveland Museum of Art depict Christian figures, including the Crucifixion. These were part of the decoration of a Coptic tunic of the sixth to seventh century.

Christianity first arrived in Britain in the Roman period, but when the power of Rome declined and the legions were withdrawn, the country and its Celtic population were left open to invasion in the fifth and sixth centuries AD by the pagan Anglo-Saxons. The newcomers were evangelized, in the south by St Augustine from Rome, who carried with him a banner embroidered with the image of Christ, and in the north by Celtic missionaries. From about the seventh century AD, Christianity became the chief stimulus to artistic expression in England. Anglo-Saxon rulers instigated and encouraged crafts and skills for the enrichment of churches and monasteries. So strongly was Christianity established in the Anglo-Saxon kingdoms that they were able to absorb and convert fresh waves of pagan invaders in Viking times. Needlework was a cherished prowess of Anglo-Saxon women, especially of noble and privileged position. There are several records of gifts made by such women, such as St Etheldreda,

1. (opposite) Part of a fine *opus anglicanum* orphrey cross showing the Crucifixion with the background worked in gold thread. English, c. 1320.

2. (above) Woolwork roundel depicting the Annunciation and Visitation. Coptic, c. seventh to tenth centuries.

Abbess and patron saint of Ely (d.AD 679) who offered St Cuthbert a stole and maniple which was finely embroidered by herself.

The earliest surviving piece of needlework in Western Europe is the much deteriorated remnant of an English chasuble at Maaseik in Belgium. Of Anglo-Saxon workmanship of about the middle of the ninth century AD, it must have once been spectacular, with coloured silks, gilt thread, and seed pearls, depicting birds, animals and monograms in interlacing roundels. The design appears to be related to the illumination of manuscripts, and this points to the fact that monks may have been responsible for the preparation of ecclesiastical needlework in the same way that it was their duty to design and oversee the construction and decoration of their abbeys. The tenth-century Archbishop of Canterbury, St Dunstan, for example is known to have designed embroideries.

Remarkable and beautiful survivals of about AD 909–16 are the stole and maniple (4) discovered in 1827 in the tomb of St Cuthbert at Durham cathedral. Both have inscriptions indicating that they were made by Queen Aelfflaed, wife of Edward the Elder, for Bishop Frithstan of Winchester. It is likely that they were made in monastery workshops in that city, then the West Saxon capital. They depict saints with inscriptions; the stole is embroidered with the agnus dei and the maniple with the hand of God issuing from clouds. The figures on both pieces are finely worked, but are of a stiff hieratic nature, Byzantine in feeling, and showing no signs of the expressiveness that was to be the special characteristic of later English work.

Other fine needlework continued to be made by noble ladies for ecclesiastical purposes and there are records of them contributing costly textile treasures for pious use. In the eleventh century, Queen Emma, wife successively of Ethelred the Unready, and King Canute, embroidered many vestments and altar cloths, and King Canute's second Queen, among other gifts, donated an altar hanging with a gold border to the Abbey of Ely. The writings of William of Malmesbury show that King Edward the Confessor's wife embroidered the mantle for his coronation in 1042.

On the continent the decorative arts reflected influence from distant lands and, following exchanges of trade and art, exotic motifs derived from imported fabrics were brought into designs. The coronation mantle of King Roger II of Sicily (1130–54) was executed in the King's Wardrobe in Palermo in about 1133 (see p. 13). It is much more Muslim in appearance than Christian with superb gold-embroidered animals on a red silk ground, and further enriched with pearls,

enamels and precious stones. The animals are paired heraldically, and stylized in Middle Eastern fashion, in this case depicting lions overcoming camels. The Arabic feeling is confirmed by a thin border of script. Equally fascinating and very bizarre in spirit is the so-called Mantle of Charlemagne of the late twelfth century which is also Sicilian. This mantle is Byzantine in appearance with large displayed eagles worked in gold, silver and silk embroidery on a silk ground. It is clearly based on Mesopotamian or Persian models but is edged with orphreys (the embroidered bands on vestments) of the traditional Christian form.

Opus Anglicanum

The high period of English medieval ecclesiastical needlework, however, is marked by the unique co-ordination of artistic and technical achievement that came together between monks who carried out designs, and professional workshops and craftsmen, usually men working mainly in Winchester and London. The vestments which were conceived and created there are among the chief glories of European needlework. Known as opus anglicanum (English work), these superb pieces were famed abroad and were the envy of popes and princes. Their quality has never been surpassed and vestments made especially around the period 1250–1350 are decorated with embroidery that is arguably the finest English needlework of all time.

The qualities of opus anglicanum were essentially two-fold. Firstly the materials used were beautiful; the embroidery was of silk worked on twill-weave silk lined with linen or on samit, taffeta, satin or camcoa (a combination of fine camel hair and wool). Secondly the design, layout, and the religious portraiture were developed by some of the finest draughtsmen – monks with exceptional artistic talents, and admirably suited to their medium. From a technical point of view, the use of underside couching, whereby gold and silk threads were attached to the material by small loops from the underneath, led to a great versatility of working. Also, the embroidery itself was executed in coloured silks worked in minute split stitch which enabled the sewer to achieve great accuracy in shading and an extraordinary degree of expressiveness.

The general designs of opus anglicanum vestments developed through several basic forms. Firstly, patterns were geometric with flowing circles containing figures or scenes. Subsequently, these became more florid and complex with different shaped panels, interflowing and comparable with the divisions in stained glass windows. Thirdly, the design might be in the form of the Tree of

3. The cope of the Passion (*opus anglicanum*) with a gold thread background. English, *c.* 1300.

Life, or Stem of Jesse pattern, with saints and narrative vignettes bound together by a scrolling branch formation. The last method of linking subjects was to show them within an orderly framework of pointed arches or niches, like sculpture on the walls of Gothic cathedrals. They were placed in rows on altar frontals, in vertical columns on orphreys or in radiating arcs on copes. These various design formats became conventions that were interchangeable though seldom combined in any one item. The cope of the Passion from St Bertrand de Comminges (3) is a charming and magnificent example of *opus anglicanum*; this shows within circles a number of saints in elegant expressive postures. The roundels are joined by smaller ones, each containing beautifully depicted birds, making the vestment more decorative, but not lessening the poignancy of the chief illustration which depicts scenes of the Crucifixion story. The delicacy of design and execution is outstanding and this must be one of the finest survivals of the early fourteenth century. Like all vestments of the period it has been altered somewhat and has been cut down so that parts of the design are missing. The vast majority of medieval vestments were destroyed in the Reformation or subsequently lost through wear; many were cut and the good parts altered for new use; some were carefully reconstructed as far as possible. A cope at Pienza and another from Steeple Aston, Oxfordshire, have silver-gilt backgrounds. Only fragments of the

one from Steeple Aston survive, but these are most beautiful, extremely charming in design and of soft, subtle colours. The Clare chasuble of a few decades earlier is characterized by the blue satin ground over which are embroidered neat but languid scrolling tendrils containing animals, while the front contains a group of scenes within cruciforms. The beautiful Jesse cope (5) depicts an elegant tendril pattern embroidered on a red silk twil ground. The recumbent figure of Jesse gives birth to a large number of descendants linked within curling vine branches. The Syon cope is in a remarkable state of preservation, albeit cut, altered and pieced together. It shows Passion scenes and saints within cruciforms and between them neat, formalized angels; the cope is borrdered with heraldic lozenges and circles. The Butler Bowden cope, of the second quarter of the fourteenth century, is an example of later *opus anglicanum*. Its complex design perhaps shows a weakening of style though the quality of workmanship and drawing remain of the highest rank. On this cope the figures are enclosed by foliate Gothic arches while a long orphrey is embroidered with a formal hieratic and jewel-like precision. Another chasuble adapted from a cope of a comparable kind is in the Metropolitan Museum of New York (7).

Orphreys were especially a focus for exquisite illustrative needlework and they were often applied and re-applied many times over to new vestments. Some magnificent examples have survived. The details of a remarkable one (8) depicts the Crucifixion of our Lord flanked by Mary and John against a background of gold

4. Part of the maniple found in the tomb of St Cuthbert, depicting St John the Baptist. English, 909–16.

drain on resources caused by the Hundred Years War, together with the domestic unrest in England itself. Quicker and cheaper methods of workmanship introduced from the continent had a new appeal, with bolder raised needlework of a more sculptural quality, but much less refinement in detail. There was also an increasing use of fine imported fabrics, figured damasks and velvets (6) from Italy. These were sometimes combined with *opus anglicanum* but the combination was not entirely satisfactory. At the same time there was a weakening of standards both in design and in manufacture. The drawing did not have the natural manner or the same charm of needle-painting and the skills used became somewhat less refined. To some extent the needlework had now become more formalized and stiff, unadventurously following continental conventions, with stereotyped imagery and repetitive patterns that included strapwork and floral motifs more suited to weaving than to embroidery. It seems that the remarkable artists had moved to other fields; figures were now often merely pricked out and pounced, a quicker and cheaper method than drawing directly and individually on to the ground material. Such short cuts as these were inevitable as a result of the excessive demands for English vestments. The embroidery itself also suffered in quality; later pieces can be seen to be worked in long and short, brick and satin stitches replacing finer embroidery. Surface couching was substituted for the more laborious underside couching and the characteristic tiny split stitch of the thirteenth century was replaced by stem stitch.

Other Remarkable Vestments

The demands for fine vestments were prodigious. The inventory of Lincoln cathedral listed over 600 vestments, all of the embroidered, and some encrusted with jewels. There were also mitres and other items, frequently of elaborate needlework, and sometimes bejewelled or decorated with pearls and seed pearls. English embroidery enjoyed extraordinary fame and, as already indicated, was treasured throughout Europe. Even in the thirteenth century Pope Innocent III saw certain vestments and orphreys and on being told that they originated in this country he exclaimed: 'Surely England must be a garden of delight.'

A remarkable set of vestments of the mid-fifteenth century is that of the Order of the Golden Fleece, probably made in Brussels and commissioned by the

thread. *Opus anglicanum* was seen, at its best from 1250 to 1350, during which time the making of vestments had become an important and lucrative industry catering for domestic and foreign orders, and paid for by rich ecclesiastical foundations, the nobility and prosperous merchants. The high standard in English workshops was founded on seven-year apprenticeships and a continuity of experience. Most of the embroiderers were male professionals, but nuns too carried out some work especially under the guidance of monks, and they also did repairs and restoration work. The vestments were sent to Flanders, France and Italy, and it is known that the Vatican in Rome had more English needlework than any other. Pope Boniface VIII made gifts of English embroidery, and is known to have held it in great esteem.

The Black Death of 1348 can roughly be said to mark the end of the flowering of *opus anglicanum*. It cost embroidery workshops, as all the other trades, horrible decimation. Another factor was the general

5. Detail of the Tree of Jesse cope showing one of the descendants, depicted within curling vine branches. English, c. 1300.

6. Chasuble of blue velvet with an orphrey cross, angels, eagles and rose slips. English, *c.* 1500.

Duke of Burgundy whose Court was renowned for its lavishness. The Duke also possessed mourning cloaks of black silk decorated with shields and his heraldic device, a fire steel with radiating flashes of sparks (7).

Heraldry played an important part in church decoration: architecture, monuments, furniture and all the furnishings were charged with coats of arms, shields, crests and badges as personal labels and for ornamentation. Vestments certainly often had such motifs on them but funeral palls especially tended to display the arms of the institution or house to which

they belonged. Religious bodies, colleges and livery companies usually owned palls which could be loaned or hired out for funerals. A few examples may be cited. The Saddlers' Company has one of crimson velvet with applied embroidery, first worked on pieces of linen, depicting angels, the sacred monogram IHS and the arms of the company. The Fishmongers' Arms of the late fifteenth century shows St Peter enthroned (he is the patron saint of fishermen) with angels, and also St Peter receiving the keys from Our Lord. The Vintners' is of Italian velvet and cloth of gold, embroidered with St Martin of Tours. Rows of kneeling figures, with a discrepancy in size usually denoting status, are a familiar feature of palls and a convention also seen on monuments and church brasses. Many churches had funeral palls St Margaret's, Westminster, charged a small fee for the use of its pall.

On the continent embroidery had a different character and was somewhat sculptural in appearance, more reminiscent of carving in wood and ivory, or of the elaborate repoussé techniques of metalwork. The padded raised forms sometimes appear cumbersome but the richness of the metal threads of different kinds and the intricate backgrounds of couched gold thread, sometimes in elaborate geometric patterns, are delightful (8) and seem to echo goldsmith's work. This technique, known as *or de chypre* was usually limited to orphreys.

Threads of Silk and Gold

Another particularly significant technique which probably originated in Flanders, but which was much used in many parts of Europe, is *or nué*. This method, 'shaded gold', allowed for a new versatility (9) in needle-painting as it enabled colours to be used in varying strengths. The

7. Cope of black velvet with the arms and fire steel device of the Duke of Burgundy. Southern Netherlands, *c.* 1475.

8. *(left)* Orphrey cross showing the Crucifixion, worked in padded relief. A rich design recalling goldsmith's work. German, late fourteenth century.

9. *(right)* Mitre with the costumes on the figures worked in the *or nué* technique. Flemish, sixteenth century.

principle of the method was a simple one; gold threads were couched down horizontally by irregularly placed coloured silk threads which gave a shaded appearance according to their density, as in painting. The effect was heightened by the metallic surface of the horizontal lines of gold thread. The straight threads of gold also gave an impression of weaving so that the needlework almost resembled tapestry, and additionally this aspect eliminated the multiple reflections caused by threads being laid at different angles. There are a number of fine survivals of *or nué* including a group of twenty-seven pieces in the Museum of Santa Maria del Fiore in Florence which were made to designs for vestments by Antonio Pollaiuolo (*c.*1431–98). Pollaiuolo was a painter and sculptor, especially in gold and silver, and it is significant that he also designed textiles. Like paintings of the period, these twenty-seven pieces show new attempts at perspective and relate in narrative form the life of St John the Baptist. Following Renaissance principles and tending towards the influence of Giotto and the theories of Florentine painters, needlework took on a new naturalism and religious scenes were depicted in more realistic terms. Figures began to reflect human nature and were more subtle than mere symbols of religious passion. A fine set of vestments of 1554 from Averbode Abbey, Brabant, South Netherlands, is typical of the best quality needlework in the Renaissance mode (10). These have deep orphrey bands

10. Cope from Averbode Abbey. Bands of embroidery illustrate the life of St Matthew. Southern Netherlands, 1554.

decorated with formalized scrolling foliage, grotesque masks, flowers and fruit, around large medallions depicting narrative subjects in superbly worked detail.

The Renaissance itself brought about great changes in religious thinking and an element of secularization that made the religious piety of the medieval period appear to be superstitious mysticism of ignorant Dark Ages. At the same time the Reformation in England caused the Roman church a substantial loss of spiritual and temporal power and brought about a new independence and secularization in social life. Revolutionary zeal in search of new truths cast out the old ways of life and it is a terrible thought to contemplate the iconoclasm that took place in ruining churches and abbeys. One dreads to contemplate how quantities of magnificent *opus anglicanum* were burned and the gold thread melted down for its material value.

With these two enormously significant developments both temperamental and political, the same importance was never again to be attached to ecclesiastical needlework, though good quality vestments of a less individual kind continued to be made from the sixteenth century onwards. These were bound much more by convention and though many were of very fine workmanship they did not compare with the earlier ones which were true works of art. Good sets of both seventeenth- and eighteenth-century vestments have survived in relatively large numbers and fine examples may be seen in many museums.

The technique of *or nué* continued in use well into the seventeenth century and was employed by Charles I's embroiderer, Edmund Harrison (1589–1666). He may have been trained in Flanders and was certainly a master of the technique. Of the many works that he supervised for the court, only some of his religious pictures survive. These are worked in silk on canvas and are in the manner of paintings; the figures were done separately and applied to the ground fabric giving them a slightly raised relief quality. His three pictures entitled 'The Visitation', 'The Betrothal' and 'The Adoration' were made for William Howard, Lord Stafford and are dated 1637.

Although we can inspect closely the few survivals of medieval ecclesiastical vestments, looking at paintings can also be invaluable. Often textiles and embroidery are depicted in minute detail and clarity and there is no reason to believe that they are not true portrayals of specific garments, in the same way that Elizabethan painters are known to have depicted real costumes very precisely.

There was a revival of ecclesiastical needlework in the seventeenth century. Archbishop Laud took office in 1633 and was instrumental in introducing High Church traditions, advocating stylized church decoration including the use of fine needlework. Several survivals of this period show an extensive use of metal thread on velvet grounds and often incorporate motifs that are not especially religious but more a feature of late Baroque decoration, such as fat cupids, sun-burst patterns and architectural forms.

Work became more pictorial and decorative with freer subjects replacing the harrowing details of the Passion, and the use of larger areas of bright colours. There was almost a sense of humour in the portrayal of the animals procession into Noah's ark as depicted in bright floss silks on a late seventeenth-century Italian altar frontal.

Much church embroidery from this period and throughout the eighteenth century shows a greater use of pattern, as opposed to picture, with contrasting stitches in silks and metal threads, and cheerful colouring. Flowers in formal and naturalistic forms also feature to a large extent and the feeling is of sophisticated decoration, much more suited to Protestantism than an almost morbid adherence to high Catholic piety.

Religious Motifs in Secular Embroidery

As a new class of wealthy merchants, manufacturers and entrepreneurs assumed the ability to patronize the luxury trades, hitherto the prerogative of the nobility of church and state, the attention of professional and

amateur embroiderers moved away from ecclesiastical display to sumptuous decoration within private households. Domestic riches were the hallmark of success and power, and patronage was directed towards a proud display of wealth in the building and furnishing of great houses. Religious iconography and metaphor, however, continued to be significant subjects; the old familiar stories being a favourite topic for constantly varied treatment in many art forms, just as much as those of the much-loved classical heroes of Ovid and Virgil. The engraved illustrations of Gerard de Jode's *Thesaurus Sacrarum Historiarum Veteris Testamenti* (Antwerp 1585) were, for example, much used, copied and adapted, for canvas-work domestic furnishings. By the late sixteenth century, beds, valances, cushions and larger hangings would show scenes from Bible stories, sometimes individually, sometimes in narrative sequence.

Around the time of Mary Queen of Scots there developed in Scotland, following a French tradition, a form of bed valance that consisted of fairly deep panels worked in tent stitch and depicting densely detailed narrative scenes, often biblical. Of complex design, these were necessarily drawn and embroidered by professional workshops. They are visually busy, often with many figures packed closely together. Usually the figures are shown in 'modern', i.e. late-sixteenth century costume; the elaborate details of ruffs, embroidered costumes, and jewellery are depicted minutely, as well as the settings – knot gardens, animals, terraces, and buildings (11). However, another form of bed hanging, perhaps marginally later in date, varied somewhat

in that it consisted of a series of scenes quite clearly derived from engravings, framed and linked by borders of flowers, fruit and animals. A set dated 1594 shows a number of rectangular panels illustrating the story of Jacob (12).

Table carpets of a similar kind of needlework were also supplied and must have been costly and highly valued. A few fine ones have survived, some showing classical scenes, but others with Bible stories, regarded as philosophical literature or quaint as much as for religious content. An entry in the 1601 inventory of Hardwick Hall, Derbyshire, notes a carpet 'of needlworke of the story of David and Saul with a golde frenge & trymmed with blew taffetic sarcenet. . .' Large cushions of similar decoration were also a feature of the lavish and sumptuous comfort that was achieved by a rich, almost profligate, use of textiles in the great houses of the new aristocracy.

Large hanging tapestries frequently depicted religious themes but sometimes colossal embroidered hangings were made as a substitute or to rival weaving. A fine set of five mid-seventeenth-century Italian hangings, in the format of tapestries, is in the Royal collection. They depict New Testament stories that include the Annunciation, the Massacre of the Innocents and Christ in the house of Simon the Leper. Each subject is derived from a painting, and each is contained within a

11. Bed valance showing elaborately dressed figures against a complicated background including formal gardens. French or English, *c.* 1590.

12. Detail from a set of bed valances showing scenes from the story of Jacob and Esau. Scottish, 1594.

border composed of arabesques, baskets of flowers and roundels with further biblical scenes. Other large Italian silk embroidered hangings depicted events in the lives of saints. An example of this type is one showing St Anthony of Padua preaching with St Francis and the Trinity above (13).

The wealthy often had private chapels in their houses and also perhaps patronized ancient churches within their estates. For both they had prayer books and Bibles bound in velvet and embroidered with heraldry or monograms. Others were covered entirely with embroidery, and sometimes carefully protected by a bag. A largish volume in the Victoria and Albert Museum, dated 1613, depicts in tent stitch Jonah and the Sacrifice of Isaac, but there were usually smaller books, mostly decorated with panels of flowers or with religious figures with a silvergilt thread background. Others had raised work in a mixture of silks and metal thread, perhaps on a velvet ground. Lastly, as made by the small community at Little Gidding, near Peterborough, there were bookbindings of silk embroidery on white satin. Some of these had floral patterns, others oval portraits or vignettes (14) within flower borders, or were worked with a high proportion of metal thread. One also finds occasional examples of covers made entirely of beadwork.

Biblical Stories

Towards the later part of the seventeenth century needlework had become an important aspect of a young girl's education and each child was expected to master several kinds of sewing and embroidery. Conventional milestones were the completion of a sampler and the perfection of embroidered pictures in tent stitch and

stumpwork, and sometimes a casket. for the last two, the subjects again were often derived from popular engravings, usually depicting well-known biblical stories, but transposed into contemporary dress and further adorned with topical images such as houses or grottoes, small animals, insects and flowers from pattern books. Most themes were taken from the Old Testament, regarded as 'historical', instead of from the New Testament — that would have seemed too close to 'graven images' for the Protestant temperament of the day. Among the most popular subjects were the History of Ahasuerus, King Solomon receiving the Queen of Sheba, the Sacrifice of Isaac, the Judgment of Solomon, and Susanna and the Elders.

Another interesting feature of these pictures, which were exceedingly finely worked by remarkably young children, is the fact that the kings and queens frequently represented are usually depicted as the late King Charles I, or the restored King Charles II, with their respective queens (15), Henrietta Maria or Catherine of Braganza. From about the beginning of the eighteenth century it seems that amateur needleworkers devoted more time to making coverings for furniture: backs and seats for chairs and stools as well as bed hangings, firescreen panels and pictures. These were frequently pictorial, especially chair backs, the seats being

13. (above) Large silk hanging of St Anthony of Padua preaching, and St Francis with the Trinity above. Italian, c. 1680.

14. Picture of Jonah and the Whale, worked in deep relief with metal threads on a velvet ground. Early seventeenth century.

15. Silk tent stitch picture of King Solomon and the Queen of Sheba with attendant figures, all represented in contemporary costume. English, mid-seventeenth century.

decorated with floral or leaf patterns. The subjects depicted were professionally drawn and derived from prints showing favourite classical or biblical stories. Large upholstered armchairs, often known as wing chairs, offered a splendid opportunity for fine embroidered coverings and many beautiful ones were made. A magnificent example in the Metropolitan Museum of Art in New York is densely covered with

images set among hillocky ground, trees and flowers. The back of the chair shows an incident from the Acts of the Apostles – the baptism of the Ethiopian eunuch by St Philip. A contemporary panel, circa 1710, probably made for a firescreen, shows exactly the same subject (16). What is especially interesting is that both the chair and the panel show the scene set amid an identical formation of trees and flowers together with a chinoiserie bird and a large exotic parrot in the composition. The St Philip scene, birds and flowers originally came from different sources but the fact that they are brought together in these two embroideries means that both

16. (above) Panel of the baptism of the Ethiopian eunuch by St Philip, and other motifs, all derived from engravings. c. 1710.

pieces of needlework must have been designed or drawn out by the same teacher, supplier or needlewoman.

Neo-classical Designs

Firescreens especially offered an opportunity for needlework, often of a purely decorative floral nature, but also sometimes with a scene. They were worked in tent stitch and many have more recently become separated from their stands and are now hung as pictures. Religious subjects remained popular motifs for working and framing as pictures, although as the century went by pastoral themes took over. By 1770, however, there was a new fashion in embroidering silk pictures, again, very often for pole firescreens. These were normally professionally drawn on silk, the flesh parts painted in and the rest left to the embroiderers to work in long and short satin stitch. They were seldom very original, frequently oval in format, and usually based on popular engravings. They were essentially neo-classical in feeling, echoing the medallions of painters such as Antonio Zucchi and Angelica Kauffmann. One difference between these and late seventeenth-century embroidered pictures is that the religious examples more often show New Testament events such as the risen Christ

17. Silk picture showing the risen Christ's meeting with Mary Magdalene in the garden. The faces and the sky are painted. Nineteenth century.

18. Woolwork picture of the Holy Family, in the style of an old master painting. The faces, hands and background are painted. Early nineteenth century.

appearing to Mary Magdalene in the garden (17). Wool embroidered pictures were also made, somewhat larger and of course more crude in workmanship, but sometimes very effective. An example of the early nineteenth century appears to imitate the style of an old master painting and elegantly depicts the Holy Family in a group reminiscent of Raphael (18).

From the early nineteenth century Berlin woolwork, a canvas embroidery worked in bright German wools, enjoyed extraordinary popularity. Pictures worked in this technique followed printed patterns exactly and were very often religious in content, reflecting the new Victorian piety that so quickly developed into prudery and sentimentality. Biblical stories were provided in thousands, in kit form, and often in colossal proportions. Of these, many were dull and unambitious but some

were elaborate and filled with historical detail. 'The Flight into Egypt' is typical of one of the most popular subjects. Others were based on well-known paintings such as Leonardo da Vinci's 'The Last Supper'; six versions were displayed at the Great Exhibition in 1851. The Berlin designs often 'improved' the masterpieces for embroidery purposes.

An Ecclesiastical Revival

From even fairly early in the nineteenth century there was a reaction against the dull standardized domestic embroidery of the Berlin fashion and equally a desire by some to seek out originality in the face of increased industrialization and general manufacturing. From about 1840 a prestigious group of architects led a considerable revival of ecclesiastical needlework. Their ambitions were to restore many aspects of medievalism; they built a large number of neo-Gothic churches and intended to furnish and decorate them in an appropriate vein and reinstate ceremonies with rich vestments.

In 1854, G. E. Street, with the help of his sister and Agnes Blencowe, founded the Ladies' Ecclesiastical Embroidery Society to provide altar cloths based on old examples, or made to modern designs supplied by architects. Among these was George Bodley whose draw-ings were closer to medieval origins than many others, in that they were largely pictorial, with figures rather than pattern alone. Bodley also commissioned work from Morris's firm and from Watts and Co., a business still operating today. There is a banner worked to his design at Peterborough cathedral. In 1841–2 A. W. Pugin, the prominent architect (and partner of Sir Charles Barry in designing the Houses of Parliament) attacked the 'prettiness' of domestic needlework in the *Dublin Review* and urged a return to serious work with 'an appropriate meaning'. He designed vestments for Roman Catholic churches and preferred a rich back-ground of velvet or cloth of gold. His set of vestments made for St Chad's cathedral, Birmingham, have a feeling of medieval richness with elaborately patterned damask and a liberal use of silver and gold thread. Sir Arthur Blomfield, another prominent architect, also designed embroideries, including some for the Radcliffe Infirmary Chapel in Oxford. Street provided designs for Newton, Jones and Willis of Birmingham, a firm that produced catalogues of designs that were popular for church furnishings for many years. But he also saw the potential of amateur embroiderers and spoke of:

> . . . the happiness which must result from employing their fingers and their eyes upon something fair and beautiful to behold instead of upon horrid and hideous patterns in cross-stitch, for foot stools, slippers, chair-covers, and the like too common objects.

Two other organizations directed towards the making of needlework for churches were the Church Extension Association and the School of Mediaeval Embroidery.

Modern Needlework

Following the cult which grew around the Arts and Crafts movement there developed again a drabness in church needlework and textile furnishings that repre-sented all too typically late Victorian taste. The Royal School of Needlework had considerable influence in exciting new ideas and stimulating work, but not very appreciably in ecclesiastical circumstances. At the

19. The Visitation, one of five panels by Beryl Dean at Windsor on the life of the Virgin Mary. English, 1973.

beginning of this century there was little development, then a world war drained Europe of resources and there was little time, money or initiative for original home or church improvements. Later, however, there was a considerable new impetus in this field and over the last fifty years a lot of good needlework has been provided for religious and especially ceremonial purposes. Many churches now have interesting and colourful hassocks for kneeling on. Mostly worked in fairly coarse canvas stitch, these make a strong and practical contribution, and with well selected colouring become a significant decoration in the often dark, sometimes dull, woodwork of church pews. Other larger panels and seat cushions, as at Wells cathedral (20) stand out against a foil of stonework in majestic surroundings. These, like kneelers, combine many kinds of pattern including heraldry,

21. Cope for the Diocese of London to mark the Queen's Silver Jubilee, 1977. Designed by Beryl Dean and executed by herself and her students at the Stanhope Institute of Adult Education.

religious motifs and narratives. The inspiration for much of this needlework spread from Winchester, as had the medieval *opus anglicanum*. At the cathedral there, in 1931, a body of about two hundred amateur embroiderers, known as the Winchester Broderers, was coordinated by Louisa Pesel on a project to make hassocks and cushions. Miss Pesel had previously done needlework for the private chapel of the Bishop of Winchester, based on seventeenth-century sampler designs. Artistically and technically she adhered to two fundamental principles, each crucial to successful embroidery: if the work is to be multi-coloured, the variety of stitches must be reasonably limited and conversely, if a variety of stitches is to be displayed, a limited range of colours should be used.

In recent years some very exciting modern needlework has been made for ecclesiastical use. Of this the most remarkable feature is a bold combination of techniques and materials making the works especially sculptural; appliqué and embroidery are used together in both angular and softer shapes and, while colours are usually carefully limited, there is a great variety of texture. Metal threads, so much a feature of *opus anglicanum* are again used extensively. Beryl Dean is well known for some remarkable pieces which combine a feeling of the times with interesting technical innovations. Modern works of art can often shock and jar, especially in conventional surroundings, but these are grand in conception and orderly in execution and fit happily into the ancient buildings they were made for. Five large panels at St George's chapel, Windsor (19)

show large figures illustrating New Testament events, all with bold seriousness, and the faces with large Byzantine eyes, but set among some gentler decorative motifs. Beryl Dean's cope, stole, mitre and morse made for the Bishop of London on the occasion of the Queen's Silver Jubilee in 1977, echo, in a collage effect of architectural motifs, a sense of the binding unity which is embodied in church and state. The design of the cope includes St Paul's cathedral and many London churches massed over each other in arc formation, so that when the vestment is worn they stand as great pillars of windows, towers, spires and cupolas. The colouring is subtle and harmonious and, unlike earlier vestments, it is limited to shades of yellow-golds and silver-greys (21).

BIBLIOGRAPHY

Carbonell, D. *Winchester Cathedral Embroideries*, Winchester, Hampshire, 1975

Freeman, M. B. *The St Martin Embroideries*, New York 1968

Hackenbrock, Y. *English and Other Needlework, Tapestries and Textiles in the Irwin Untermeyer Collection*, London 1960

Higgin, L. *Handbook of Embroidery*, ed. Lady Marion Alford, London 1880

King, D. *Opus Anglicanum*, London 1963

Macquoid, P. *A Record of the Collections of the Lady Lever Art Gallery*, Vol. III, London 1928

Wills, K. C. A. *The Quire Embroideries*, Wells, Somerset, 1976

20. The fourteenth-century choir stalls at Wells cathedral have fine modern embroidered cushions. English, c. 1937.

GLOSSARY

Blackwork (Spanish work) Monochrome embroidery, usually in black, sometimes enriched with metal threads, fashionable in sixteenth century. Brought to Europe through Spain by the Moors.

Bobbin lace Lace made by weaving with a number of threads on bobbins.

Boxers Outline figures depicted in early samplers, possibly derived from a European motif of lovers exchanging gifts; small naked or costumed boys with wings, holding up a large hand or bunch of flowers.

Burato work Woven cloth, one vertical thread interwoven with two twisted horizontal ones, with darned designs.

Burse Ecclesiastical: stiff, square pocket to contain linen cloth (corporal) used at Holy Communion; also formal bag, for example as carried by the Lord Chancellor, often elaborately embroidered and containing an official seal.

Chasuble Vestment worn by priest officiating at the Eucharist; a large almost circular garment. In the Middle Ages often magnificently embroidered; in the sixteenth century the shape altered to a long round-ended vestment, leaving the arms free of the heavy material.

Chinoiserie European imitation of Chinese decoration in laquer, needlework, etc., often recognizable by caricatured features.

Coif (quoif) Close-fitting cap worn by men and women from the Middle Ages to the early seventeenth century, latterly finely embroidered; worn on semi-formal and domestic occasions.

Col rabat Gentleman's large flat square collar of bold gros point with narrow strip of lace hidden behind the full wigs of late seventeenth century.

Cope Ecclesiastical cloak worn by dignitaries on festal occasions, a large semi-circular garment often of rich materials or fine embroidery.

Couching Technique whereby a thread is laid over fabric and attached to it by an additional one sewn over it. Technique especially used for metal threads.

Crewel (crul, cruel, crewels etc)-work Strong two-ply lightly-twisted worsted yarn of home manufacture, extensively used for domestic embroidery of hangings, furnishings and costume since the Norman Conquest.

Cut-and-drawn-work Fore-runner of needlepoint laces in sixteenth and seventeenth centuries and extensively revived in the nineteenth century. Parts of white fabric are cut away and then infilled by patterns of crossed threads with elaborate variations.

Dalmatic Ecclesiastical vestment worn by deacon at Eucharist, normally a short tunic. Also, an historic garment worn by the sovereign at coronation ceremony, and by a bishop under his chasuble.

Engageantes Shaped sleeve ruffles.

Filet Hand-knotted cloth, like a traditional fishnet, with darned designs (*see* **Lacis**).

Gros point Cross stitch. Also loosely used as term for coarser canvas work.

Lacis Handmade netting darned with patterns, with coarse lace-like appearance, but very ancient in itself, and often highly complex. Designs often in squares, of a stylized nature,

following pattern books. Also known as filet, guipure d'art, etc.

Maniple *En suite* with a stole, a shorter strip of material, sometimes embroidered, worn by a priest over his left forearm at the Eucharist. Symbolizes the towel used by Christ at the washing of the feet of His disciples.

Mantua Eighteenth-century court dress with extremely wide skirt, exaggerated hips and displaying magnificent fabric or embroidery.

Mezzo punto Boldly patterned furnishing lace made with bobbin lace tapes laid on a parchment pattern, finished with needlelace and no raised work.

Needlelace Lace made by sewing with a needle.

Or nué Shaded gold embroidery. Technique whereby gold threads are laid horizontally, couched down with coloured silk threads, at densely close intervals where dark shades are required, and sparsely for lighter areas, forming shading in a pictorial design.

Orphrey Band, usually of embroidery, superimposed in cross or 'Y' formation, or as border, on chasuble, cope, etc.

Palampores Indian dyed, painted (latterly printed) cotton hangings and covers made for export to Europe.

Passementerie Earliest narrow pointed edgings which appeared in fashion after the development of *punto in aria*.

Pillow shams Decorative cover laid over a pillow while not in use, often with whitework embroidery such as a coat-of-arms.

Point de gaze Elaborately patterned fashion lace sometimes with raised flower petals.

Point de neige Minutely detailed lace based on gros point, with layers of tiny picots to resemble snowflakes.

Point plat Flat needlelace based on gros point, but with a smaller design and no raised work, giving it a draping quality.

Pulled work Drawn thread work, sewn and embroidered.

Punto in aria Earliest form of needlelace made on a parchment pattern – literally 'stitches in the air'.

Reticella Needlelace worked on a geometric grid formed by drawing threads from a woven cloth, the patterns formed with buttonhole stitches.

Roundels Circular panels of decoration.

Pole screen Fire screen whereby the shield is fixed to a pole or stand so that the height can be altered.

Stumpwork Embroidery with raised padded motifs, especially for pictures and boxes made in the second half of the seventeenth century.

Tambour work Embroidery worked with a tambour hook or needle on muslin or other fine material, the stitches resembling chain stitch, in a continuous line.

Trapunto Form of quilting where a soft padding is inserted through the under material, after the quilting stitches have been done, to emphasise a relief design. In Italian quilting a cord is inserted in the same way between parallel lines of stitching.

Trompe l'oeil Pictorial deception making the spectator think he is seeing the actual subject depicted, rather than a representation. For example, playing cards, counters, etc, are sometimes embroidered on the lining of card tables.

A select list of places where
fine needlework may be seen
in museums and private
collections open to the public
at certain times.

PUBLIC AND PRIVATE COLLECTIONS

Private collections marked
with an asterisk are National
Trust properties.

PUBLIC COLLECTIONS

United Kingdom
The American Museum in Britain, Claverton Manor, Bath
The Ashmolean Museum, Oxford
Bethnal Green Museum, London
Bowes Museum, Barnard Castle, Co. Durham
The British Museum, London
The Burrell Collection, Glasgow
Castle Museum and Art Gallery, Nottingham
The Cecil Higgins Art Gallery, Bedford
Fitzwilliam Museum, Cambridge
The Gallery of English Costume, Manchester
Lady Lever Art Gallery, Port Sunlight, Cheshire
Leicester Museum
The Museum of Costume, Bath
The Museum of London
The National Museum of Antiquities, Edinburgh
Royal Scottish Museum, Glasgow
Strangers Hall Museum, Norwich
The Ulster Museum, Belfast
The Victoria and Albert Museum, London
The Whitworth Gallery, Manchester
William Morris Gallery, Walthamstow, London

United States of America
Art Institute of Chicago, Chicago
Boston Museum of Fine Arts, Boston
Brooklyn Museum, New York
Colonial Williamsburg Foundation, Virginia
Cooper-Hewitt Museum of Decorative Arts and Design, New York
The Frick Collection, New York
The Henry Francis du Pont Winterthur Museum, Delaware
Isabella Stewart Gardner Museum, Boston
The Metropolitan Museum of Art, New York
Old Deerfield, Massachusetts
Philadelphia Museum of Art
Smithsonian Institution, Washington

Europe
Bayerisches Nationalmuseum, Munich
Germanisches Nationalmuseum, Nuremburg
Kunsthistorisches Museum, Vienna
Museé du Louvre, Paris
Museé Historique des Tissus, Lyons
The National Museum of Ireland, Dublin
Österrecisches Museum für Angewandte Kunst, Vienna
Rijksmuseum, Amsterdam

USSR
Kremlin Museum, Moscow

PRIVATE COLLECTIONS

United Kingdom
Alnwick Castle, Northumbria
Anglesey Abbey, Cambridgeshire
Arundel Castle, Sussex
Aston Hall, Birmingham
Belvoir Castle, Leicestershire
Blair Atholl Castle, Perth, Scotland
Blickling Hall, Norfolk*
Boughton House, Northamptonshire
Burghley House, Stamford, Cambridgeshire
Castle Ashby, Northamptonshire
Castleton Manor, Oxfordshire
Clandon Park, Guildford, Surrey*
Cogenhoe Church, Northamptonshire
Coughton Court, Warwickshire*
Doddington Hall, Lincolnshire
Dorney Court, Buckinghamshire
Drayton House, Northamptonshire
Drumlanrig Castle, Dumfries and Galloway, Scotland
Durham Cathedral
Fenton House, Hampstead, London*
Gawthorpe Hall, Burnley, Lancashire*
Glamis Castle, Angus, Scotland
Hardwick Hall, Derbyshire*
Holyrood House, Edinburgh, Scotland
Houghton Hall, Norfolk
Knole, Kent*
Little Gidding Church, Cambridgeshire
Longleat, Wiltshire
Mellerstain, Borders, Scotland
Montacute House, Somerset*
Packwood House, Warwickshire*
St Georges Chapel, Windsor, Berkshire
Scone Palace, Perth, Scotland
Snowshill Manor, Gloucestershire*
Squerryes Court, Westerham, Kent
Sudeley Castle, Gloucestershire
Syon House, Middlesex
Temple Newsam, Leeds, West Yorkshire
Traquair House, Peebles, Borders, Scotland
Waddesdon Manor, Buckinghamshire*
Wallington Hall, Northumbria*
Winchester Cathedral
Woburn Abbey, Bedfordshire

Europe
Averbode Abbey, Brabant, Belgium
Cathedral de Saint-Bertrand-de-Comminges, Haute Garonne, France
Chinese Pavillion, Drottningholm, Sweden
Sens Cathedral, France

NT: National Trust

Prelims
Half-title, title page: Private Collection; *Contents page:* Collection Esther Fitz-Gerald (*see also* 5, *p.* 219).

Introduction *Lanto Synge*
1. The Royal School of Needlework (photo Nick Meers); 2. Private Collection; 3. The Royal School of Needlework (photo Nick Meers).

Embroidery: One Thousand Years of History *Rosemary Ewles*
1. By courtesy of the Board of Trustees of the Victoria and Albert Museum; 2. The Bridgeman Art Library; 3–4. Kunsthistorisches Museum, Vienna; 5. Bayerisches Nationalmuseum, Munich; 6. Museo degli Argenti, (Scala), Florence; 7–9. By courtesy of the Board of Trustees of the Victoria and Albert Museum; 10. Museé de Cluny, Paris (Documentation Photographique de la Reunion des Musées Nationaux); 11. Museum für Kunst und Gewerbe, Hamburg; 12–13. By courtesy of the Board of Trustees of the Victoria and Albert Museum; 14. Historisches Museum, Basel, Switzerland; 15. Narodini Galerie V. Praze, Prague; 16. By courtesy of the Board of Trustees of the Victoria and Albert Museum; 17. Kunsthistorisches Museum, Vienna; 18. Chapel of St George of the Generalitat, Barcelona (The Bridgeman Art Library); 19. The British Museum, London; 20–21. Embroiderer's Guild Collection, Hampton Court (photo Dudley Moss); 22–7. By courtesy of the Board of Trustees of the Victoria and Albert Museum; 28. Museo Diocesano, Trento; 29–30. By courtesy of the Board of Trustees of the Victoria and Albert Museum; 31. Hardwick Hall, Chesterfield, Derbyshire (NT); 32–5. By courtesy of the Board of Trustees of the Victoria and Albert Museum; 36. Rijksmuseum, Amsterdam; 37. Embroiderer's Guild Collection, Hampton Court; 38. Rangers House, Blackheath, The Greater London Council as Trustees of the Iveagh Bequest, Kenwood; 39. Private Collection; 40. By courtesy of the Board of Trustees of the Victoria and Albert Museum; 41–4. Private Collection; 45. Embroiderer's Guild Collection, Hampton Court; 46. Bowes Museum, Barnard Castle, Co. Durham; 47. Embroiderer's Guild Collection, Hampton Court; 48. Private Collection; 49. Photo copyright Museé de L'Armée, Paris; 50. By courtesy of the Board of Trustees of the Victoria and Albert Museum; 51. Embroiderer's Guild Collection, Hampton Court; 52. By courtesy of the Board of Trustees of the Victoria and Albert Museum; 53. Bath Costume Museum; 54–5. Embroiderer's Guild Collection, Hampton Court; 56–7. By courtesy of the Board of Trustees of the Victoria and Albert Museum; 58. Embroiderer's Guild Collection, Hampton Court (photo Dudley Moss); 59. Bowes Museum, Barnard Castle, Co. Durham; 60. By courtesy of the Board of Trustees of the Victoria and Albert Museum; 61. Embroiderer's Guild Collection, Hampton Court; 62. Canon's Ashby, Northamptonshire (NT); 63–4. Private Collection; 65. The Henry Francis Du Pont Winterthur Museum, Delaware; 66. Metropolitan Museum, New York (Rogers Fund); 67. The Museum of London; 68. Embroiderer's Guild Collection, Hampton Court (photo Dudley Moss); 69–70. The Henry Francis Du Pont Winterthur Museum, Delaware; 71. Mallett and Son Ltd, London; 72. Embroiderer's Guild Collection, Hampton Court; 73. Embroiderer's Guild Collection, Hampton Court (photo Dudley Moss); 74. The Art Institute, Chicago (gift of Mr Frank D. Loomis); 75–6. The Embroiderer's Guild Collection, Hampton Court (photo Dudley Moss); 77. Plumpstead Embroiderer's Guild Collection, Hampton Court (photo Dudley Moss); 78. Embroiderer's Guild Collection, Hampton Court; 79. Buckinghamshire County Museums; 80–81. By courtesy of the Board of Trustees of the Victoria and Albert Museum; 82. Christie's, Fine Art Auctioneers, London; 83. Embroiderer's Guild Collection, Hampton Court (photo Dudley Moss); 84. By courtesy of the Board of Trustees of the Victoria and Albert Museum; 85–6. Glasgow Museums and Art Galleries; 87–8. Embroiderer's Guild Collection, Hampton Court (photo Dudley Moss); 89. Embroiderer's Guild Collection, Hampton Court; 90–92. Embroiderer's Guild Collection, Hampton Court (photo Dudley Moss); 93. Embroiderer's Guild Collection, Hampton Court; 94. Private Collection; 95. Embroiderer's Guild Collection, Hampton Court; 96. Royal College of Needlework, London; 97–8. Embroiderer's Guild Collection, Hampton Court (photo Dudley Moss).

Canvas Work *Carol Humphrey*
1. By courtesy of the Board of Trustees of the Victoria and Albert Museum; 2. Traquair House, Peeblesshire (photo Kenneth Martin); 3–4. Hardwick Hall, Chesterfield, Derbyshire (NT; photo Andrew Haslam 1985); 5. Hardwick Hall, Chesterfield, Derbyshire (NT); 6. Burrell Collection, Glasgow; 7. By courtesy of the Board of Trustees of the Victoria and Albert Museum; 8. Hardwick Hall, Chesterfield, Derbyshire (NT; photo Andrew Haslam 1985); 9. Hardwick Hall, Chesterfield, Derbyshire (NT); 10–11. By courtesy of the Board of Trustees of the Victoria and Albert Museum; 12. By kind permission of the Earl of Mansfield, Scone Palace, Perth (photo Jarrold & Sons); 13. Burrell Collection, Glasgow; 14–15. Fitzwilliam Museum, Cambridge; 16. By courtesy of the Trustees of the British Museum; 17. By courtesy of the Board of Trustees of the Victoria and Albert Museum; 18. Clandon Park, Guildford, Surrey (NT; photo John Bethell); 19. Aston Hall. By courtesy of Birmingham Museums and Art Gallery; 20. The Bowes Museum, Barnard Castle, Co. Durham; 21–22. Temple Newsam, Leeds

(photo R. Collier; 23. Arniston House, Lothian (photo Joe Rock); 24. Temple Newsam, Leeds (photo Ron Collier); 25. Saltram House, Devon (NT; photo Robert Chapman); 26. Arbury Hall, Nuneaton, Warwickshire; 27. Mellerstain, Gordon, Berwickshire. By kind permission of Lord Binning (photo Hector Innes); 28–29. Wallington Hall, Cambo, Northumberland (NT; photo A. C. Cooper); 30. City of Birmingham Museums and Art Gallery; 31. Montacute House (NT; photo B. S. Evans); 32. Montacute House (NT); 33. Clandon Park, Guildford, Surrey (NT); 34. Merseyside County Art Galleries, Liverpool; 35. Saltram House, Devon (NT; photo Robert Chapman); 36. Temple Newsam, Leeds (photo Ron Collier); 37. Aston Hall. By courtesy of Birmingham Museums and Art Gallery; 38. Musée des Arts Décoratifs, Paris; 39. Metropolitan Museum of Art, New York (gift of Irwin Untermyer); 40. Metropolitan Museum of Art, New York (gift of Mrs J. Insley Blair); 41. Museum of Fine Arts, Boston (Babcock Bequest); 42. Museum of Fine Arts, Boston (Seth K. Sweetser Fund); 43. Museum of Fine Arts, Boston (gift of Mrs Samuel Cabot); 44. The Bowes Museum, Barnard Castle, Co. Durham; 45–46. Strangers Hall, Norwich; 47. Fitzwilliam Museum, Cambridge; 48. By courtesy of the Board of Trustees of the Victoria and Albert Museum; 49. Embroiderer's Guild Collection, Hampton Court (photo Dudley Moss); 50. Embroiderer's Guild Collection, Hampton Court; 51. Wisborough Green Tapestry, Church of St Peter, West Sussex, Wisborough Green Trust; 52. Fitzwilliam Museum, Cambridge; 53. Embroiderer's Guild Collection, Hampton Court (photo Dudley Moss).

Embroidery and Dress *Imogen Stewart*
1. Musée de Louvre, Service Photographique des Musées Nationaux; 2. Museum of Costume and Textiles, Nottingham (Lord Middleton Collection); 3. By courtesy of the Board of Trustees of the Victoria and Albert Museum; 4. The Royal Library, Windsor Castle; 5–6. By courtesy of the Board of Trustees of the Victoria and Albert Museum; 7. Aston Hall. By courtesy of Birmingham Museums and Art Gallery (Aston Hall); 8. Kunsthistorisches Museum, Vienna (photo Meyer); 9–14. By courtesy of the Board of Trustees of the Victoria and Albert Museum; 15–16. Rangers House, Blackheath. Reproduced by courtesy of the Greater London Council (© Woodmansterne Ltd, Watford); 17–18. Parham Park, Pulborough, West Sussex (photo Walter Gardiner); 19–20. By courtesy of the Board of Trustees of the Victoria and Albert Museum; 21. The Museum of London; 22. Museum of Costume, Bath (© Bath Museums Service); 23. Burrell Collection, Glasgow; 24. By courtesy of the Board of Trustees of the Victoria and Albert Museum; 25. Rijksmuseum, Amsterdam; 26–27. The Museum of London; 28. Courtesy of the Cooper-Hewitt Museum, The Smithsonian Institution's National Museum of Design; 29. The Museum of London; 30. By courtesy of the Board of Trustees of the Victoria and Albert Museum; 31. The Royal School of Needlework, London; 32. The Museum of London; 33. By courtesy of the Board of Trustees of the Victoria and Albert Museum; 34. The Royal School of Needlework, London; 35–36. By courtesy of the Board of Trustees of the Victoria and Albert Museum; 37. Royal Scottish Museum, Edinburgh; 38–40. By courtesy of the Board of Trustees of the Victoria and Albert Museum; 41. Glasgow School of Art; 42. By courtesy of the Board of Trustees of the Victoria and Albert Museum; 43. The Brooklyn Museum, New York; 44–47. By courtesy of the Board of Trustees of the Victoria and Albert Museum; 48. Courtesy of Sue Rangley; 49. By courtesy of the Board of Trustees of the Victoria and Albert Museum.

Samplers *Anne Sebba*
1. By courtesy of the Board of Trustees of the Victoria and Albert Museum; 2. Goodhart Collection (photo Derrick Witty); 3. Museum of London; 4. The Dorset Natural History and Archaeological Society, Dorset County Museum, Dorchester, Dorset; 5–6. Goodhart Collection (photo Derrick Witty); 7. By courtesy of the Board of Trustees of the Victoria and Albert Museum; 8–9. Goodhart Collection (photo Derrick Witty); 10. Royal Scottish Museum, Edinburgh; 11. By courtesy of the Board of Trustees of the Victoria and Albert Museum; 12. Royal Scottish Museum, Edinburgh; 13–14. Goodhart Collection (photo Derrick Witty); 15. Royal Scottish Museum, Edinburgh; 16. By courtesy of the Board of Trustees of the Victoria and Albert Museum; 17. Courtesy of the Cooper-Hewitt Museum. The Smithsonian Institution's National Museum of Design; 18. Goodhart Collection (photo Derrick Witty); 19. By courtesy of the Board of Trustees of the Victoria and Albert Museum; 20. Goodhart Collection (photo Derrick Witty); 21. Courtesy of the Essex Institute, Salem, Mass.; 22. The Henry Francis Du Pont Winterthur Museum, Delaware; 23. Museum of the City of New York; 24. The Henry Francis Du Pont Winterthur Museum, Delaware; 25. Courtesy of the Museum of Fine Arts, Boston; 26. Sotheby's, New York; 27–28. The Henry Francis Du Pont Winterthur Museum, Delaware; 29. Mary Grierson Collection; 30. Mrs Syrett's Collection; 31. Welsh Folk Museum; 32. Goodhart Collection (photo Derrick Witty); 33. Anne Sebba Collection.

Patchwork and Appliqué *Shiela Betterton*
1. Cheltenham Art Gallery and Museums (The Bridgeman Art Library); 2. Blickling Hall (NT); 3. The American Museum in Britain, Bath; 4. Kilkenny Design Workshops; 5. Schecter Lee (© 1985, all rights reserved); 6. The American

Museum in Britain, Bath; 7. Ulster Folk and Transport Museum, Co. Durham; 8. By courtesy of Portsmouth City Museums; 9. Bath City Council (The Pump Room; photo Unichrome); 10. Bowes Museum, Barnard Castle, Co. Durham; 11. Collection of Pat Novy; 12. North of England Open Air Museum, Beamish Hall; 13–14. The American Museum in Britain, Bath; 15. The Baltimore Museum of Art (gift of Mr and Mrs Lester N. Towner); 16. The Bowes Museum, Barnard Castle, Co. Durham; 17. Mrs Helen Kelley, Minneapolis, Minesota; 18. Sainsbury Centre for Visual Art, University of East Anglia, Norwich; 19. Royal Ontario Museum, Toronto (gift of Mrs Edward Martin Stubbs); 20. National Trust of Scotland, Edinburgh; 21. Welsh Folk Museum, Cardiff.

Needlelace and Whitework *Audrey Field*
The author's special thanks are due to Miss Santina Levey and Miss Margaret Simeon for their generous encouragement and to Miss Bartlett of The Royal School of Needlework, Miss Anne Marie Benson of Phillips Fine Art Auctioneers, Miss Esther FitzGerald, Mrs Fulvia Lewis, Mrs Joan Pendle and Mrs Alison Walford for the loan of books, photographs and lace, and for the pleasure that they generate in sharing their knowledge.
1–2. National Portrait Gallery, London; 3–4. Collection Audrey Field (photo Martin Dohrn); 5. Collection Esther FitzGerald; 6. Collection Audrey Field (photo Martin Dohrn); 7. Private Collection; 8. National Portrait Gallery, London; 9. Collection Audrey Field (photo Martin Dohrn); 10. Collection Fulvia Lewis (Peter Greenland. Photography, Abingdon); 11–15. Collection Audrey Field (photo Martin Dohrn); 16. Collection Joan Pendle (photo Martin Dohrn); 17. Collection Audrey Field (photo Martin Dohrn); 18. Phillips Fine Art Auctioneers, London; 19. Collection Audrey Field (photo Martin Dohrn); 20. Collection Joan Pendle (photo Martin Dohrn).

Ecclesiastical Needlework *Lanto Synge*
1–2. By courtesy of the Board of Trustees of the Victoria and Albert Museum; 3. Le Curé de Saint-Bertrand-de-Comminges; 4. Durham Cathedral, Northumbria; 5–6. By courtesy of the Board of Trustees of the Victoria and Albert Museum; 7. The Bridgeman Art Library; 8. Benedictine Abbey, St Peter, Salzburg; 9. By courtesy of the Board of Trustees of the Victoria and Albert Museum; 10. Averbode Abbey. Brabant (The Bridgeman Art Library); 11–12. Private Collection; 13. Victor Frances Gallery, London; 14–15. Mallett and Son Ltd. London; 16–18. Private Collection; 19. St George's Chapel, Windsor; 20. Wells Cathedral, Somerset; 21. The Museum of London.

INDEX